"We always knew something stunk about basketball and the sneaker business, and SOLE INFLUENCE lets us know where the stench is coming from. . . . A most revealing and insightful book."

—Jackie MacMullan, *Sports Illustrated*

"Wetzel and Yaeger make a disturbing case. . . . with an outrage tempered by realism, [the authors] mount a case that corporate money and the sneaker wars are bad for basketball and, more importantly, bad for the thousands of athletes who want to be like Mike."

—*Publishers Weekly*

"A sobering look at the shoe business . . . offers insight into the solution of how to stop the madness that, sadly, has become commonplace."

—*Northern Virginia Daily*

"Highly recommended. . . . The story is very convincingly laid out and makes the ironic point that the phenomenon of Michael Jordan so changed the world that there probably never will be another player with the same drive and relative innocence who so appeals to such a wide demographic."

—*Library Journal*

"Revealing . . . the authors present a view of basketball that will change the way we view the game as they expose its seamy side, which is far removed from the glamour of the NCAA Final Four and the public relations spectacle of the NBA." **—***Abilene Reporter News* **(TX)**

Sole Influence

BASKETBALL, CORPORATE GREED, AND THE CORRUPTION OF AMERICA'S YOUTH

DAN WETZEL AND DON YAEGER

WARNER BOOKS

A Time Warner Company

WARNER BOOKS EDITION

Cover design by Caroline Lechter
Cover photograph by Herman Estevez
Book design by H. Roberts Design

Warner Books, Inc.
1271 Avenue of the Americas
New York, NY 10020

Visit our Web site at
www.twbookmark.com

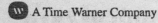 A Time Warner Company

Printed in the United States of America

Originally published in hardcover by Warner Books.
First Paperback Printing: November 2000

10 9 8 7 6 5 4 3 2 1

For my parents,
Mary Ellen and Paul
——DW

To my son, Billy:
You have so many talents,
so many gifts,
so great a future.
I'm counting on you to change the world.
——DY

Acknowledgments

I n the course of some two hundred interviews for this book the authors benefited from the assistance, professionalism, honesty, and courage of people from throughout the world of basketball who were willing to talk about a tough subject. Some of the people quoted in this book we know well, while for others we were just a voice on the phone asking a lot of questions. To thank all of those who helped would be impossible, but know that we are indebted to all of you.

Of course, many of the interview subjects would prefer to keep their identity private and for that we understand. Basketball is a lucrative, powerful, and cutthroat multibillion-dollar industry and one which values loyalty and an adherence to a certain code of silence that, unfortunately, prevents some from speaking out even for the common good. In the course of this book we attempted to keep the use of off-the-record quotes and assertions to the bare minimum, preferring instead to remain on the record at all times. While this toned down some of the more eye-popping allegations, we believe it gives the reader a more balanced perspective.

We also drew on our experience of many years covering high school and traveling team basketball at the national level. We did not descend upon this world for a few weeks to write a snapshot. Rather, we believe our thorough coverage of grassroots basketball over the years allowed us to view things with a broad perspective. We gratefully thank the high school and traveling team coaches and players, not to mention college head and assistant coaches, we have spent many days and nights watching and talking basketball with. Of particular note we would like to thank the following for their contributions to this effort.

Rick Wolff, our editor at Warner Books, believed in this project from the start and kept us sharp and honest from proposal to final draft. Thanks also to his assistant, Dan Ambrosio. Basil Kane is more than a tremendous agent, he is also a friend.

Special recognition to *Sports Illustrated* editors Greg Kelly, Craig Neff, and Rob Fleder, fellow writers Chris Stone, Alex Wolff, and Seth Davis, and research staff Linda Ronan and Linda Wachtel, all of whom make life at *Sports Illustrated* the best job in the business.

We must also thank *Basketball Times* publisher Larry Donald for his support of this project, as well as Dan's colleagues Mike Sheridan and Joe Kyriakoza.

A number of journalists provided great help, moral support, and guidance and may find some of their work reflected here, including Jeff Manning of the *Oregonian*, Mike Marshall of the *Huntsville Times*, Taylor Bell of the *Chicago Sun Times*, Pat Forde of the *Louisville Courier-Journal*, David Scott and Norb Garrett of *Sport*, Dick "Hoops" Weiss of the *New York Daily News*, Mike DeCourcy of the *Cincinnati Enquirer*, Andy Katz of the *Fresno Bee*, Jack Ebling of the *Lansing State Journal*, Steve Lopez of *Sports Illus-*

trated, Rome Hartman and Lesley Stahl of *60 Minutes,* Sonja Steptoe of CNN/SI, Constance Johnson of HBO Sports, Michael Morrissey and Sean Hayden of the *Northwest Indiana Times,* Oscar Avila of the *Kansas City Star,* Chris Fusco of the *Arlington* (Illinois) *Daily Herald,* James Ahlers of the *Mesa Tribune,* and Rick Notter of *Inside Indiana.*

Also thanks to recruiting scouts Clark Francis, Stephen Wacaser, Dave Tellep, Van Coleman, Tom Konchalski, Bob Gibbons, and Vince Baldwin: We like you no matter what Bob Knight says.

Special thanks goes to Armen Keteyian, who along with the aforementioned Alex Wolff, authored the trailblazing 1989 book *Raw Recruits,* which was a tremendous help. Keteyian's 1997 effort, *Money Players,* which he wrote along with Harvey Araton and Martin F. Dardis, was just as valuable.

Also to our friends and family who helped us through the process, most notably Jan Wilson, whose daily encouragement of and patience with Dan made this possible, Paul and Mary Ellen Wetzel, Rich Cohen, Daniel Strikowski, Paul Connolly, Howard Ziff, Russ Pulliam, Bill Strickland, Brian Murphy, Paul and Matt Tryder, Eric Hynes, Pat Mungovan, and John Berry.

From Don goes thanks to his greatest partner, Denise, and children Billy and Katie, who always have the book advance spent before the ink on the contract is dry.

Contents

Cast of Players

The Kingpins

George Raveling: Longtime college basketball coach, now the director of Nike grassroots basketball, which funds and runs talent camps, tournaments, all-star games, traveling teams, and high school programs.

Sonny Vaccaro: Held Raveling's current job at Nike throughout the 1980s, now has a similar position at adidas America. Runs and sponsors the adidas ABCD Camp and Magic's Roundball Classic, as well as numerous AAU and high school programs.

The Coaches

Joel Hopkins: Head coach of Durham (North Carolina) Mt. Zion Christian Academy. Has made a name for himself for his aggressive recruiting tactics, his rhythmic speech patterns, and, according to Sonny Vaccaro, an approximate $150,000 a year he receives from Tracy McGrady's contract with adidas.

Myron Piggie: Gold-toothed former crack dealer who rose to power in Kansas City AAU circles behind heavy Nike funding and a talented team that became notorious in the world of traveling basketball.

The Players

Kevin Garnett: South Carolina native who spent senior year of high school in Chicago before becoming the first player in twenty years to enter the NBA directly from the prep ranks. Now an All-Star with the Minnesota Timberwolves.

Kobe Bryant: Currently an All-Star guard with the Los Angeles Lakers, was the first academically qualified player to turn pro out of high school. In 1996, inked a five-year, $5 million sponsorship deal with adidas before ever playing a minute in the NBA.

Tracy McGrady: Followed Bryant's footsteps in 1997 and was drafted by the Toronto Raptors out of Durham (North Carolina) Mt. Zion Christian Academy. Signed a six-year, $12 million deal with adidas that included six-figure payments to his high school coach and the scout who discovered him.

Dermarr Johnson: Lithe, 6-foot-9 forward considered one of the top players in the class of 1999. Originally from Maryland, rose to fame in the adidas grassroots system, starring at the ABCD Camp and for D.C. Assault traveling team. Finished high school career at the prep school Maine Central Institute.

Wesley Wilson: Powerful 6-foot-10 center from northern California, attended the prep school Maine Central Institute during the 1998–99 season, in part because they wear Nikes.

Marvin Stone: 6-foot-10 center from Huntsville (Alabama) Grissom High, considered one of the top players in the class of 1999. His career fractured a basketball-mad city.

Marcus Taylor: Number one prospect nationally in the class of 2000, the guard has long been compared to fellow Lansing, Michigan, native Magic Johnson. He and his family have deemed AAU, and other forms of nonscholastic basketball, unnecessary, preferring instead that Marcus live a traditional teenager's life.

Shortly after graduating from Georgetown in the spring of

Sole
Influence

CHAPTER 1

Unlike Mike

His hair perfect, smile polished, and wardrobe impeccable, Kobe Bryant sprang to his feet with the enthusiasm of the eighteen-year-old kid he was. His name had just been called by National Basketball Association commissioner David Stern as the thirteenth pick of the 1996 draft. The Charlotte Hornets had selected the precocious recent graduate of Lower Merion High School in suburban Philadelphia, who just weeks before had taken recording sensation Brandy Norwood to his prom. Now it was time to celebrate in the recesses of New Jersey's Continental Airlines Arena.

Bryant quickly hugged his father, former NBA player Joe "Jellybean" Bryant. Then his mother, Pam, and other assorted family and friends.

With TNT television cameras rolling live, he stepped over and embraced a middle-aged white man named Sonny Vaccaro. It would prove to be a momentous hug, one ignored by the commentators, the fans, and the media assembled to cover the draft that night. The hug, though, wasn't missed by executives at Nike and adidas, shoe companies sitting just miles apart in Beaverton, Oregon. In so many ways, it was a hug that changed the way the business of basketball is conducted in this country.

Vaccaro is the legendary basketball character and marketing guru who during the 1980s and early 1990s helped make Nike synonymous with the game. Now working for adidas after a bitter 1992 breakup with his former employer, Vaccaro needed to deliver a special kind of endorser to his new company, the kind who could establish adidas—a German-based corporation that was big in worldwide soccer but had become a nonfactor in hoops—as a player in the lucrative basketball market. Just as in 1984 when he delivered Michael Jordan, then merely a promising shooting guard from the University of North Carolina, to Nike despite concerns from his superiors and competitors alike. That marriage didn't just make Nike—then a company that was popular in track and field circles but, like adidas in 1996, a sideline player in basketball—competitive with basketball industry leader Converse, it changed nearly everything in sports.

"The marriage of Michael and Nike is the biggest story in the history of sports marketing," says Vaccaro now. "[If it hadn't happened] everyone's lives would have changed. Nike would never have been Nike. I certainly wouldn't have been this person. And maybe Michael's persona and his marketing thing might have taken longer. It was a three-fold thing there. Everyone benefited."

And so as Vaccaro and his young star hugged on national television that night in 1996, the similarities were endless: two young and somewhat unproven players—Bryant nothing but a high school kid, Jordan an early defector from college who went third in the draft; two companies both desperately turning to Vaccaro to get them a share of the multibillion-dollar basketball market. Vaccaro, though wiser in 1996, was still the consummate insider, armed with his famed guile, street savvy, and a generation of contacts throughout the game. He was still a gambler years after he bottomed out as a card player in Las Vegas.

Thus it came as no surprise that within weeks, Bryant had signed an exclusive five-year, multimillion-dollar endorsement deal with shoe and apparel manufacturer adidas, the company that employs Vaccaro to run its grassroots basketball operations. Bryant chose adidas after hearing Nike's pitch, but not spending a great deal of time deliberating over the particulars. Vaccaro's loyalty to and history with Bryant was enough. It was Vaccaro who had allowed Bryant to shine on the national stage the previous two summers at his adidas ABCD talent camp, invited him and his parents to his postseason all-star game in Detroit, Magic's Roundball Classic, where Bryant was named MVP, and sponsored his traveling basketball squads for two years. It was Vaccaro who had known his father since 1972, when Joe was the MVP of the Vaccaro-run Dapper Dan All-Star Game, the forerunner to Magic's Roundball Classic. It was Vaccaro who had known Kobe's uncle, Chubbie Cox, the brother of Kobe's mother, Pam, since Cox also played in the 1974 Dapper Dan.

"I knew this family," Vaccaro says. "They knew me. Ever so slightly, but they did. So when we got down to the personal stuff, I was way ahead of the game."

The only difference in how Vaccaro signed Jordan and how he signed Bryant or other young stars such as Tracy McGrady, Antoine Walker, or Tim Thomas is how much more work it took to get it done in 1996. As much as the game of basketball has changed in the twelve years since Jordan invited the world to come fly with him, the game of identifying and signing pitchmen has changed even more.

This is fact: Jordan brought Nike to inconceivable levels of popularity and worldwide dominance. This too is fact: The battle to find similarly effective stars to endorse products—to find "The Next Jordan"—has intensified with frightening seriousness. Where once a player, after being drafted or even a few years into his career, reviewed some solid business presentations before choosing a potential endorsement, now a young player can be slotted for a shoe company—particularly either Nike or adidas—as young as twelve years old.

Vaccaro knows if he tried to sign a Kobe Bryant the same way he tried to sign Michael Jordan . . .

"Impossible," he says. "Impossible. Can't happen now. You have to identify them early, you got to talk to all the necessary people. There's got to be a foundation. You have to identify him and say who you want. And you have to have a relationship. You don't go in cold on anybody today."

Which has left basketball in the middle of a major war for the hearts and soles of its young players. Because just as Vaccaro and Bryant's hug flashed back to Beaverton and the headquarters of Nike, the war for allegiances of the nation's young players was officially underway. Nike knew that Vaccaro had found a way to beat the well-heeled industry giant at its own game. By getting in early with young players, he proved loyalty could outmuscle money.

Four months later Nike CEO Phil Knight summoned twenty coaches of Nike-sponsored traveling basketball programs—generally regional all-star teams that play in tournaments around the country during the off-season—to Nike's headquarters to map out a battle plan. On Saturday,

October 19, 1996, with thirty or so people sitting in one of the company's posh conference rooms with stadium-style seating, across the stage strolled Knight—decked out in blue jeans, T-shirt, light-colored sport coat, and a pair of Nike running shoes—who told them in no uncertain terms that this was a fight Nike had to win.

"We never want another kid to go pro out of high school again without Nike being involved," Knight said, according to Tom Floco, a Nike summer coach from Philadelphia, and a half dozen other people present that day. Knight, through a spokeswoman, denied having made the statement, but Floco and others were crystal-clear. "There was no doubt what he said and what he meant," Floco said.

When Knight's quote was printed a week later in the *Chicago Sun-Times,* a chill ran through high school basketball coaches from coast to coast. It was suddenly apparent that if one of the most recognizable and powerful CEOs in America was stating that high school sports was now an important battlefield for business, the future of the game played in every community in America was up for grabs.

Knight's monumental statement, coupled with a broad-based and heavily financed campaign to identify young prospects and feed them into Nike's grassroots basketball program and compete with adidas' similar grassroots system, brought big money, big egos, and hypercompetitive recruiting to the high school and junior high level.

Nike repeated its message to its grassroots coaches scattered around the country over the next year, in teleconferences and letters: Establish relationships early and steer players to the company. All this so a certain company can have the inside track on landing the mythical next Michael Jordan, a player who would not only be considered among the game's greatest talents, but become indisputably the most powerful and effective endorser of products in American history.

The first company to find that next Jordan would, if Jordan's success was a yardstick, be set for the next decade. By setting an unbelievable standard—at his peak Jordan's annual endorsements earned him $16 million from Nike, $5 million from Gatorade, $5 million from Bijan Cologne, $4 million from MCI, $2 million from Ray-O-vac, $2 million from Hanes, $2 million from Ball Park Franks, $2 million from Wheaties, $2 million from Wilson, $2 million from Oakley, $1 million from AMF Bowling, $1 million from CBS Sportsline, and $1 million from Chicagoland Chevrolet—the greatest endorser of all time made the business of hawking products more lucrative than playing the game.

The irony is how easy it was for Nike to sign the original.

It was the summer of 1984 and Vaccaro was waiting at a Tony Roma's restaurant in Santa Monica, California, for his then best friend George Raveling, the head coach of the University of Iowa and an assistant on the U.S. Olympic men's basketball team, to bring Michael Jordan to lunch.

Vaccaro was a marketing guy for Nike, charged with the concept of getting the company involved in the world of basketball. At the time Converse, whose stable of endorsers included Earvin "Magic" Johnson, Larry Bird, Isiah Thomas, and others, was the industry leader. But Nike had decided that what would truly work is developing a signature shoe for an athlete. By creating for a player his very own shoe, named and marketed just for him, Nike was hoping that said player's popularity would spur sales.

Vaccaro liked the concept of the signature, just as he had liked the concept of signing college basketball coaches to exclusive endorsement contracts and assuring that the nation's top collegians—all amateur athletes prohibited from signing individual endorsement deals—would have his brand-name shoe on their feet. Converse had almost all of the NBA's top talent locked up, but, Vaccaro figured, wasn't using them as effective pitchmen. In Converse's most popular television commercial, a series of NBA stars, including Johnson, Thomas, and Bird, passed a Converse shoe to each other. Vaccaro wanted to eliminate the clutter and instead focus on one player, with one niche and one message. He needed someone who had the kind of game that everyone could relate to, regardless of what NBA team the player played for.

Big men, including 1984's top two draft picks, the University of Houston's Akeem [later Hakeem] Olajuwon and the University of Kentucky's Sam Bowie, were out because few street players or young kids envisioned themselves as centers. Vaccaro wanted a guard or a small forward. Someone who could shoot from outside, handle the ball, and make the kind of athletic plays—particularly dunks—that were causing the NBA's popularity to surge.

He thought he wanted Michael Jordan.

Now he had to meet him. Vaccaro knew almost everyone in basketball but it was easy to see how Jordan eluded him. Vaccaro had run summer instructional camps and his Dapper Dan All-Star game in Pittsburgh since the early 1970s and thus met most of the nation's top young talent—both players and coaches.

But Jordan had taken a different route to the brink of superstardom. Cut from his high school varsity team as a sophomore at Laney High School in Wilmington, North

Carolina, Jordan was hardly a can't-miss prospect. Instead he became a self-made player, using the disappointment of being cut to rededicate himself to the game. As a junior he made the team and as a senior became a schoolboy star good enough to attract the attention of Dean Smith, the head basketball coach of the North Carolina Tar Heels, an hour-and-a-half drive up the road in Chapel Hill. Smith offered a scholarship, Jordan accepted, and although he went on to an all-state season as a senior, he finished second in the voting for North Carolina Mr. Basketball to future UNC teammate Buzz Peterson.

Regarded as only the second-best player in his own state, Jordan was never invited to the Dapper Dan.

But when, as a freshman, he hit the game-winning jump shot to lead the Tar Heels over the Georgetown Hoyas in the 1982 NCAA Championship Game, Vaccaro couldn't help but notice the thin 6-6 guard. He left college two years later, as the consensus national player of the year in college basketball. And Vaccaro was determined to get to know the young phenom.

"I never had anything to do with Michael," Vaccaro recalls. "He never went to a camp, he never played in the Dapper Dan. My first identity with him—obviously I knew who he was when he started playing college basketball—was when he beat Georgetown in the game in '82. But there was never any personal contact there.

"But the game plan was set in motion from Nike's standpoint in November of 1983 when we were identifying the college players and then solidifying them in January or February of '84. We knew Michael could come out and that was the year of [Charles] Barkley and Olajuwon. That was a pretty good class."

It was a class that would go on to win the 1984 Olympic

gold medal—although Barkley was cut by U.S. and Indiana University coach Bob Knight and Olajuwon was then a Nigerian citizen (he later became a U.S. citizen and played on the 1996 U.S. National Team)—which was why Jordan was in Southern California. He was practicing for the Olympic team, after being selected number three overall by the Chicago Bulls in the NBA's amateur draft. And on this off-afternoon, he agreed to meet Vaccaro at Tony Roma's.

Vaccaro, Jordan, and Raveling had lunch and talked hoops. Through college Jordan had worn Converse at North Carolina because of the company's endorsement deal with Tar Heel coach Dean Smith. Off the court, Vaccaro says, Jordan wore adidas.

"Michael had never seen nor ever played in a Nike shoe until then," Vaccaro said.

Vaccaro touched lightly on Nike's ideas and they agreed to another meeting just before the Olympics with Jordan, his agent, David Falk, Vaccaro, and Nike executive Rob Strasser. That time they met at the exclusive L'Ermitage Hotel in Beverly Hills. Strasser was one of the creative geniuses behind Nike until he left the company in 1988; he later ran adidas America until his death in the mid-1990s. He and Vaccaro laid out the plan for the signature shoe— the Air Jordan, a phrase Falk and Strasser coined. Jordan and Falk were intrigued and although Converse was signing most of the game's top talents Jordan seemed uninterested in endorsing the company.

"We presented a plan to him," Vaccaro said. "It was a detailed plan. The whole plan was how we were going to market Air Jordan, how we were going to make it different."

Jordan was interested enough about Nike to come to Portland, Oregon, in the fall with his parents to learn more about the Air Jordan. There the Jordans were given a tour of the city, wined and dined, and showed repeatedly that Nike considered the Air Jordan to be the highest of priorities.

"It was very formal," Vaccaro said of the meetings. "It was a recruiting trip because I think signing him had a lot to do with what we said we were going to do and the relationship I established with him early. He felt comfortable once he came to Oregon." Although, Vaccaro admits, there really wasn't much to show the Jordans. Phil Knight's company was nowhere near the corporate giant it is now, so he couldn't offer much of a tour.

"There was no plant," Vaccaro said. "There was no NikeTown. There was no Nike campus. We were in cubbyholes, a bunch of cubbyholes in leased office space. We didn't have a building. Michael built the Nike buildings."

Although Michael sat in on every presentation, it was his parents who did most of the talking, Vaccaro said. "I think they were more in tune with what we were trying to do than even Michael," Vaccaro said. "I think Falk had a lot to do with convincing them this was a landmark thing. I think David did a good job preparing him and getting him ready for this thing."

At one meeting the Jordans were shown the Air Jordan logo—then a pair of wings similar to the kind airline pilots wear. They were also shown a prototype of the Air Jordan shoe. "He was excited about having his shoe, but it wasn't like we had this prototype thing that was the most innovative shoe in the world," Vaccaro said. "In fact, the first Air Jordan was pathetic."

It didn't matter. Jordan was interested and Nike was more interested than adidas, which was the only other company to make a bid for his services.

Vaccaro had convinced Nike officials, including Phil Knight, that Jordan was the complete package: a fundamentally sound player with the kind of breathtaking athleticism that would appeal to all players. His game was street enough to be legit on city playgrounds, yet his personality and speaking ability were polished enough to work in suburban living rooms. In a league that is predominately black but plays to a majority white fan base, he was perfect. He was a gamble, but it was one Vaccaro was willing to take.

Others at Nike weren't so sure. There was a movement to sign Olajuwon or Barkley, a powerful forward from Auburn University. Other players were also mentioned. Vaccaro was so convinced he had the right guy that when Nike executive Howard Schulser asked him if he was willing to bet his job on Jordan, Vaccaro never hesitated.

"I said, 'Yeah.' "

Why?

"Because I wasn't making a lot of money anyway. What difference did it make?"

So Nike laid out its plan: a signature shoe, with the athlete sharing in the profits. Adidas offered $500,000 according to Vaccaro. Nike countered with $250,000 and a percentage of the shoe revenues. Falk wanted a half million guarantee and the percentages. Nike came back with the $500,000 but a smaller cut. They had a deal.

"David Falk elected to take more guaranteed money and less revenue percentage," said Vaccaro. "So out of the chute he lost himself a lot of money. But in retrospect, it really amounted to nothing. It wasn't a big-time bidding war. Probably the most determining thing was adidas wasn't going to offer him a lot of money. It was the first time that the athlete was going to share in the royalties of the shoe. That was the gamble."

To say it paid off wouldn't begin to describe it. In 1985,

with total sales slumping at around $900 million and Reebok surging to become the industry leader behind the sale of its aerobics shoes for women, Nike experienced a "belt tightening to bring down general administration costs and reduction in inventory," according to company documents.

In 1986, in his second season as a Chicago Bull, Jordan scored 63 points in a heavily watched playoff game against the Boston Celtics and his popularity began to soar. Sales of his black and red shoes and apparel followed suit.

"Then [sales] went off the wall," said Vaccaro. "It was the popularity of the kid that carried everything. It got so popular that, I'll never forget [Nike executive] Jack Joyce, he was in charge of production at that time of the Jordan line, said, 'Let's just make everything black and red and sell it. T-shirts, everything. Just paint bricks black and red and sell them.' That's how popular it became."

Two years later, after Spike Lee's ad campaign featuring Jordan and Lee himself (playing Mars Blackmon) hit the airwaves, declaring "It's gotta be the shoes," stores couldn't keep Air Jordans on the shelves. Nike sales soared past the $1 billion mark and the company assumed its spot as number one in the industry, a mantle it has yet to give up.

By 1997, Nike's worldwide sales hit a record high of $9.19 billion, more than a 1,000 percent increase from sales of $877 million in 1987. Although 1998 sales stalled—causing some layoffs and a reduction in stock prices—its hold on number one in the shoe and apparel industry is still considerable. During fiscal year 1998, according to Nike, gross sales hit $9.89 billion, highest in industry history.

Meanwhile Jordan went on to win five NBA Most Valuable Player Awards, six NBA Championships for the

Chicago Bulls, and established himself as the greatest basketball player of all time. He has also become a pitchman without peer, proving he could be both Everyman and Superman at the same time. Despite links (described in the 1997 book *Money Players*) to heavy illegal gambling losses—both in card games and golf matches—and associations with some less than reputable people, his public persona has not wavered. Even an eighteen-month retirement stint where he played minor league baseball didn't affect his Q rating.

He is, and will likely remain even in retirement, the most popular athlete in the world.

All this is only part of the reason the search for the next Michael Jordan is so cutthroat. For a contending company such as adidas, Converse, Fila, or Reebok or an upstart such as And One, executives need only look at the Nike story to realize that finding the perfect athlete could change everything.

Nike's numbers explain why others are looking so hard today and why Vaccaro says the rules of the game have changed so drastically. While targeting the athlete is still a key to the business, no longer can a shoe company wait until the player is a junior in college. Now waiting until a player is a junior in high school can be too late.

As a fifteen-year-old freshman at Benton Harbor (Michigan) High School, 6-9 Robert Whaley made an immediate impact on the local high school scene. With extraordinarily long arms, big broad shoulders, and tremendous agility, Whaley cut an imposing figure on the court despite his tender age. An accomplished shot blocker with polished post moves and an unstoppable hook shot, he became one of Michigan's most dynamic high school players as a mere freshman.

Midwest talent scout Vincent Baldwin—who owns the college scouting service Prep Spotlight—began hearing whispers about this western Michigan man-child in December 1997. When he decided to check up on the rumors later that winter, he was shocked at how good Whaley was.

"His talent level was incredible," Baldwin said. "He could do everything on the court. I couldn't believe he was fifteen years old. The next day I called both Sonny [Vaccaro] and Nike's George Raveling and left messages saying, 'There's a fifteen-year-old in Michigan named Robert Whaley that you guys need to check out.' I called them both to be fair."

Within a week Whaley had heard from Vaccaro and received a package full of complimentary adidas gear and shoes. He was also contacted by Christopher Grier, the coach of the Michigan Mustangs, an adidas-sponsored traveling basketball team from Southfield, Michigan, some two hundred miles away. Whaley began playing for the Mustangs after his high school season and was quickly signed up for the 1998 adidas ABCD Camp, which Vaccaro oversees.

"Adidas has been good to me," said Whaley. "They started sending me stuff and everyone around me was wearing adidas. I just got used to it. I know Sonny will be good for me."

How good is the question. In the cutthroat competition to lock up young Robert Whaleys—in hopes they become a Jordan, or at least a Kobe Bryant—it is clear that shoe companies and the high school coaches, scouts, and summer ball organizers that they sponsor or employ will do just about anything to be good enough.

Raveling, by the way, didn't return the call, leaving Vaccaro with an open lane into Whaley's heart. Vaccaro jumped because he knows if he is ever going to sign another MJ, he'll lay the groundwork when the player is fourteen, not twenty-one. And if he's right, Vaccaro might be smiling again for the cameras on draft night.

CHAPTER 2

Shoes to Fill

The sight of a 7-foot-2, 280-pound basketball player passing by would normally not elicit even a furtive second glance from Nike employees, who had long grown accustomed to having the world's greatest athletes touring the shoe manufacturer's Beaverton, Oregon, campus. But this day in the late spring of 1992 was different, for the visiting athlete, twenty-year-old Shaquille O'Neal, was wearing a jacket bearing the logo of Nike's most despised rival, Reebok. Nike executives, who since the company's beginning in the early 1970s had taken great pride in their iconoclastic, nonconformist sensibilities, ordinarily might have been amused by the chutzpah of the former Louisiana State University basketball star. However, the unsmiling, almost belligerent looks O'Neal and his father had worn during the entire visit suggested anything but humor.

The men in charge of trying to sway O'Neal to the swoosh held little hope of signing him to an endorsement deal. Nonetheless, they felt obligated to try, especially since Reebok—with whom Nike had been waging a jihad for nearly a decade—had mounted an all-out campaign to woo

O'Neal into its fold. Though Nike had recently reasserted its supremacy in the athletic shoe industry, Reebok had managed to stay within striking distance of number one thanks to the immense popularity of its line of women's aerobics shoes.

When O'Neal signed a five-year, $15 million contract with Reebok that summer, Nike officials would grumble that he wasn't "a Nike guy" anyway. Nonetheless, the signing was still cause for alarm at the Beaverton campus, where many believed in the idea that one basketball superstar could change the balance of power in the world of athletic shoes. Nobody understood this better than Nike chairman and CEO Phil Knight, who had wrested the top spot in the industry back from Reebok in the late 1980s largely on the strength of a single personality, Michael Jordan. With Jordan, who was growing increasingly weary of the demands of his ethereal celebrity ("How does it feel to be God?" a Japanese reporter would ask him at that year's Summer Olympics in Barcelona), hinting at retirement, the always-intense search for the next Jordan would gather fresh urgency.

O'Neal, whom the Orlando Magic would select with the first pick in that summer's NBA draft, appeared a logical choice to fill that void. Though he would not turn twenty-one until the following March, he had already demonstrated a savoir faire about the endorsement market that was far more advanced than any Jordan had demonstrated during his earliest days in the NBA. Before his rookie season was over, O'Neal would cut a rap album, agree to a movie deal, and put out his autobiography. In addition to his deal with Reebok, he signed endorsement contracts with Pepsi ($13 million), Kenner toys, Spalding, and Scorecard trading cards (worth approximately $25 million). "He's tough but not nasty," said James Mullen, a Massachusetts-based marketing expert, at the time, "the spokesman of the next generation."

Reebok officials were downright giddy. "How much longer has Michael Jordan got?" Tom Carmody, a former Nike exec who had recently defected to Reebok, crowed to a *Vanity Fair* interviewer the following summer. "Two, three years tops? And already kids are putting up Shaq posters, and they'll go through a glass wall for their Reeboks. You know what we're going to do this summer in Japan? You know that sumo wrestler in Japan, whatshisname, Hawaiian descent? We're going to bring Shaq to Tokyo and have them meet in public. We have to get permission. You know why? Because it's going to shut down Tokyo in August when we do this. It is going to shut down the city. The sumo wrestler and the Shaq, just standing there."

At the 1993 Super Show in Atlanta, the world's largest sporting goods convention, Reebok CEO Paul Fireman would ebulliently proclaim: "I think Jordan has three or four years of significance left at the top. Shaq is next. We will use Shaq to catapult to leadership throughout the world."

This was the power of a basketball shoe in fin de siècle America. Gone were the days when the basketball player made the sneaker famous. Now it was the sneaker that would make the basketball player famous.

In the beginning, there was no Shaq, Mars Blackmon, or li'l Penny, just Chuck and his Chucks. We're speaking, of course, of the Chuck Taylor All-Stars by Converse. Even today, some seventy-five years after the first pair of Chucks was manufactured, the hightop bearing the patch with the blue star and the Chuck Taylor autograph remains a symbol of retro cool, an emblem of sartorial hipness as much as a mere basketball shoe. Little is known about the small-town Indianan for whom the famous Converse shoe is named (his plaque in the Basketball Hall of Fame in Springfield, Massachusetts, which inducted him as a member in 1969, reads only "contributor"). But this much we do know: In 1920, Taylor, a sweet-shooting hoops junkie who barnstormed the country with semipro teams nearly a quarter century before there was an NBA, showed up at the offices of the Converse Rubber Co. in Malden, Massachusetts, and offered to drive around the U.S. on the company's behalf, giving basketball clinics to coaches and trumpeting the virtues of the canvas sneakers he stuffed into the trunk of his car (usually a big Cadillac). In contrast to the image we commonly ascribe to today's street-hustling athletic shoe representative, Taylor would typically show up at a gym, give his clinic, a small plume of smoke coming out of the pipe that never seemed to leave his mouth, and casually close the deal before exiting the building.

Thus began Converse's dominance of the basketball shoe market, which stretched across much of the century. Bill Russell wore them. So did Wilt Chamberlain, Bob Cousy, Jerry West, and Elgin Baylor. And one day so too would Julius Erving, Magic Johnson, and Larry Bird. Tradition and Taylor's legendary salesmanship, however, were not enough to sustain Converse's preeminent position in the industry. Perhaps having grown fat on its success, Converse appeared disinclined to introduce any new innovations to its product, even as new competitors appeared on the horizon in the 1960s.

"They hadn't improved the insole; the cushion in the heel hadn't been improved; and the area around the little toe was a problem," said famed UCLA coach John Wooden in 1984, recalling a conversation he had with his good friend Taylor in the late 1960s. "Even though my players wore them, I had to use a razor blade myself on every new pair to cut the seam that would be right over the little toe. If I didn't do that, the players would all have blisters."

By the early 1970s, Converse had been supplanted by adidas as the shoe of choice among college and professional basketball teams. While Chuck Taylor, with his door-to-door salesmanship, brought to mind a picture of the kindly mom-and-pop proprietor, adidas founder Adolf "Adi" Dassler conjured images of the ruthless corporate takeover artist. Founded in post–World War II West Germany, adidas quickly established its dominance of the European and, soon thereafter, the global marketplace, its three-stripe emblem becoming as familiar to sports fans as the five rings of the Olympic logo. By the early 1960s, the majority of top soccer players and Olympic athletes were wearing adidas; at the 1968 Summer Games in Mexico City, an astounding 85 percent of the medalists wore the shoe.

Superior technology enabled adidas to quickly gain a firm foothold in the basketball shoe industry (when UCLA switched from Converse to adidas in 1970, Wooden no longer had to worry about cutting holes in his players' shoes). But while basketball players were certainly appreciative of the vulcanized nylon soles, rubber toe caps, and other innovative wrinkles the mad German scientists back at the adidas plant were dreaming up, they were also starting to receive a far more juicy inducement to wear Adi Dassler's kicks: They were free.

For most college and professional players today, it is inconceivable that there was a time when you actually had to pay for your sneakers. But until Adi Dassler and his son and successor, Horst, came along, that is exactly what most college and NBA teams did. (The Dasslers didn't mind giving away the shoes. In fact, it beat having to pony up hundreds of thousands of dollars to keep Olympic athletes in their shoes, which was the strategy adidas had been forced to adopt in the late 1950s when Adi's estranged brother, Rudolf, started paying Olympians to wear his Pumas.) By 1976, the company estimated that more than 80 percent of NBA players were wearing its shoes. And let us not forget Michael Jordan's long-forgotten declaration to Nike representatives in the summer of 1984 when they first approached him about becoming a swoosh guy. "I've never worn Nike. I'll probably sign with adidas."

Phil Knight wore adidas too. Like most serious runners of his generation, he had grown up competing in Adi Dassler's shoes, and as a student at the University of Oregon had even kept a pair of them on a shelf above his desk for inspiration. In the early 1960s, fresh out of Stanford School of Business, Knight traveled up and down the West Coast attending local track meets, where he gave away free pairs of a Japanese shoe called Tiger, which was essentially a knockoff of an adidas sneaker.

But as he built his fledgling shoe business from a $3,240-a-year operation known as Blue Ribbon Sports into a billion-dollar colossus called Nike, that admiration quickly turned to outright disdain, a hatred no doubt stoked, in part, by the memory of adidas representatives laughing at him and his early business partners as they tried to foist their Tigers off on any runner who would take them. Blue Ribbon Sports, Knight and his earliest business associates determined, would be the antithesis of Adi and Horst Dassler's Goliath. Adidas was formal and elitist. Nike would be irreverent and anti-establishment. Adidas executives sipped Chardonnay with the patrician aristocrats who ran the International

Olympic Committee (indeed, Horst Dassler is widely credited with delivering the votes Juan Antonio Samaranch needed to be elected as IOC president in 1980). Nike execs, most of them former athletes themselves, would turn the board room into a locker room; high-level meetings would be called "buttfaces," a tequila fountain would replace the water fountain at large sales conferences. They would hang out with the actual jocks, preferably the ones most likely to rattle the china, iconoclasts like legendary long-distance runner and notorious rules breaker Steve Prefontaine and volatile, profane Romanian tennis star Ilie Nastase.

In the eight years following the launch of the shoe under the name of Nike in 1972, revenues grew from $3.2 million to $270 million and profits doubled every year. But even as Nike was becoming the shoe of choice for the millions of Americans who were taking to the streets during the nascent jogging boom, adidas remained firmly entrenched atop the U.S. market throughout most of the 1970s, thanks in large part to its booming sales of basketball shoes. Nike was not completely behind the curve—as early as 1975, Knight had launched a major promotional campaign centered around the NBA and convinced a handful of top NBA players to wear his company's shoes—but Nike executives for the most part were runners, hopelessly out of touch with the basketball players the company so coveted. In *Swoosh,* a best-selling history of Nike written in the late 1980s, the authors recall a retreat at an Oregon resort in which a handful of Nike's NBA clients approached John Phillips, an early company consultant. "You know, are these white guys OK?" Phillips, who is African-American, recalls them asking. "They seem a little nervous."

Knight clearly needed somebody who knew and felt comfortable around basketball players.

Enter John Paul (Sonny) Vaccaro, a western Pennsylvania native who had washed up on the Las Vegas Strip in the early 1970s, a small-time sharpie destined it seemed to fail at the various enterprises he undertook. Vaccaro likes to tell how, as a rock and roll promoter in the 1960s, he had turned away both Elton John ("This four-eyed wimp?" he recalls asking rhythm and blues artist Edgar Winter, who had brought the British musician to his attention in 1969) and Simon and Garfunkel ("We kicked their butts out [of a meeting]").

What brought Vaccaro to the Beaverton campus in the first place was yet another cockeyed idea: a backless sneaker, which was, in effect, an athletic sandal.

"Nobody was very interested in it," the authors of *Swoosh* wrote. "They were fascinated, however, by Vaccaro. . . . With his accents, his looks and gestures, and his way of making them feel he was giving them insider information on the world of basketball, they believed he had Mafia written all over him. Maybe they had seen too many movies, but their suspicions deepened when they heard that Vaccaro lived part-time in Las Vegas, and that his friends all seemed to have last names that ended in vowels."

Nonetheless, it was abundantly clear that Vaccaro knew hoops; if there was one positive credential on his résumé, it was his success in attracting the top high school players in the nation to the annual Dapper Dan Roundball Classic in Pittsburgh, which he founded in 1965. Borrowing on his vast network of connections with college coaches, Vaccaro proposed to take adidas' policy of giving college teams free shoes one step further: Nike would pay college programs to wear its shoes. Knight hired Vaccaro as a part-time consultant.

"I was charmed by Sonny," Knight has said. "We had

been beating our brains in trying to get a foot in the door in [basketball]. Then this little portly Italian fellow comes around and says he's going to burn down the walls for us. When we saw his relationships with coaches in action, that he could produce. . . . And then these massive orders for shoes began pouring in. We gave him all the room he wanted."

Almost instantly, Vaccaro signed up more than a dozen coaches, including the late Jim Valvano, then a little-known coach at Iona, Maryland's Lefty Driesell, Duke's Bill Foster, South Carolina's Frank McGuire, and UNLV's Jerry Tarkanian. Within a year, he would add such prominent coaches as Georgetown's John Thompson and Washington State's George Raveling. As textbook as it seems now—convince a coach to put his players in your company's shoes—it was a revolutionary concept at the time.

As Vaccaro tells it, the game started innocently enough.

"When I first told Nike that we had to get involved in colleges, they had the University of Oregon, which, no one knew they were playing basketball," Vacarro recalled in a 1998 interview. "I said we needed to have coaches preaching our gospel all over the country. They said, 'Well, how do you do that?' I said, 'You pay them.' These guys, in the 1970s, were making nothing and some were buying their own shoes. So Nike said, 'What do you need? How do you pay them?' I told them to leave that to me, I'll go to each coach and say, 'Listen, we're going to give you the shoes for nothing. Your administration is going to love you, because you'll no longer have that expense. Then I'm going to give you $5,000 or $10,000.' That was the maximum number.

"With that very small commitment, I went out on the road—here's the irony of it all, the simplicity of this. It's not like they gave me money to go out and sign like they gave me this bundle of cash. I would go out—I'd go to [UNLV coach Jerry] Tarkanian, okay? 'Jerry, are you coming with me?' I'd ask. Immediately, he said, 'Sonny, we can do this.' Then I wrote him a check out of Sonny Vaccaro's account, my very own personal checking account. Then I'd call Rob Strausser at Nike and he'd wire into my account the money to cover the check. So I was writing these checks to these coaches on my personal account. There was no Nike budget. I paid the coaches and Nike reimbursed me. It wasn't like I had a satchel. Everyone has always tried to say that's how it happened.

"Tark was a key guy because I had known him for years. I knew him since the beginning of the Dapper Dan. There was an easy comfort level. He made it easy for me. Other than Tark, I had no contacts on the West Coast. I knew the guys on the East Coast. I took the next year and I drove around making deals. Literally I did all this stuff on the phone or driving in a car going—I went to meet Joe Foster when he was at Duke at a summer camp and I did a deal with him. I met Jimmy Valvano at La Guardia Airport and did a deal with him.

"In that way, a lot of this is my fault. I did all of this—I created this whole industry. The funny thing, as you get deeper into it, this is almost creating part of Microsoft. Instead of Windows, this was 'Doors' or 'Shoes.' It's a billion-dollar industry now. Paying these coaches and owning the universities, a lot of money is spent on the idea. It went from $5,000 to signing these other coaches to much bigger deals to eventually getting John Thompson on the board of directors of Nike. That's how it has escalated."

"Picture this," Jim Valvano, who later won the 1983 National Championship at North Carolina State, told *Sports Illustrated* in 1988. "Two guys named Vaccaro and Valvano meeting at [New York's] La Guardia Airport. Vaccaro reaches into his briefcase. Puts a check on the table. Like we were putting a contract out on somebody. He says, 'I would like your team to wear this shoe.' I say, 'How much?' He says, 'No, I'll give you the shoes.' You got to remember, I was at Iona. We wore a lot of seconds. They didn't even have labels on them. I say, 'This can't be anything legal.' "

It was perfectly legal, though ethical questions would soon arise about whether Vaccaro—who continued to hold the Dapper Dan tournament—was steering high school players toward colleges that were affiliated with the swoosh. By 1980, Nike's entrée into college hoops, combined with the continued jogging boom, enabled the company to replace adidas as the number one sneaker company in the U.S. By 1984, more than 60 percent of Division I teams were wearing the swoosh, compared to roughly 6 percent who were in adidas. Some would even argue that the college basketball dynasty of the 1980s wasn't Georgetown, North Carolina, or Michigan, but Nike, which put its sneakers on the feet of five national champions during the decade. That was no small feat for Nike, which stood to gain millions in free advertising from its shoe exposure in the multimillion-dollar television orgy known as March Madness, a stage Knight would later describe as "better than any fashion runway in Paris."

In the meantime, the swoosh was rapidly becoming ubiquitous in the NBA. Of the 273 players in the NBA in 1984, 135 were under contract to wear Nikes. By contrast, adidas, which only eight years before had shod more than four-fifths of the NBA, had less than 7 percent of its players under contract and had effectively been boxed out of the basketball market altogether. The reason for this dramatic swing in loyalty among professional basketball players? Whereas adidas signed only superstars to lucrative shoe contracts, Nike started giving out generous sums to scrubs and stars alike. And while its chief competitor might hand out the occasional free tote bag to its client, Nike was flooding players and coaches with its bags and apparel, in addition to shoes.

"I've worn Converse, Pony, adidas, Brooks, and Nike," said Milwaukee Bucks guard Junior Bridgeman in 1984, "and Nike is the leader in fringe benefits. They sent me jogging shoes, tennis shoes, warmups, T-shirts, shorts, everything. They even sent my kids at basketball camp things like bags and key chains."

Nike's rise to preeminence in the NBA could not have happened at a more opportune time, for the 1980s would witness a confluence of two of the greatest cultural forces of the twentieth century: Michael Jordan and television. David Stern, who was installed as the league's commissioner in 1984, saw television possibilities in everything from All-Star Game halftime slam dunk contests to the league's lottery draft to, of course, Jordan, the most telegenic athlete of our time. From the start, nobody could replicate the young Jordan's contortions and airborne magic. "It must be God disguised as Michael Jordan," Larry Bird said after Jordan hung 63 points on his Boston Celtics in a 1986 playoff game.

To consumers, it hardly seemed to matter that Jordan played on some terrible teams (the Bulls would not even have a winning record until his fourth season). Watching him fly through the air resonated with the public, even those who cared little for basketball, in a way that the more pedestrian, less flashy styles of Bird and Magic Johnson—or anybody else for that matter—never would. In its first year of production, the new line of sneakers called the Air Jordan grossed $100 million. Despite Knight's distaste for advertising ("Hi, I'm Phil Knight and I don't believe in advertising," a Portland advertising executive recalls Knight once saying to him by way of introduction), Nike would pour millions into clever ad campaigns that featured Jordan and eventually other lesser-known NBA stars like Charles Barkley, Jordan's teammate Scottie Pippen, and David Robinson. The latter three individuals were certainly very good players well known to even casual NBA fans, but it was their shoes that made them celebrities. Soon Nike would hold screenings—screenings!—of its commercials for journalists.

That was the power of a basketball shoe. Several years later, even Jordan, by then perhaps the world's most recognizable face, would admit: "Nike has done such a good job promoting me that I've turned into a dream. In some ways it's taken me away from the game and turned me into an entertainer. To a lot of people, I'm just a person who stars in commercials."

Imagine, if you will, a company so powerful that its CEO could say "Michael Jordan without Nike won't mean a damn thing" and still be reasonably certain that the Chicago Bulls superstar would remain in the Nike fold. So powerful that a just-graduated college star felt empowered enough to declare—even before he had played a single professional game—that he "worked for Nike," not the NBA team that had made him the second pick in the 1992 draft. Or so powerful that its clients would be willing to absorb a major hit to their public image rather than wear the Reebok logo at the Olympics, an event that is supposed to transcend corporate pettiness.

Between 1980 and 1993, Nike's revenues grew from $270 million to just under $4 billion, more than $800 million of which were revenues from sales of basketball shoes. In 1992, Knight was named "the most powerful man in sports" by *The Sporting News*. Around the same time, a survey of Chinese schoolchildren placed Michael Jordan alongside Zhou Enlai, China's premier at the time, as the two greatest men in history. Though Nike still fervently cultivated its contrarian, Everyman image, it was no longer possible to think of Nike as the rebellious, grassroots company it once was—no matter how much attitude its commercials exuded or how many international sports federations it tweaked. As its influence widened to all corners of the globe, Nike was being increasingly viewed as a less-than-benevolent monolith, guilty of the same excesses, callousness, and arrogance other corporate behemoths like IBM and General Electric were. Critics spoke of Nike with the same vitriol that Knight and his early associates had once reserved for Adi Dassler and his elitist cronies.

For Nike, the early 1990s would at once be a period of unprecedented sales and immense backlash against the company. No longer a mere sneaker or corporation, Nike had become a social and, to a degree, even a political entity. In 1990, the public would be bombarded with stories of inner-city youths killing each other over basketball shoes. In several of the documented cases, blood was shed over Nikes (which, of course, wasn't such a surprise given the fact that an estimated 70 percent of all money spent on footwear by American boys between the ages of thirteen and eighteen was spent on the swoosh). Could the shoe companies, columnists asked, be indirectly responsible for this violence? By employing African-American superstars like Jordan, Pippen, and Barkley to pitch their $175 sneakers, were they unfairly targeting inner-city youths who could not afford them? In a diatribe directed at Spike Lee, whose Mars

Blackmon character had become almost as familiar as Michael Jordan himself, *New York Post* columnist Phil Mushnick wrote: "It's murder, gentlemen. No rhyme, nor reason, just murder. For sneakers. For jackets. Get it, Spike? Murder." Opined *Sports Illustrated*: "Something is very wrong with a society that has created an underclass that is slipping into economic and moral oblivion, an underclass in which pieces of rubber and plastic held together by shoelaces are sometimes worth more than a human life."

While other companies, including Reebok and adidas, had also come under fire for their alleged exploitation of young American consumers, only Nike would have to answer to charges of worker exploitation. In the late 1980s, Nike had closed its last U.S. footwear factory, in Saco, Maine, and taken its business overseas to Asia, where nonunionized labor worked for a small fraction of the $6.94 an hour that unionized American workers in the rubber-shoe industry averaged. And if any Asian workers showed an inclination toward unrest, the company would simply seek out more malleable employees. For example, when South Korean laborers gained the right to unionize and strike, Nike simply sought a cheaper labor pool elsewhere in Asia, eventually settling in places like Indonesia, where the average wage for a worker could be as low as fourteen cents an hour. With such inexpensive labor available to it, Nike cruised through the recession of the early 1990s with profits approaching $300 million. That such bounty came from the hands of cheap foreign labor further heightened the perception of Nike as just another cold, carnivorous multinational.

Meanwhile, Nike's own "laborers"—that is, its NBA endorsers—were pulling in such a healthy wage that some of them were brazenly threatening to sit out entire seasons. Shortly after graduating from Georgetown in the spring of

1992, Alonzo Mourning was selected by the Charlotte Hornets with the second pick of the NBA draft. The negotiations with Hornets management would quickly become nasty, the likelihood of resolution becoming less and less likely with each passing day. That, however, did not appear to concern Mourning, who had already signed a five-year $16 million (all of it guaranteed) contract with Nike as part of the company's "total career management program."

Under the terms of the deal, Nike would have complete control over an athlete's endorsements and marketing activities that did not relate to the team for which he played. Soon thereafter, Mourning would deliver his memorable line when asked who he intended to work for during the coming 1992–93 NBA season: "I work for Nike."

Of course, by the time Mourning made that declaration, the public had long grown accustomed to such proclamations and behavior by Nike athletes. The outcry against Nike's corporate arrogance had become deafening, even angry. How angry? Even Michael Jordan was not immune to it.

By the early 1990s, the athletic shoe wars had essentially been distilled to a two-company war between Nike and Reebok, though the competition for the soles of high-profile athletes was strictly a one-horse (i.e., Nike) affair. In 1990, Reebok, which had wrestled the top spot in the athletic shoe market away from Nike in the mid-1980s on the strength of its women's aerobics shoes, saw its revenues fall behind those of Nike for the first time in four years. Reebok CEO Paul Fireman decided it was finally time to vigorously court some marquee name athletes. It signed tennis star and 1989 French Open winner Michael Chang, promising Chicago

White Sox slugger Frank "The Big Hurt" Thomas, and All-Pro Dallas Cowboys running back Emmitt Smith.

It would also sign a few rising NBA stars like the Seattle SuperSonics' Shawn Kemp. However, it would barely make a dent into Nike's near-monopoly in the NBA. But in 1991, Reebok would execute a major coup when it attained exclusive rights to attire the greatest collection of basketball players to ever be assembled on one team.

As part of a multimillion-dollar deal Reebok had struck with the United States Olympic Committee, the members of the so-called Dream Team—which included Jordan, Magic Johnson, Larry Bird, and David Robinson to name just a few megastars—would be obligated to wear warmups bearing the Reebok logo when they received the gold medals they were certain to win at the 1992 Summer Olympics in Barcelona.

This, of course, infuriated many of the Dream Teamers, most notably Nike guys Jordan and Barkley. "We won't wear Reebok," Jordan said. Barkley declared that "he had two million reasons not to wear Reebok," referring to the number of dollars Nike was paying him to wear its shoes. Even after USOC officials informed the Dream Teamers they would not be permitted to participate in the medal ceremony, Jordan and Barkley refused to budge.

Nike executives were similarly alarmed by the USOC decree, but while no doubt moved by the loyalty of Jordan, Barkley, and their other swoosh brethren, they were caught in a tight spot. As the Nike clients became increasingly defiant in their stand against the USOC, especially in the days leading up to the gold medal ceremony, public opinion turned against the swoosh. In the past, the public had wholeheartedly embraced Nike for its stands against the establishment. To wage war against the NBA by refusing to let it use

Michael Jordan's likeness (as it had in 1988), or to tweak a bunch of stodgy tennis officials by tacitly endorsing the roguish behavior of a John McEnroe or Ilie Nastase conformed to a baby boomer's sense of cool. But to refuse to attend the medal ceremony out of loyalty to one's corporate sponsor did not. Certain moments were adjudged to transcend the marketplace, and even Michael Jordan. This was one of them.

In the end, Jordan, Barkley, and the other swoosh guys grudgingly wore the Reebok warmup suits. Determined to get the last word, however, Jordan rolled back the collar of the suit to obscure the Reebok name and draped a flag over the emblem. The letters poured into the Beaverton headquarters—roughly two hundred decrying Jordan's lack of patriotism for every supportive missive—and Knight reveled in the controversy. "That moment," Knight later said, referring to Jordan and Barkley placing Old Glory over the Reebok logo, "was by no means orchestrated from headquarters, but I thought it was great."

This was the power of Nike, where loyalty to company over country seemed to make perfect sense to the men who ran it and the celebrities who endorsed its products. "We see a natural evolution . . . dividing the world into their athletes and ours," Knight would tell the *New York Times* years later. "When the U.S. played Brazil in the World Cup, I rooted for Brazil because it was a Nike team. America was adidas."

"Five years from now maybe I will say we should have gotten Shaq," Knight said not long after O'Neal signed with Reebok. "You roll the dice and you take your chances. After all, I am the guy who said a college player named Magic Johnson's professional future was in doubt because he was a player without a position. But remember that we didn't have

Magic and we didn't have Bird [both of whom were Converse clients], and we still did pretty well."

In fact, in July 1998, a little more than five years after Knight rued the loss of O'Neal to his most reviled competitor, Reebok, citing sluggish sales of its basketball line, announced that it would not renew the contract of its onetime would-be savior. It was a staggering event considering that O'Neal, at twenty-six, was not only one of the game's most dominant players but also one of its most recognizable figures, a player whose celebrity and marketability the NBA was undoubtedly banking on as it prepared to make the transition to the post–Michael Jordan era.

Ordinarily such a momentous event would be cause for celebration at Nike headquarters, a confirmation of the earlier suspicion among the company's executives that Shaq wasn't Nike material, that he didn't embody the essence of cool that, say, Jordan, Charles Barkley, or Scottie Pippen had. Alas, it was not a time for jubilation. Not at all.

As they had in the early 1990s, protectionist groups were again decrying the fact that Nike did not have a single factory in the United States, though it held a better than 40 percent share of the domestic market for athletic shoes and apparel. But this time, human rights groups had joined the debate and were leveling far more serious allegations at Nike than had any previous group. They painted pictures of Nike factories in China that were akin to forced labor camps, where children as young as thirteen were being beaten and forced to work for wages below China's already absurdly low minimum wage levels. They told shocking stories of Vietnamese workers being hospitalized after their supervisors forced them to run laps because they had failed to meet their production quotas. They pointed to footage of Knight answering "No," when noted filmmaker Michael

Moore asked the Nike CEO if he was bothered by the fact that fourteen-year-olds were working in his company's Indonesian factories.

From a strictly economic standpoint, things were starting to come apart for the swoosh as well. After another period of seemingly runaway growth from 1993 to 1997, when revenues increased from $3.8 billion to over $9 billion, Nike's sales, not to mention its already somewhat sullied reputation, started to go into free fall in 1998. On the same day Reebok said it was cutting Shaq loose, Nike—which had already laid off 7 percent of its workforce only a few months earlier—revealed it had lost nearly $68 million for the fourth quarter of its 1998 fiscal year. It was the first quarterly loss for the company in thirteen years, and with the Asian economy in the throes of collapse, even bigger losses appeared on the horizon. Less than a week later, NBA commissioner David Stern announced that the league's owners would begin their long-threatened lockout of the league's 350 players. With Jordan already having strongly hinted at retirement even before the start of the lockout, Nike faced, for the first time since Knight pulled out his first waffle shoe, an uncertain future.

Nike wasn't alone. Converse, which as recently as 1996 had paid New York Knicks forward Larry Johnson $800,000 per year to star in those famously clever "Grandmama" commercials, was now giving Johnson only free gear to wear its shoes. In fact, the same company that only a decade before had shod the feet of Dr. J, Magic, and Larry now had only five NBA players on its payroll, three of them rookies. Reebok, in addition to severing ties to Shaq, had also axed such big names as Glenn "Big Dog" Robinson of the Milwaukee Bucks and had seen its roster of NBA players go from more than 130 in 1995 to less than twenty. Among heavily promoted signature lines of shoes named for stars like Grant Hill (a Fila client) and Shawn Kemp (Reebok), only the surefire Air Jordans weren't a flop. "We don't have a lot of heroes out there," said Josie Esquivel, an analyst with Morgan Stanley Dean Witter and longtime watcher of the sneaker wars.

But the search for heroes, for that elusive "air apparent" to Michael Jordan, would rage on, more intense than ever. With the NBA draft classes getting increasingly younger—since 1995, eleven players have been drafted straight out of high school, compared to only three in the forty-seven years before that—shoe companies were stepping up their efforts to find would-be Jordans at a younger and younger age. With much of the shoe companies' focus turning toward high school gyms and the local city playground, it was the perfect time for an old hand at the game, Sonny Vacarro, to reassert himself in the war for the soles of young athletes.

CHAPTER 3

Sonny and George

As an assistant coach at Villanova and the University of Maryland back in the 1960s, George Raveling was one of the pioneers of modern recruiting. At the time, most college programs spent minimum time on player procurement, usually scouting the high schools of their home city, relying on friends in high school coaching ranks to send along recruits.

The head coach at, say, Villanova would scour Philadelphia's public and Catholic leagues, maybe look to a few South Jersey high schools, and hope a coach out of state might call with a tip. Recruiting trips that required more than a hour drive were unusual. Coaches often were home in time for dinner with their families.

There were no national scouting services, no national prep tournaments, and no summer talent camps. July was a good month to schedule a couple weeks on the Jersey shore, not jet around the country in search of long-armed seventeen-year-olds.

Because of that, few fans and even fewer media paid attention to recruiting. No 900 lines, no Internet, not even any local news accounts. Recruits signed with little or no fanfare. Even the best prospects would cause only the slightest public stir.

When University of Kansas coach Phog Allen, in one of the boldest recruiting moves ever, convinced Philadelphia prep standout Wilt Chamberlain to leave the East Coast and head to the Plains it happened with minimum fanfare. Even as Chamberlain tore up the competition on the Kansas freshman team, causing large crowds to flock to the usually ignored games, Allen barely acknowledged Chamberlain's existence. Asked by the media about this star 7-footer on the freshman team, the legendary coach merely shrugged and said, "If he's as good as you say, I hope he comes out for the varsity."

In the dark ages of recruiting, George Raveling wanted to turn the light on. He was one of the first coaches who spent considerable effort trying to upgrade his program's recruiting efforts. Then, as now, the most valuable commodity in the recruiting game is information, and Raveling stockpiled it.

He worked the phone to gain scouting information from contacts throughout the country. In his office he kept a detailed file on nearly every player he heard of, jotting down on index cards key information about a player. He wanted to know not only whether a point guard could go to his left, or how soft a big man's hands were, but the names of parents, siblings, and pets. Who was his coach? Did he have a girlfriend? What school's pennant hung on his bedroom wall? Who was going to influence his college decision?

It mattered not whether the school Raveling was working at would recruit a player in, say, Denver; he wanted the information. You just never knew when it might pay off. As he enjoyed increased success as a recruiter, it didn't take long before Raveling's index cards and horizonless system of identifying prospects became the rage.

Not surprisingly, in the course of finding reliable scouts and sources in high school basketball, Raveling came upon a hoops junkie from Pittsburgh named Sonny Vaccaro.

In 1965, Vaccaro had just started the Dapper Dan Round-ball Classic in his native Pittsburgh. Then just a twenty-five-year-old with a lot of energy, Vaccaro's life was in transition. Growing up in the hardscrabble mining town of Trafford, Pennsylvania, he had been a star athlete. He was a good enough pitcher to be drafted by the Pittsburgh Pirates and a fast enough tailback to be offered a scholarship to play football at Kentucky. Vaccaro decided to play football, although a lackluster academic transcript sent him to junior college first.

A back injury killed his playing career, although Youngstown State offered a scholarship if he became a student assistant coach in football and basketball. Vaccaro accepted and later moved on to Wichita State as an assistant basketball coach.

Vaccaro's natural recruiting charm worked for Shockers coach Ralph Miller until a car accident derailed Vaccaro's career. Now back in Pittsburgh, the Roundball, as he still calls it, became his passion. It started small, with local players forming two all-star teams, and Vaccaro hustling around the city looking for funding and sponsors. A year later he took a job as a physical education teacher and assistant basketball, football, and baseball coach at Trafford High School, his alma mater, which gave him a base salary and a foothold in the community.

He worked at Trafford during the day and on his Roundball Classic at night. In 1965 the Classic sold out the Pittsburgh Civic Arena, and quickly became a spring staple for the area. A few years later he began running basketball camps in Silver Spring, Pennsylvania. As he looked to expand both his camp and the Roundball to players throughout Pennsylvania, the East Coast, and, eventually, the nation, he developed his own network of coaches, scouts, and movers and shakers.

Hence Raveling's index cards and Vaccaro's network became fast friends. The two gym rats talked on the phone endlessly, comparing notes, news, gossip, and their own dreams of making it big. They ran into each other at high school games, like the night in 1965 they sat together at Maryland's Cole Fieldhouse and watched 7-foot Lew Alcindor lead Power Memorial of New York against Maryland's DeMatha Catholic. Rav wanted Alcindor to come to Maryland and lead the Terrapins to the national title. Vaccaro wanted the big guy to play in the Roundball, giving the young tournament the ultimate in credibility.

Alcindor said no to both invitations, choosing to stay home instead of taking a weekend in Pittsburgh, and heading to UCLA for college. The two just moved to the next prospect. And they became the best of friends.

When Raveling would be in Pittsburgh recruiting, he often took up residence in Vaccaro's parents' home, sometimes even sleeping in Sonny's bed. One day Sonny's younger brother, Jimmy, who now runs the sportsbook at the Mirage Casino in Las Vegas, peeked into Sonny's room expecting his brother and found Raveling sleeping under the covers. As Raveling recalls, Jimmy called out, "Mom, some black guy's sleeping in Sonny's bed."

As both moved up in the world of basketball they were a constant. They helped each other find young talent and introduced each other to recruiting contacts. And by having

Vaccaro's ear, Raveling had some recruiting juice that all kids wanted, a shot at playing in the Roundball.

It was no surprise, then, that when Vaccaro took his job at Nike in 1978 and began signing up college coaches, Raveling, then at Washington State, was one of the first to agree to a deal. When Rav was an Olympics assistant in 1984, he introduced Vaccaro to Michael Jordan. And when Vaccaro was married in 1984, "There was no one more logical to be best man than George," Sonny says. "He was the one person I'd gone through basketball with to that point."

How times have changed.

Today, they work not with each other, but against each other. Professionally they are bitter rivals, with Vaccaro running the grassroots basketball operations at adidas and Raveling doing the same at Vaccaro's old place, Nike. Personally, although only Sonny will admit it, they are cutthroat enemies.

The two former friends and confidants are locked in a heated test of wills, using millions of shoe company dollars to out-recruit, one-up, and embarrass each other in a competition everyone in basketball is watching. They fight over young players to stock their summer camps. Try to put on better all-star games. Battle over which AAU team or high school squad to outfit with their respective gear. Call each other names in coaching circles. It's the nastiest feud in all of basketball and your average fan has never heard of it.

"I just don't like George Raveling," says Vaccaro. "I don't like what he does or what he says or the hypocrisy in his life. He disgusts me."

"People just keep bringing it up and bringing it up," says Raveling. " 'Oh, you were the man at his wedding, now you don't speak.' Well, hell, people marry each other and then don't speak. That's life. It's human personalities and differences of opinion along the way. That's why you have di-vorce in America because people can't agree."

The breakup of a friendship would, indeed, be easy to shrug off as a natural course of human relations, if the resulting feud wasn't being fought with fourteen-year-old basketball studs as pawns. The rivalry has caused amateur basketball to spin out of control. Players, high schools, and traveling teams are hotly contested for, with sponsorship deals bid and counterbid, partly because the companies want them, but partly because Raveling and Vaccaro seemingly will do almost anything to best each other. More than just a battle between two multinational corporations fighting over shares of the lucrative sports shoe and apparel market, the war ripping apart youth basketball is personal.

"It's Sonny vs. George," says Gary DeCeasare, head coach of adidas-sponsored St. Raymond's High School in the Bronx. "And it's insane."

"Do I want to beat Nike?" says Vaccaro of his professional competition with the swoosh. "Yes. They're the biggest and the best. But this one's personal, see. This one's like, 'Okay, throw the ball up. Let's play the game.'"

Raveling laughs at his old friend's fighting words. Vaccaro grew up in that mining town in the hills outside Pittsburgh and has been everything from a pool hustler to a skid row Vegas gambler. The only thing he likes more than a good fight is challenging someone to it. Raveling won't bite at the taunts of the man he used to call "Pear."

"I don't have any rivalries with Sonny," he says. "Personally, I think this thing is overdone."

Hardly.

The genesis of the feud dates to the 1990 recruitment of highly decorated prep star Ed O'Bannon. The gifted 6-9 forward from suburban Los Angeles had signed with UNLV in the fall prior to his senior year of high school, but with the stipulation that if the Runnin' Rebels were placed on any type of NCAA probation, he was free to go elsewhere.

When Jerry Tarkanian's Rebels program was slapped by the NCAA in the spring of 1990, just as O'Bannon's senior year was ending, his recruiting process was suddenly reopened. Vaccaro, who was then at Nike, was very close with the O'Bannon family. Ed, as well as younger brother, Charles, were always welcome at Vaccaro's Pacific Palisades condo and Vaccaro got along well with their parents and the coaches at Mater Dei High School, which Nike sponsored.

Raveling was the head coach of USC at the time and in dire need of an impact recruit—particularly an impact local recruit, who was also considering UCLA. In recruiting battles against its mighty crosstown rival Bruins, USC and Raveling were something like zero for life. O'Bannon was the signature recruit that could change that.

Raveling, who had moved from Washington State to Iowa in 1984 before coming to USC in 1987, was still the tenacious recruiter of his youth. In 1992 he would earn national publicity when it became public that he had written California high school stud Avondre Jones nine hundred recruiting letters in an effort to show his commitment to the player. By the time the Trojans got Jones's signature, Raveling had started another trend. Assistant coaches throughout the country began wearing recruits' local postmen ragged with correspondence. (Raveling's onetime record was easily eclipsed in 1996 when USC's new coaching regime led by Henry Bibby sent more mail than Ed McMahon. Setting the pace was maniacal assistant David Miller, who on two occasions sent five hundred handwritten, hand-addressed recruiting letters in a single day to Kevin Augustine, a point guard from Santa Ana (California) Mater Dei. Augustine signed with USC that fall. When all was said and done, Augustine estimated he received nearly four thousand letters from USC, the vast majority of which he never opened.)

In 1990, O'Bannon was the recruit that Raveling had to have. Vaccaro says Raveling called him up and asked him to influence O'Bannon's decision and steer him to USC.

"Losing him to Vegas had been okay," Vaccaro says. "But George couldn't lose him to UCLA."

In July, Vaccaro says he met with Raveling and their then mutual friend, Georgetown coach John Thompson, and Rav begged him to send O'Bannon his way. Vaccaro took umbrage at the request.

Just two years earlier he had been at the center of a storm of controversy when he paid a visit to Chesapeake, Virginia, the hometown of top recruit Alonzo Mourning, on the eve of the spring national letter of intent signing period. Although it was a dead period when college coaches were forbidden by NCAA rules to contact recruits, Vaccaro, living outside the Association's regulations, could speak freely with the 6-10 prep All-America, although he denies he ever saw Mourning that day.

Still, when later that week Mourning chose Georgetown over Maryland and Georgia Tech, critics howled that Vaccaro had helped recruit Mourning to the Hoyas because of Georgetown's lucrative contractual arrangement with Nike and the fact that Thompson was not only a member of the shoe company's board of directors, but at the time a close personal friend of Vaccaro's.

Vaccaro vehemently denied he did any recruiting, saying he was there merely to make sure Mourning was set to attend the Roundball. He insisted he would never steer a player to a particular school.

At the time, Raveling came out and defended Vaccaro, saying, "I've known him longer than anyone. If Sonny was steering players, he'd be steering them to the guy he's known the longest and needs them the most—me."

Now, just two years later, Vaccaro says he was shocked to hear Raveling ask for just such a favor. Vaccaro says he looked at Thompson, shook his head and said, "You and I know I didn't deliver Alonzo to you. Now George wants me to do what I've told the world I never do."

A few days later Vaccaro says Raveling approached him again seeking help, this time with tears in his eyes. Then Vaccaro received a telegram stating: "Desperately need your help. Please don't let me down on this one. George Raveling." (Vaccaro keeps a copy of the telegram to share with reporters.)

O'Bannon, of course, picked UCLA over USC. Charles followed three years later. In 1995, with Ed a fifth-year senior and Charles a sophomore, they led the Bruins to their eleventh national championship and first since the John Wooden era of the 1960s and 1970s. By then Raveling was out at USC, a combination of never getting the Trojans on track and a terrible 1994 car accident that affected his health.

Raveling admits he hoped Vaccaro would provide O'Bannon with a good word about USC, but he disputes that he ever begged for help and said he doesn't remember the telegram. At the very least, he says, he wishes Vaccaro had remained neutral. Instead, Raveling is convinced, Vaccaro told the O'Bannon family that Raveling would never win at USC and that UCLA would be a better option.

Whether or not Vaccaro steers players to particular colleges has been a source of debate since he rose to influence. Certainly his close, personal relationships with so many top stars leaves the possibility open. When a top young player gets close to Vaccaro, he is treated as a member of the family, doted upon by Sonny and his wife, Pam. One of the class of 1999's top players, Maryland's Dermarr Johnson, recalls meeting Vaccaro for the first time. He had just arrived at adidas' ABCD Camp as a sixteen-year-old sophomore-to-be, but was already regarded by scout Bob Gibbons as one of the best players in the country.

"Sonny came over to where I was standing, gave me a hug and a kiss on the cheek, and said, 'Welcome,' " Johnson says. "I just laughed. I was like, 'Who is this guy?' "

However, because Vaccaro no longer controls many schools—adidas has only eight colleges under contract—there is no way he could place his best players along shoe affiliation lines. Consider the college choices of two of his favorite adidas players in 1999. Johnson, a slashing 6-9 small forward, chose Cincinnati, over Connecticut and Maryland, all Nike schools. Alaska's Carlos Boozer, Jr., a bruising 6-9 power forward, picked Duke over St. John's, both flagship Nike programs, and over the adidas-sponsored UCLA program.

Still it stands to reason shoes play some factor.

"Every adidas kid we recruited this summer, something happened to make it difficult," said one coach who tried to recruit adidas players to his Nike program. "The four kids we signed early were Nike players. I have no idea if that's a coincidence or not. I just found it interesting. I'm going to recruit players who are talented, good students, and good people. I'm not going to recruit players based on what kind of shoe they wear. I don't think Sonny hurt us at all, I'm not saying that. I like Sonny. I just found it interesting."

Certainly if Vaccaro was regularly steering players to certain schools, he would have been run out of the business long ago. However, he does wield a quiet, behind-the-scenes influence. Coaches who are close to him often ask for particular housing assignments at the adidas ABCD Camp or Magic's Roundball Classic, looking for Vaccaro to put a player who is already verbally committed to their program in the same hotel room with another top prospect they are recruiting in hopes that a friendship is struck.

Vaccaro is also still that great source of information that Raveling found so useful twenty-five years ago. His personal relationship with players allows him to know their families, their backgrounds, their hopes and dreams. Wise assistant coaches pick his brain for clues on the best way to recruit a kid.

If a player is shy, he might be turned off by too much mail or long phone calls. Others desire the attention recruiting brings. Some have overbearing fathers, some have no parents at all but a minister who calls the shots. Vaccaro usually knows the secrets to success.

Some coaches also say Vaccaro subtly directs recruiting traffic, telling coaches where to recruit and where to lay off. Say a coach close to Vaccaro has a local prospect he really needs. Vaccaro will tell other programs to back off and let the kid go in exchange for a favor in the future.

"Sonny will say to a coach, 'Hey, let that kid alone, Jimmy really needs him,' " said one ACC coach. "He'll protect you. It's all part of it. That's why you stay on good terms with Sonny."

But the outright dealing of a player? Obviously when his then best friend Raveling needed a player, Vaccaro didn't come through. And from there, things between the two went downhill.

In 1991, still smarting from O'Bannon's enrollment at UCLA, Raveling became active in the National Association for Basketball Coaches campaign to reform the summer recruiting season that Vaccaro had helped create in the 1980s. Raveling—who by this time wasn't speaking to Vaccaro— argued that the proliferation of talent camps and traveling summer teams had brought a "sleazy" atmosphere to recruiting and if the game was going to continue to thrive, it needed to be cleaned up.

"It's a cancer which needs to be cut out of the game," said Raveling in 1991. "Kids are flying all over the country to attend specialized camps and they're being influenced by certain people to go to these camps. As a result of these summer activities, college coaches are having to deal with these middle people. The summertime is the most unregulated aspect of basketball. It's no wonder you see increasing abuses taking place. When you leave the doors unlocked and the windows open in the summer, some of the wrong people will get into the house."

Raveling was more than willing to talk to the media about "street people" and "unsavory elements" and left little doubt he was referring to his onetime friend. Always a great quote, Raveling became a favorite of the basketball media. In 1994 he was even honored by the United States Basketball Writers Association for "rendering special service to the USBWA." The group described him as "an accessible and thoughtful individual in his dealings with the media." It was no surprise he was extensively quoted on the subject of summer basketball and shoe company involvement in the game in newspapers and magazines around the country. He routinely offered gems such as, "In the summer, everybody's on vacation. That's the time to rob the house."

Vaccaro never doubted why there was a sudden attack on the system he helped create and run.

"The O'Bannon thing would have passed over time," says Vaccaro about why he and Raveling don't speak almost ten years later. "What did it was when George feared he was going to be fired by Southern Cal and campaigned for the executive directorship of the NABC and stood up on his soapbox. That's when the dislike in me for this man turned into hate.

"George has a very, very fine way of accusing everybody of everything without ever identifying the problem or taking these people to task. The worst person in our society is the accuser. Those people are without redemption and that's the way I feel about George Raveling. He accuses everybody of everything and does nothing to stop it.

"In fact, now he's condoning what he discredited."

Raveling's attacks on the summer basketball influence peddlers continued until 1995, when now out of coaching, he took over Vaccaro's old position with Nike as head of grassroots basketball.

In 1992, Nike sent shock waves through amateur basketball when they fired Vaccaro. Why, remains one of the better kept secrets in basketball. The company refuses to provide a reason for firing a man who assisted in their dominance of the lucrative basketball market and will not comment at all on any aspect of Vaccaro's dismissal. For his part, Vaccaro says it was never explained to him, either, and he remains puzzled by it to this day.

"They fired me and I can't explain it," Vaccaro said. "They fired me. The biggest mistake they ever made, you can quote me on this, was firing me. It has literally cost them millions and millions of dollars to compete against me. So I can't answer why they did things."

Indeed, Vaccaro was down, but never out. He managed to keep the rights to his Dapper Dan game and his ABCD Camp and as he and his wife, Pam, opened a marketing firm in Los Angeles, he kept his hand in basketball by running both.

In 1993, under the sponsorship of Converse, Vaccaro ran the ABCD Camp on the campus of Eastern Michigan University in Ypsilanti. He did it during the same week as the Nike All-America Camp. A year later, he moved it to Irvine, California.

Suddenly the Nike Camp had competition and Vaccaro was landing his share of the top prep players. Nike needed an insider to compete. They turned to Raveling.

"They never thought my camp would get off the ground," says Vaccaro. "The camp is the battleground. That's the one [thing] that's very obvious to [media] people and the kids. They can buy the whole Brazilian soccer team but they can't beat me in a week-long basketball camp."

By the time Raveling came on board at Nike, Vaccaro had taken a full-time position at adidas and the stage was set. Raveling, once a critic of summer basketball and shoe companies, now controls the largest pot of gold in youth basketball—a reported $3.5 million budget—which covers high school and AAU team sponsorship as well as funding for certain tournaments. That does not include Nike's nearly two hundred deals with college coaches and programs.

Nike's deal with Raveling easily outdistances Vaccaro's $1 million budget at adidas.

With thousands of kids in his grassroots programs, Raveling is now every bit the basketball middleman Vaccaro is. If he's less popular among college coaches, it's only because he lacks the effusive personality of Sonny.

Although Vaccaro loves pointing out how Raveling has

changed his tune now that he's got a paycheck riding on it—in the 1995 adidas ABCD media packet Vaccaro even reprinted a 1992 article from the *Des Moines Register* where Raveling ripped shoe-company-sponsored summer camps—Raveling insists he is still the same man and that what Nike does, although outwardly similar to adidas, is actually very different.

"There's this myth out there that I've changed," he says. "I've only changed my employment, not my philosophy. I still say summer basketball is the most unregulated aspect of the game. We're trying to be part of the solution, not the problem."

In fact, although Vaccaro is the first to admit that adidas is in the game to sell shoes, Raveling says Nike's concern is much more altruistic. "We provide a positive role in the lives of young athletes," Raveling says about Nike grassroots efforts. "We are involved in the summer because we see a sense of obligation to provide events and resources that allow young people to compete successfully in the summer at the highest level and to provide them with the footwear and apparel to excel at the maximum level.

"What we say at Nike is, 'We have an obligation to grow the game, to take it to the next level of excellence,' " Raveling continued. "And I think we take that mission seriously."

While Raveling says Nike has noble intentions, the objects of his affections, the young players excelling with the best footwear and apparel, see it differently.

"They run camps because they are basically trying to get you down for a shoe contract," said Kevin Gaines, a freshman at Michigan who attended the 1998 Nike Camp prior to his senior year at Clark High School in Las Vegas. "It's for the guys who are going to college and hopefully the NBA.

Then [once you are in the NBA] they'll get you down for a shoe contract."

Is this the positive message Nike is trying to get across?

"The thing about trying to find [the next] Michael Jordan, that's the biggest joke at Nike," says Raveling. "Everybody laughs about that. That's all we ever hear.

"There's a lot of myths out there," Raveling said. "A lot of times we get a lot [more] credit than we deserve. I think people think we sit around in a room in the basement with the war boards dreaming up all these ways we can dominate things."

It's clear now, however, that Vaccaro and Raveling, Nike and adidas are locked in a battle for the souls, if not the soles, of the best high school players in the nation. Raveling admits that his job at Nike has effectively ended his friendship with Vaccaro forever, although he claims he possesses no ill will. Raveling says he believes in the power of reconciliation, something he may have learned from one of his heroes, Dr. Martin Luther King, Jr.

In a Forrest Gump–like brush with history, Raveling, a Washington, D.C., native, was working a security detail during the civil rights march on Washington and was standing just behind Dr. King when he gave his famous "I Have a Dream" speech. When King finished his rousing talk, he turned around and Raveling asked if he could have King's speech. The Nobel Prize winner complied, handing the few pages to Raveling, who today keeps the historic document in a safe. "At the time, we had no idea it was going to be such a famous speech," says Raveling.

"I tried twice to make up with Sonny," Raveling says. "Once I had a meeting with him in Las Vegas. We sat down [and talked] and I thought it was solved. I met with Sonny another time in Seattle and I thought it was solved.

"And it probably would have been solved if I hadn't taken the job with Nike. I think we probably would have been back as friends. But then, when I took the job at Nike, although I don't know, I never had a chance to talk to Sonny, but I think maybe Sonny took it personally. That it was a personal affront to him. I really don't know."

Vaccaro says he knows. He considers Raveling's actions since the O'Bannon recruitment to be obvious, first as vocal critic of what he does, then as a competitor in that very business. Raveling's goal since O'Bannon signed with UCLA, Vaccaro is convinced, has been to beat him at his own game, something Vaccaro revels in preventing.

"I've never been more happy with the success we've had [at adidas]," said Vaccaro. "Even signing Michael [Jordan] wasn't as enjoyable to me as what I do today. Kobe and Antoine [Walker] and these kids have given me a special direction.

"I embarrassed Nike," Vaccaro continued. "Kobe and I embarrassed them in front of the world. They're spending all their money, and I found this gem."

Raveling denies he is motivated by Vaccaro, says he isn't in a competition with his old friend, and insists that Nike isn't concerned with adidas. Yes, he wants to run the best camp possible, but not because of Sonny. In fact, he says he gives virtually no thought to Sonny Vaccaro. If it weren't for the media, he says, it would be no thought.

"I don't have any rivalries with Sonny," Raveling says. "I can't speak for Sonny. I think Sonny has done a lot for basketball at the high school and college level. I don't have anything against Sonny and I mean that from the bottom of my heart. Sonny might have something against me, but I don't have anything against Sonny.

"I'm sixty-one years old and I'm setting a goal to live fifteen more years and I can't afford to be stressed out worrying about Sonny and adidas. I don't know how this thing keeps getting promoted about me and Sonny. Personally I think it's overdone because I don't hate Sonny. I don't dislike Sonny. If God came down here right now I'd say right in front of Him just what I said to you. I like Sonny. I respect him. I don't have any hatred in my heart for Sonny Vaccaro and I mean that sincerely."

Vaccaro isn't buying that.

"George, he has changed drastically in my eyes," Vaccaro says. "I thought the world of him. He was with me in the early years. He was my best man. It took me a long time to understand George Raveling. He just speaks so many different languages.

"I always run into him. I always see him. But I have no desire to speak to him. He is one of the few human beings I don't care if I ever see again and I know I will probably never speak to the rest of my life."

Although Raveling says he doesn't pay attention to Vaccaro, he is as quick to criticize adidas operations and decisions as Vaccaro is to hammer Nike. He likes to mention that he fields calls from adidas-sponsored high schools and traveling teams who are fed up with Vaccaro.

"I can think of a traveling team [that called]—I won't name the name—and they said, 'I was talking with this guy from such and such team and he's really unhappy and he'd like to be with Nike.' Or sometimes they will call us and say, 'We were promised this or that and we never got it.' "

He mocks adidas' decision to give Tracy McGrady a $12 million endorsement deal, complete with payments to prep coach Joel Hopkins and talent scout Alvis Smith.

"It's all money down the drain," Raveling says, with glee. "We weren't going to do that. We weren't gonna do it.

So if they wanna make a bad business decision, that's up to them. We just didn't think it was a good business decision for us."

Vaccaro says Raveling is a man who subscribes to his own form of revisionist history. "For him to say they didn't want McGrady is funny," Vaccaro says. "The irony of this thing with McGrady was there was a courtship. They flew McGrady up to Portland and took him to NikeTown. They had him up there for three days. They brought Alvis [Smith] and Joel [Hopkins] in. They flew to [McGrady's agent Arn] Tellem's office [in Los Angeles] and basically discussed contracts. So there was a courtship. They wanted Tracy. There was a bidding situation. So Tracy benefited because the price was higher than what it really would have been."

And when asked about some of Nike's signature prep-to-pro players, like Detroit Pistons rookie Korleone Young, in 1998 Vaccaro was quick to criticize. "He's not very good, that's what everybody says," Vaccaro says. "He's a waste of time for Nike." Not that Vaccaro is one to hold a grudge with a player. Just a year after ripping Young to the media throughout the country, he invited him to the formal banquet of the 1999 Magic's Roundball Classic and picked up the cost of Young's meal.

Though he denies the rivalry, Raveling's desire to distance himself from Vaccaro has even taken a ridiculous twist. In 1996, Raveling told *Basketball Times* publisher Larry Donald that he would increase Nike's advertising deal with the monthly tabloid on one condition: Donald accept no advertising from adidas. That included dropping the highly popular one-page column Vaccaro writes for the magazine in space paid for by adidas.

"He said he would make it worth my effort, he'd buy out all of adidas' advertising space," said Donald, who declined

Raveling's offer. Nike, a longtime advertiser in *BT,* hasn't bought space since.

It doesn't surprise Vaccaro that Raveling wants to downplay the rivalry and usually shuns questions about his former pal.

"There's nothing to talk about," says Vaccaro. "What can they say, except that I kick their ass."

CHAPTER 4

This Little Piggie Went to Nike

Twelve inches. That is the distance between Myron Piggie, Nike pitchman and AAU coach, and Myron Piggie, inmate in the federal penitentiary.

Piggie, who today is one of Nike's most influential summer league coaches, was a self-employed painter and a simple crack cocaine dealer in the summer of 1987 when federal Drug Enforcement Administration agents began work with one of the best undercover informants to hit the drug-infested streets of middle America.

At about 8:30 P.M. on September 17, DEA agents were preparing to leave the home of their informant when the phone rang. It was Myron Piggie and he was calling to say he had "the package" that the informant was waiting for. The package contained three ounces of crack and Piggie wanted $3,600 for its contents. Piggie told the informant he and his brother Brian were just a few blocks away and would be pulling up in a matter of minutes.

The agents had to scramble. They weren't prepared for this deal, but it was the one they had been waiting for. Piggie had been known as an area crack hustler and, working with the informant, the DEA had made three previous crack buys from Piggie. The buys—3.66 grams on June 22, 6.03 grams on July 1, and 9.6 grams on July 31—were small potatoes compared to this purchase. By federal law, anyone convicted of delivering two ounces of crack goes to the penitentiary for a mandated minimum of ten years. If Piggie delivered, he was headed to the Big House.

As promised, the Piggies arrived a few minutes later, Myron riding shotgun in Brian's red 1985 Chevrolet Cavalier. As the police informant walked from her apartment, Myron jumped out of the passenger seat of the Cavalier and showed off a bag he said had the informant's "package." The woman told Myron she would go inside to get the money and after she ducked behind closed doors, the DEA sprung into action.

DEA special agent David Major gave the signal to other agents in the area to "take them down." In a flash, Agent Carl Hicks pulled his car in behind the Cavalier. Special Agent Ronald Wright raced in from the opposite direction, hoping to pin the Cavalier against the curb. But Wright made a mistake. He stopped his car too far away from Piggie to hem his car in.

Twelve inches.

"If Ron had pulled twelve inches closer to Piggie's car, we would have had him right there," one federal agent at the scene said. "But in the rush to get out of the car and apprehend the Piggies he gave Piggie enough room to angle out of there."

As Brian Piggie jammed his foot to the gas pedal, Wright pulled his gun and yelled "Police, don't move." Brian Piggie paid no attention and as he spun out of the area, his car rolled over Wright's lower leg. Wearing Nikes (the DEA, ironically, once had a discount buying program with Nike) offered Wright no protection and the weight of the car left him with two broken bones in his foot and ankle. Injured, he couldn't give chase.

The Cavalier took off down Armour Boulevard. Special Agent Major pulled up, intentionally hitting Brian Piggie's car on the driver's side. The collision sent the car spinning before it took off at top speed again, passing Wright, who was sprawled out on the ground. Wright fired two shots, one hitting the car in the bumper, just barely missing the gas tank.

The DEA agents, worried more about Wright's injuries than catching Myron and Brian Piggie, didn't pursue the brothers. The Piggies sped away and it wasn't until several days later that the police picked them up. When they did, police took a bag from Myron Piggie containing a fully loaded six-shot .38 caliber revolver.

According to court records, police also reported that Myron Piggie bragged that "if he found out where the informant is now living, he is going to kill her."

A federal grand jury indicted the Piggie brothers— Myron faced six counts, Brian three, for assorted drug charges and "assaulting a special agent of the Drug Enforcement Administration with a dangerous weapon." On November 30, Myron entered a plea agreement, acknowledging he had sold crack to the informant in the June 22 deal. In exchange, prosecutors dropped the remaining charges. On January 5, 1988, he was sentenced to four months in a community treatment center and was placed on federal probation for five years. As is customary, Piggie was ordered never to carry a weapon again and told he'd see the jail time he was avoiding if he was arrested while on parole.

"At the hearing where he got probation, he turned

around and he apologized and made a big scene crying and everything, saying he really felt bad that I was hurt," Agent Wright said. "He told me he had learned his lesson and was really sorry. I took it for what it was worth, but I don't know how sincere he was. The funny part is that if we had gotten him at the informant's house, he would have been headed for prison, no question. So by driving away, his brother not only broke my leg, he kept Myron out of prison for ten years. That should have been a Nike commercial because his wheel was spinning right on my ankle and it burnt a hole right through the Nike. I guess their escape was pretty fortuitous for Myron. But I believed him when he said he learned that lesson."

Within twelve months, the lesson must have been forgotten.

Early in the morning of February 12, 1989, Piggie and several other men got into a shoving match inside the Epicurean Lounge, a popular nightspot in South Kansas City. Employees of the bar bounced the troublemakers out, but two bar patrons, off-duty Kansas City police officers Daniel Billberry and Frederick Lewis, felt further trouble brewing.

Billberry and Lewis walked outside and saw two of the men speeding off in a blue Cadillac, then watched as the car turned around and headed back toward the bar. From the southeast corner of the bar, the officers saw Myron Piggie pull out an automatic pistol and start shooting at the Cadillac. Billberry and Lewis pulled their guns, announced they were police officers, and ordered Piggie to drop his gun.

Piggie would have none of that. Instead, he started shooting at the two officers, then took off running. "These guys were only thirty feet away and he missed wildly," one officer said. "But he was sure as hell trying to get them."

On foot, Piggie headed up 75th Street. As the two officers chased him, he turned and shot at them again. Piggie was darting through backyards in the neighborhood when he inadvertently got boxed in by a chain link fence. Officer Billberry again yelled at Piggie to stop and drop his gun, telling Piggie that he was a police officer. Instead, Piggie aimed his gun at Billberry, prompting the officer to shoot and nail Piggie in the shoulder. Wounded, Piggie finally gave up, surrendering the 9mm semiautomatic pistol he had been carrying.

During questioning by police, according to the report, Piggie admitted shooting at the officers, but said he didn't hear any of the three warnings they gave him identifying themselves as police.

Prosecutors in Jackson County, Missouri, charged Piggie in October 1989 with five felony counts ranging from assault in an attempt to kill to unlawfully exhibiting a firearm. In January 1990, Piggie made a deal with prosecutors to drop four of the five charges in exchange for a guilty plea to the least serious of the charges.

Because he also had violated his probation in the crack cocaine conviction, Piggie finally found himself facing real jail time. He was sentenced to one year's imprisonment in the Jackson County Department of Corrections.

What made Piggie successful was understanding how to take advantage of opportunity. So it shouldn't have shocked anyone when the slick-talking, fast-walking Piggie seized another opportunity just a few years later.

This time, the opportunity was packaged as a 6-foot-3 junior high school stud who was one of the best young basketball players in the land and also just so happened to be teammates and best friends with Piggie's son, Myron Piggie, Jr. Piggie Senior befriended the budding basketball legend Jaron Rush, and when Jaron was invited into the elite basketball program funded by Kansas City millionaire Tom Grant, both Piggies came along. Once there, they were joined by another phenom, Korleone Young, who, it just so happens, turned out to be Myron Piggie's second cousin once removed.

Myron Piggie the opportunist understood what this relationship to two great young stars could mean. Though he had almost no real basketball coaching experience, it didn't take long for Myron Senior to work his way up the ladder and suddenly he was the head coach of Grant's team, the Kansas City Children's Mercy Hospital 76ers.

An old basketball axiom: Load a team with talent and the talent compensates quickly for a lack of coaching. Myron Piggie knew and understood that axiom. His 76ers were loaded. Not only did the team boast Young, Jaron Rush, and his younger brother Kareem, but Piggie branched out and recruited players from throughout the country. Chicago's Corey Maggette signed up for duty and at various times other prep stars did, such as Baltimore's Kevin Braswell, South Dakota's Mike Miller, and Connecticut's Ajou Ajou Deng, among others. All that talent didn't just win Piggie games, it won him "friends," the kind of people trying to gain access to the talent Piggie was connected to.

One of Piggie's new best friends became George Raveling. Raveling adopted the 76ers, promising to support the program as he would only a handful of others throughout the United States. Raveling also made Piggie Nike's only paid "consultant," paying him $70,000 a year, Piggie told friends in Kansas City.

According to Raveling, Piggie took it upon himself to share his background with Nike's staff. "He told me what happened," Raveling said in a 1998 interview. "First of all, it happened fourteen years ago, and second of all, it was a drug charge. My understanding of what happened was, him and his brother went to buy some drugs and the narcotics people came, his brother knocked down one of the narcotic guys and they ran. They were eventually accosted and arrested and convicted. He told me that the first time I met him. He said, 'You need to know this.' It wasn't like the guy was trying to hide anything."

Told that nearly every fact he shared was wrong—most significantly that Piggie was selling crack to police informants, not buying it—Raveling seemed slightly shocked, but not enough to slow his defense: "Well, I know the Myron Piggie of today," he said.

Bobby Dodds, national president of the AAU, had a similar impression of Piggie's background. "Myron had a criminal record as a young person," Dodds said. "The story I was told was that Myron was involved in either marijuana or something like that as a young person in college and got arrested. He doesn't shy away from discussing it."

Told the true nature of Piggie's criminal history, Dodds was reduced to two words: "Oh, my."

It is tough to blame Nike or the AAU for not grasping the seriousness of Piggie's background if all they did was interview him. The authors of this book did just that, but had prepared for the conversation by pulling indictments, court records, and police reports, all of which were publicly available and not pulled by Nike or the AAU. The following is an exchange with the silver-tongued Piggie:

Q: Didn't you shoot at a police officer?

A: No. See, people don't know what the whole thing was. If I shot at a police officer, why am I on the streets?

Q: Well, I read the police report. It said there was no question you were shooting at him, and he kept yelling, I'm a police officer.

A: Well, bottom line is—okay—why did them police officers, why did they drop the case if I did that?

Q: They didn't drop the case. You pled guilty.

A: On what?

Q: You pled guilty to unlawful use of a firearm, didn't you?

A: Okay, is that shooting an officer? No, you got to realize what the case was.

Q: Well, what was the case?

A: The only thing I was charged [with] was a D felony [for] shooting a gun in public. It was never shooting a gun at nobody. So bottom line is, if I was shooting at a police officer, I would have been charged with shooting at a police officer.

Q: You were charged with it. You just pled guilty to something lower, and they reduced it. Isn't that the truth?

A: No, no, no.

Q: That's what the records say.

A: Well, if you look at the police record—

Q: I am looking at the police records and they say you were indicted on five counts, one of which was shooting at a police officer.

A: No, see, there you go. You don't even know what the fuck you talking about now. Because bottom line is I wasn't indicted on five counts. What are you talking about?

Q: Myron, I've got the records right here.

A: What are you talking about, state or feds?

Q: Well, the state one you were charged with assault with—

A: I was never indicted in state.

Q: Here it is right here. The charges were Count I, assault in second degree for "attempting to kill or cause serious physical injury to Daniel Billberry, a Kansas City police officer . . ."

A: Okay, then why did we go in front of the federal judge and a federal judge didn't believe him, and why, why, why, why did I do no time? Tell me why did I do no time?

Q: You never went to the Jackson County Correctional Facility?

A: That is—do you know what the Jackson County facility is?

Q: Go ahead, tell me.

A: You don't—see, that's the thing about it.

Q: What's the thing about it? You're asking me a question?

A: If you don't know what you're talking about, then you don't have the information right.

Q: Did you go to the Jackson County Correctional Facility?

A: Only on a probation violation.

When Piggie was asked about his good fortune that DEA agent Wright had not pulled twelve inches closer to his brother's car during the crack bust, Piggie said, interestingly:

A: The bottom line with the whole thing was it went like the Lord wanted it to go. It didn't go like you wanted to go, or the critics wanted to go. It happened the way it was supposed to happen. That's why I didn't go to prison, because the Lord didn't have that in His plan for me.

Q: The Lord wanted you to be able to get away and run over that DEA agent?

A: No, I'm saying the bottom line is the Lord had another plan, and the other plan was to come back and do the right thing.

Q: I guess, Myron, I'm wondering if there are crimes that can be committed by adults that should prohibit them from being around kids?

A: Yeah. Sexual harassment—when they do things to a kid. Sodomy, all that type of stuff.

Q: But not crack dealing?

A: It was never, ever crack dealing.

Q: You were dealing crack.

A: Never dealing crack. Where did I—you must have my fed thing?

Q: I got your fed thing. You dealt crack to them three times. You pled guilty to one of them.

A: I did for three times?

Q: Yeah. June 22, 1987. July 1, 1987. July 31, 1987 . . . None of this is true?

A: Okay, my thing is this.

Q: You pled guilty to it, Myron.

A: What year is this?

Q: 1999.

A: What year was that?

Q: 1987.

A: Okay. Why are you trying to go back eleven years? Let me ask you a question. Are you a perfect man?

Q: Am I a perfect man? No. Have I ever dealt crack? No.

A: Hold it, no. Are you a perfect man?

Q: No.

A: Have you committed sin?

Q: I'm sure I have, yes.

A: Okay. If you are a perfect man, then you can talk to me. When you ain't a perfect man, you cannot talk to me.

"Nike takes care of me like nobody could ever believe," Piggie said. "Nike has been behind me 100 percent. I'm behind Nike 100 percent. Every day I wake up, I walk out of the house with Nike on. Nike shoes, Nike shirts, Nike this, Nike everything. I'm loyal to Nike. Me and Nike are family. We're always going to be family.

"I don't burn bridges and I don't have enemies," Piggie said. "I try to treat people the way I want to be treated. That's my goal in life. Just to do right by people. I really don't give a damn about what people say. Because bottom line is this, I can go to a neighborhood where they sell drugs and talk to kids and get them out of there. Where they can go in there, if they could in there and they white, and they go in there in their suits and all that, they run their ass up out of there. So I can communicate with kids who have bad backgrounds better than guys that supposed to have degrees and all that type of stuff. My thing, I learned my degree on the streets, and where they had to go spend all that time in classrooms, and all that.

"A lot of people misread me because of all the bad publicity I've gotten. If anybody ever knows me, and if you ask anybody who knows me about Myron Piggie, they would tell you that I would give my shirt off my back for them. I would give you my last dime in my pocket if you needed anything."

It shouldn't come as a surprise that Nike didn't know much about the background of a man it was so closely aligning itself to. You see, Nike didn't do background checks on the coaches it gave its seal of approval to. But neither does adidas or any other shoe company.

Most troubling, though, is that these checks aren't even done by the Amateur Athletic Union. "You have to understand that the AAU charters teams from coast to coast in thirty-two sports in a number of age groups," Dodds said. "We'd love to, but we can't know everything about every coach of every team. When we learn of problems, we have a system in place to act and act quickly."

That was not good enough for the mother of one thirteen-year-old from Brockton, Massachusetts. During the spring of 1998, her son played for the Nike-sponsored New Bedford Buddies before she discovered that the team's longtime coach, Jim Tavares, was watching the young boys as they took showers.

The mother, who agreed to an interview for this book only if she could remain anonymous, said she knew something was wrong when her hoop-mad thirteen-year-old told her he wanted to quit basketball.

During a break in a Converse Tournament in Massachusetts, the mother was sharing her concerns with another parent when an off-duty police detective told the pair that he had heard Tavares was a convicted sex offender. Rumors like that surface occasionally in a world where grown men travel with young boys, but seldom is there anything to them.

"Sometimes that is just what a jealous losing coach says about a rival," the mother said. "But I saw the look in my son's eyes and I knew there was something there."

This mother took control. She went to the library and started scouring the police blotter in the local paper. She went back years, looking through the small type. What she found confirmed her worst fears. Two stories, both in the *New Bedford Standard Times,* told her that Tavares had, in fact, been charged with indecent assault and battery in 1968 and sodomy and unnatural acts on a child under fourteen back in 1974. The second charge stemmed from the rape of a young boy in a swimming pool. Tavares agreed to plea-bargained convictions in exchange for reduced charges in both cases.

"I couldn't believe my eyes," the mother said. "I couldn't believe that someone like this was in charge of kids . . . and that no one knew about it. Where were the people who are supposed to check these things?"

She wrote the AAU and called Nike. Within days, both groups had moved to distance themselves from Tavares.

"I will say that Nike was great when I wrote them a letter," the mother said. "They dumped Tavares immediately. That made me feel good until a friend pointed out that someone—the AAU, Nike, someone—should have done this checkup before a guy like Jim Tavares got to the position he was in."

"The man had a problem," Raveling said, explaining the speed of Nike's decision. "We are not equipped to deal with his problem."

"When parents associate their kids with AAU teams, they have to have a level of trust in a coach," Nike's

Vizhier Mooney said. "When Nike associates itself with a coach, we have to have a level of trust with the coach."

"When I look back on what happened, I cringe," the mother said. "My son, who loves basketball, was trying to send me a message. But I didn't get it, because while I loved going to his games, I didn't see what happened in the locker room. I didn't know until another boy stepped up that this coach had these boys in the hot tub with him, no clothes allowed. I didn't know that he walked around hotel rooms in front of them naked.

"This coach had it all. He was successful, had Nike's blessing. His program was one everyone wanted to play in because he promised parents he'd get their kids scholarships. I counted on someone to know his background. But no one else seemed to worry about that because he won and his players went to college. This is a major hole in the AAU system, if you ask me. And while they did the right thing by tossing him after I found the information, the system hasn't changed. They still don't do background checks. They still don't know who is coaching our children."

Tavares, in an interview for this book, denied he ever did anything improper while a coach for the New Bedford Buddies, noting that if he had done something wrong, someone would have gone to the police. Tavares also said he has never denied his past when confronted by a parent. Like Myron Piggie, he argued that his past should not be held against him.

"I don't see why anyone should have a problem with me," Tavares said. "All that happened twenty-seven years ago [actually twenty-five]. I've coached hundreds of boys since then and no one has ever accused me of anything.

Should I be punished for something twenty-seven years ago for the rest of my life?

"I never lied to anyone," he said. "The AAU never asked me about my background until that woman wrote a letter. There was never a box I should check or anything on a form where they asked for that information."

Asked if maybe the AAU should ask those kinds of questions on its application, Tavares paused: "Maybe. I guess. Yeah, they probably should. But they don't, and that's not my problem.

"There are a lot more people out there who have good things to say about me than bad things," he said. "You have to look at me today, not twenty-seven years ago."

Tavares suggested several parents who would speak up for him, all of whom did. "I had heard rumors about him," one mother said. "And I was concerned at first. But we got to know him and believed all that was in the past. Besides, he's a great coach and my son is much better because Jim Tavares worked with him."

Sonny Vaccaro admits adidas is as far behind as Nike and the AAU in this area. "There definitely is a vacuum," Vaccaro said. "That is clearly a weakness in the summer coach system. None of us invest in those background checks, I guess because we believe good guys are the ones getting in this business. Sometimes we're wrong."

Vaccaro should know. He was "blown away" when one of the coaches adidas helped sponsor, Jack McMahon, was alleged to have molested one boy and had improper conversations about sex with another during the summer of 1998. The charges came to light in stories published by the *Boston Globe*. Players and parents signed complaints that were forwarded to the AAU's national offices alleging that McMahon had been "inappropriate" with the boys he was coaching. McMahon, who denied the allegations, was suspended by the AAU and was dropped by adidas.

In separate articles, the *Atlanta Journal-Constitution* and the *Los Angeles Times* posed questions about the off-court lives of two other AAU coaches in 1998. Henry "Scoobie" Richardson, who occasionally coached with the AAU-sanctioned Team Georgia, pled guilty to charges of contributing to the delinquency of a minor and furnishing alcohol to a minor after the parent of one player accused Richardson of plying her fourteen-year-old son with cognac, liquor, and beer before driving the boy and two teammates to a motel where they all spent the night. Richardson, who has ties to NBA stars Allen Iverson, Shareef Abdur-Rahim, and Kevin Garnett, was listed as Team Georgia's "VP of Recruitment" on the all-star team's letterhead. After the charges were leveled, Team Georgia's chief executive, Al Outlaw, said Richardson "was no longer involved with us."

In Los Angeles, the *Times* discovered that an assistant to Nike's top West Coast program had been convicted of unlawful sexual intercourse with a sixteen-year-old girl and of embezzling $9,000 from a private account used by parents and students for school sports. The thirty-five-year-old coach, Richard Prospero, was hired by Nike consultant Pat Barrett to help handle the thirteen- and fourteen-year-old players in Barrett's Orange County Hoops. Prospero told the *Times* that it was his use of cocaine that led to his criminal charges. He was released after seven months in prison and lived in a halfway house when Barrett chose him to help coach the Hoops. "He's paid his debt and he deserves a second chance," Barrett told the *Times*. The newspaper noted that Prospero's conviction for sex with a minor disqualified him from ever working in the California public school system.

But it didn't stop him from coaching Barrett's young all-stars.

The problem, some summer basketball critics say, is that as the power and influence of summer coaches has increased in recent years, parents hopeful that the coach can help get their son a scholarship have been blinded to suspicions that otherwise would be natural.

"We're talking about a basketball god here," the father of one player told the *Boston Globe* when describing how his family viewed Jack McMahon. "All my son ever wanted to do was play basketball. It was his whole life."

Nike's concern over cases like that of Jim Tavares led the company to begin a program in 1998 that required coaches working the Nike All-America Camp to sign a release allowing the company to do a background check. "If we have some reason to believe that a background check is necessary we'll do it," Raveling said, noting that Nike hadn't actually done a background check under the new policy. "But don't put this on Nike. Are Little League coaches subject to background checks? No. There's no level in America where coaches are subject to a background check. That's just some fantasy thing. Come on now. I coached thirty-one years. I was never subject to any background check."

"You don't think the University of Southern California, before they hired you, did a background check?" Raveling was asked.

"No. I bet you any amount of money they didn't."

USC spokesman Tim Tessalone said Raveling was wrong. The university did an extensive check of his background—as it does any coach—when it hired Raveling in

1987. "We didn't hire the FBI, but we know a lot about people before we hire them, that's for sure," Tessalone said.

"At some point the past has got to be the past," Raveling said. "I guess the question is, how long does the person have to pay—especially a guy like Myron Piggie who comes back and is willing to work with kids and openly admits that I made a mistake and tells kids, 'Hey, I was convicted.' It wasn't like anybody was trying to hide it. He told people. He told the kids that. He's trying to say, 'Hey, yo, don't make the same mistakes that I made.' So it wasn't like he tried to fool anybody.

"Should there be a statute of limitations on what a person does? Oh certainly. Certainly I think there should be a statute of limitations. Let me say this to you, and this goes back to Julius Caesar and one of the great quotes that— 'the good that a man does is often turned into the bone and the bad lives on forever.' A man could lead sixty years of a virtuous life and he does one dastardly act and, all of a sudden, people forget about the sixty years of virtuous life that he led and all they focus on is this one mistake that the person made. So certainly there has to be a statute of limitations. Common sense will tell you that. Either that, or we don't live in a rational society. Sure, there are some crimes that should stick with you, but maybe not others."

In Raveling's book, charges of sexual misconduct with a minor provide a "clear-cut" reason to keep someone from coaching kids. Thus, Nike immediately cut Jim Tavares when it got the letter from the player's mother.

Crack dealing and shooting at a police officer, though, must have a different statute of limitations. As of the publishing of this book, Myron Piggie was still one of Raveling's "key guys" and remained on Nike's payroll.

"I don't know about Myron, but I have a real problem with Nike if that's their attitude about crack cocaine," DEA agent Wright said. "It's a highly addictive form of cocaine, and there has been a lot of violence associated with it. The people involved in crack were never role models, that's for sure."

CHAPTER 5

Romancing the Stone

Things were rolling along quite nicely for the people of Huntsville, Alabama, a quaint Southern town in the foothills of the Appalachian Mountains. The late 1990s economy was bustling, adding to the steady flow of NASA jobs and associated money that routinely pour into Huntsville.

Things were rolling along quite nicely for Johnny Gilbreath too. He had taken the love of his children and the love of the sport of basketball and combined them into one of the better traveling basketball teams in America, the Alabama Aces.

It was a good, small-time operation. A bunch of local Alabama kids piling into vans and driving through the South in search of some competition. For ten years Gilbreath's Aces were among the best in the game, even capturing the fifteen-and-under national championship in 1995.

But then along came a new era in AAU basketball, high-powered shoe-company-financed teams that will do anything to snatch the top talent. And about that time along came Mark Komara, owner of several taverns around town, the area's largest bingo hall, and a number of side businesses. Komara loved basketball too. He loved basketball players more.

"He loved to hang out with anyone he thought was a star," said Komara's longtime friend, Kent Looney.

And one afternoon, Mark Komara saw the fifteen-year-old basketball star he wanted to hang out with the most. And basketball in this quaint Southern town was turned upside down.

Although the state of Alabama is widely hailed as football country, basketball has always been the most popular sport in Huntsville, a town of 170,000 in the northern part of the state. It's a hoop oasis in the land where gridiron reigns supreme.

Nearly two dozen Division I prospects have emerged from the city, and within high school circles, basketball games have always been the most hotly contested events.

But never has a player come along like Marvin Stone. By the time Stone was a senior in high school he was 6-foot-10 with broad shoulders and a soft touch. He was so physically imposing, people in Huntsville had dubbed him "Tree" years ago, and Tree had such a promising game it wasn't that unusual to see Tubby Smith, Cliff Ellis, or some other famous coach hanging around town. And by the time he was done with Huntsville he would not only be regarded as perhaps the city's finest talent ever, but also the person who most changed the way the game is played there.

Huntsville is a long way from the streets of New York, Chicago, or Los Angeles, places where shady school transfers, dodgy hoop middlemen, and out-of-control traveling teams seem more at home. Here in the buckle of the Bible Belt, a town tucked one hundred miles south of Nashville and one hundred miles north of Birmingham seems an odd place for amateur basketball to be at its worst. But it is.

Stone became a local celebrity as a youth, when the oversized kid showed his knack for scoring baskets. It was only natural he began playing on a youth team for Gilbreath, the local hoops maven and his adidas-outfitted Alabama Aces traveling team.

Gilbreath is the father of two basketball-playing boys and operates a screen art shop on the south side of the city. He's run the Aces since the late 1980s as a way to give Alabama kids a chance to compete with players throughout the nation, and as a way to better his own sons' careers. (His eldest, Lance, after helping Huntsville Butler win a state championship in 1995, played some small-college ball before becoming a student coach at South Alabama. His youngest, Zack, is a potential Division I recruit from the class of 2000.)

Growing up between Lance and Zack, Marvin Stone became a close friend to the Gilbreaths. So close, Stone often ate dinner and even slept over at the Gilbreaths' home.

"He was like another son," says Gilbreath.

In 1995, the Aces, starring Stone, traveled to Kingsport, Tennessee, to compete in an eighty-eight-team field for the fifteen-and-under AAU National Championships. At the same tournament, Mark Komara entered his own upstart team, the Alabama Lasers, in the tournament. It wasn't a bad squad of locals, but according to Komara's friend Kent Looney, who was also one of the Lasers' coaches at the time, Komara spent most of his time trying to figure out how to get Stone to play for him.

"As soon as we started putting [our] team together . . . before we went to state, he started talking about it," said Looney. "He was trying to get Tree to leave Gilbreath."

And how did he say he was going to accomplish that?

"I think buying him," Looney said. "Giving him some things he wasn't getting from Gilbreath. Like tennis shoes, [a] job. I think that's when the influence started. At the time Gilbreath had a real close tie with him [Stone]. He wouldn't leave Gilbreath at first, he wouldn't leave him."

Komara eventually convinced Stone to travel to a tournament in Memphis, Tennessee, later that summer with the Lasers. Stone came but refused to play. Komara, though, found it a good way to get to know the player.

"He made him [feel] very special because anything he needed at the time, a few dollars in his pocket, tennis shoes, Mark would give him," Looney said. "He basically looked at it and said, if we can get Marvin over at our team, then Marvin's our ticket to stardom.

"What he said to me was, 'Think about it, we could get your son [James Looney], Marvin, the kids from Boab,' and we had a couple more kids he mentioned. He was just thinking, we could get them on the same team and nobody but nobody could beat him. I didn't have any idea what he was trying to do. But then, as it went on, he definitely got Marvin's attention."

Stone played his freshman season at Johnson High School, which sits in Stone's district in northwest Huntsville. At some point the following summer, Stone began working for Komara at the Sports Page Lounge & Deli, a bar on Huntsville's south side, though he played the summer of 1996 for Gilbreath's Alabama Aces.

Komara, however, spent the summer shopping Stone around to Huntsville high schools. About the only thing that was clear was that Stone wanted out of Johnson and told his friends that he liked Butler High School, a city power, which under veteran coach Jack Doss had won two state titles and produced eighteen Division I players.

According to Looney, Komara also thought Butler High was the best place for Stone.

"He wanted [Stone] to play for Jack Doss because Jack traveled and they thought Marvin could be seen more and [play] against top competition," Looney said. "And so my understanding was that he was going to Butler."

Today Doss refers to Komara, a man he has no lost love for, as Stone's "street agent." He said Komara told him that if Butler could get $5,000 together to help Stone's family move, the future McDonald's All American was his.

"Mark said they needed $5,000 to move into the Butler school district," Doss said.

Doss declined—"I've never given any player money like that, I'm sure as heck not going to start now"—but it appeared he would get Stone anyway. Stone worked Doss's summer camp in June, and later traveled to Cincinnati with Doss and the Butler players to take part in a team camp, even though he was technically still enrolled at Johnson High.

Meanwhile, Stone's game was blossoming with the Aces. During a late July tournament in Bloomington, Indiana, Stone played so well that word came down that Indiana coach Bob Knight wanted to meet him. Gilbreath says he and Stone went to Knight's office and although he had just completed his freshman season the General offered a scholarship slot in the Hoosiers' 1999 recruiting class on the spot.

Stone didn't accept but was feeling good that evening when he and his teammates played basketball in the parking lot of a Days Inn in Bloomington. Gilbreath and assistant coach Neil Ferguson—whose son, Trey, ironically later became a member of the 1999 IU recruiting class—were in their hotel room when Doss called. The low-key but respected Butler coach told them he had just heard from Mark Komara that Stone was going to enroll at Grissom High School, a predominantly white school on the far southeast side of Huntsville, which had enjoyed only moderate success on the basketball court.

"I was shocked," said Doss.

According to Gilbreath and Ferguson, Marvin Stone was shocked too when they called him in and told him the news.

"I thought Marvin was going to cry," said Ferguson. "He called his parents, and we could hear only one side of the conversation but it was clear he was surprised. He didn't want to go to Grissom."

"Until that point," Gilbreath said, "Grissom High had never come up. I don't think Marvin had any say in the transfer."

Stone may have been surprised, but he accepted the decision. "He cried basically," said one of Stone's friends, Adrian Davidson, who is a football and basketball star in the class of 2000 at Butler High and was with Stone that night. "He cried the whole night. He was upset. You don't ever see a kid transfer from his neighborhood to Grissom. Never. He said, 'I guess I'm going to Grissom. I'll deal with it.' "

Stone wasn't the only one who still had to deal with it. Not surprisingly, when the transfer of the best player in city history takes a sudden and unexpected turn everyone has an opinion.

Huntsville was buzzing with transfer talk and the role that Komara played. When contacted by the authors of this book, Komara refused to go on the record, but said he did nothing unsavory in helping Stone transfer to Grissom.

And that was just the beginning. The move caused such a furor in Huntsville that for the only time anyone can remember the superintendent of schools himself handled the decision on the transfer of a student. It went through despite the fact that superintendent Ron Saunders was concerned with the activity of Komara.

To add to the confusion, Saunders told the *Huntsville Times* that when he asked Grissom coach Ronnie Stapler about the first contact he had concerning the potential transfer of Marvin Stone, he was told this: "He said he was contacted by Marvin or Marvin's mother and was asked, 'What can you give me?'" Saunders told the *Times*. "He said, 'I can't give you anything. I'm not going to give you jack.'"

Then, when the Stone family, Marvin, father Marvin Senior, and mother Lois, met with Saunders on August 20, 1996, the day before school was to begin, Komara, the bar owner, sat in on the session. Allowing a summer league coach to join the meeting was a highly unusual move, the superintendent admitted.

The Stones argued that they wanted Marvin at Grissom because of its high academic standards and not because of basketball. Because of federal school integration laws, a minority student such as Stone was eligible to transfer to majority-white Grissom without moving into the school district. To go to Butler, which like Johnson High is predominantly minority, the Stones would have had to move.

That's partially why the city's most closely watched high school enrollment since school desegregation in the late 1960s was granted.

The problem was getting Stone, then just fifteen years old, from his modest home in northwest Huntsville to Grissom High in southeast Huntsville, a half hour drive each way. Komara, who lives near Grissom, solved that problem by volunteering to drive across town, pick Stone up, and drive back to Grissom each morning.

During those days Komara, who also owns a local realty company, Polk Realty, as well as the Army-Navy Union Bingo Parlor in the nearby, poverty-stricken town of Triana, continued to use Marvin Senior, a maintenance man for a local real estate company until his death in January of 1999, to perform odd jobs at his businesses. It's a practice, Komara said, he has done for a decade.

Suddenly, Johnny Gilbreath and the Alabama Aces were out of Marvin Stone's life. When the Aces headed to a tournament in Tennessee on a Friday afternoon, Stone, who was scheduled to come, stayed home. He arrived the next day by bus. He then played the following weekend for the Lasers in an Alabama tournament.

Komara, according to Looney, was in heavy courtship mode, dropping large amounts of money on the Laser program and bringing not only players, but their families on the road.

"What was happening is this," Looney said. "Johnny [Gilbreath] was with adidas. And adidas was giving him bags and their uniforms and whatever it took because it was Marvin playing. And so Mark [Komara] decides he's gonna spend whatever it took to get Tree up under his wing. And he did. He spent $10,000 during the little time we had a team. We traveled to two or three different places."

The weekend Stone played for the Lasers in Birmingham, he informed Gilbreath he couldn't play with him the upcoming summer.

"I guess I shouldn't have been surprised, but the look on the kid's face told me it wasn't what he wanted," Gilbreath said. "He had been at my house just about every day since he was twelve and suddenly he can't talk with me. He even slept there before a Grissom playoff game his sophomore season. It made no sense."

Stone, though, was now a member of the Lasers. Komara had gotten the kid he coveted the year before.

But new competition was coming. Being the big fish in Huntsville's small waters was one thing. It doesn't necessarily prepare you for the sharks.

April 1997, lobby of the Marriott Hotel in Troy, Michigan. It was Saturday night before Magic's Roundball Classic, and during cocktail hour before the formal banquet, everyone from Bobby Cremins to Dick Vitale was chatting, laughing, and sharing tales of the season.

The lobby was alive with the machinery of college basketball. Here tonight were twenty-four of the nation's finest players, including studs such as Tracy McGrady, Lamar Odom, and Khalid El-Amin and their families. It's a dream room for a recruiter, not to mention a sports agent, who can bump his way into half a dozen conversations with players, moms, aunts, AAU coaches. Which is why a dozen head coaches and a couple dozen assistants were there working the scene.

The shock of the night, however, was about to stroll in. Just prior to dinner, through the revolving door and into the Marriott's bright lobby walked Durham (North Carolina) Mt. Zion Christian Academy coach Joel Hopkins, wearing a flashy, white double-breasted suit. At his side were two players, Mt. Zion junior Corey Hightower, a native of nearby Flint, Michigan, and Huntsville Grissom High sophomore Marvin Stone.

It was a recruiting trip for Hopkins too, and Stone was his number one focus. He introduced him to McGrady, Mt. Zion's poster boy for success, Vitale, the biggest name in basketball media, and Sonny Vaccaro, the man capable of making dreams come true. Later, Stone even met the man the game is named after, Earvin "Magic" Johnson, whose spellbinding speech about his love of the game captured the audience.

Later Stone and Hightower fooled around the Marriott with the players, including McGrady, and Tree learned first-hand what an association with adidas can bring.

It was more than a fifteen-year-old could be expected to handle. Stone's recruitment to Mt. Zion began about six weeks before when Hopkins called him in Huntsville and told him about the school. He called another time and put the suddenly famous McGrady, who, thanks to adidas and Mt. Zion, had gone from unknown small-town Southerner to national media darling, on the phone. He made all the normal pitches about exposure, travel, and fringe benefits. Grissom High and the Lasers no longer seemed so desirable.

Tree, according to his friend Adrian Davidson, even mentioned the possibility of uprooting to Durham. But not for long.

"That spring he told me that he was going to get a new car," Davidson said. "He knew. He told me two weeks before he was going to get it, he was going to get an Explorer. I was like, 'What? Where are you going to get a car?' He just said, 'Don't worry about it.' "

Sure enough, in early June, just after Stone's sixteenth birthday, he called his friend and told him he was coming by to pick him up and go for a drive. The two teenagers cruised Huntsville all night in a black 1992 Ford Explorer, complete with a custom, high-powered stereo system.

"I was there the first night," said Davidson. "The whole night we just drove around town."

Davidson said he was surprised that Tree had a nice Explorer while his parents were driving less stylish vehicles.

(His father drove a fifteen-year-old pickup to work right up to the day he died.)

"If his parents can really afford a Ford Explorer, why aren't they driving a Ford Explorer?" Davidson said. "Why are they driving an old van and a truck and he's driving a nice Explorer? That doesn't make no sense."

Davidson said Stone told him he earned the money to pay for it working at Komara's Sports Page Lounge & Deli as a cook.

"I was like, 'Damn, I need a job like that,' " Davidson said.

Komara meanwhile says Stones' parents financed it.

That night with Davidson, Stone also began talking about his summer schedule. Adidas and Mt. Zion were no longer on the radar screen. The Nike Camp in Indianapolis and a full season of AAU ball with the now Nike-sponsored Alabama Lasers was in.

Not even a June 1997 visit to Huntsville from Mt. Zion's Hopkins—just days after the keys to the Explorer came into Stone's possession—could turn the tide. Hopkins told the *Huntsville Times* that he and the Stones "had a good time, a wonderful Bible study," although he admitted there was time for some hoop talk. Dozens of calls by the authors to Hopkins and Mt. Zion seeking comment went unreturned.

Stone, meanwhile, in a very unusual move, did not speak to the media his senior year of high school, not even his hometown paper, becoming one of the first teenage stars ever who apparently was uninterested in talking about himself.

About a week after Hopkins's "Bible study," George Raveling arrived in Huntsville and met with Komara, Stone, and Grissom coach Ronnie Stapler. Nike later signed a five-year sponsorship deal with Grissom High, a team which prior to Stone's crosstown transfer had been an afterthought on the city hoops scene. In comparison, Butler High had a five-year deal with adidas in the early 1990s.

"We sponsor Grissom because they are a good program, one of the best in the state," said Raveling. "It's a five-year deal, not just a Marvin Stone deal. Grissom will be with Nike long after Stone leaves."

After Raveling's trip Komara told Stone and Boaz, Alabama, forward Derrick Underwood, also of the Lasers, that all three of them had been invited to head to Santa Barbara, California, in August to work as counselors at the Michael Jordan Flight School.

The Flight School proved better than Stone could have imagined. At George Raveling's behest, sources at the school said, Stone and Jordan worked closely together, even playing spirited games of one-on-one. According to the *Huntsville Times,* Stone and Underwood were both paid "a couple hundred dollars" for their efforts. But it was Jordan, not money, that sealed the deal.

And later that summer Stone played for a Nike all-star team that toured Europe.

Mt. Zion was never remotely considered again. Fending off the adidas courtship, Nike had brought out its trump card, Michael Jordan.

Komara's problem with the Alabama Lasers was no longer keeping Marvin Stone, it was paying for all of the team's surging expenses. The costs of travel, uniforms, and training were piling up. He did have a plan, according to Looney. Following a trend of many traveling basketball teams, Komara created Laser Youth Inc. and made it a nonprofit organization. This allowed the team to offer corporate sponsors like Nike a tax benefit while also creating a charity for Komara to funnel funds from his Army-Navy Union Bingo Parlor.

Alabama law requires bingo parlors to donate a portion of their profits to charity, and with the Lasers now enjoying 501(C)(3) tax-exempt status, money was no longer a problem. Laser Youth Inc. is one of nine charities the bingo hall provides funding for, Looney said.

"Mark came in," Looney said of the day Komara set up the nonprofit, "and said, 'Ya'll can have money to travel wherever you want to travel.' "

A team photo of the Lasers hangs in the lobby of the unspectacular bingo parlor, just one Lasers-Stone link to Komara's business.

Another time, Komara bought some local cable advertising time for the Sports Page Lounge & Deli and playing on one of the televisions in the background was a Grissom High highlight tape featuring Marvin Stone.

Komara also worked himself a significant sponsorship deal with Nike to help offset costs and give the program cachet as an important member of the swoosh's stable. Alabama Lasers president Ronnie Flakes told the *Huntsville Times* that Nike provided upward of $15,000 in cash as well as shoes, gear, and bags.

Never one to give up on a top player, Vaccaro took charge of the Stone front and during January of 1998 called Komara a few times to discuss what adidas could do to make the Lasers wear their gear and get Stone to Teaneck, New Jersey, that summer for the adidas ABCD Camp.

"I called Mark, he runs the show down there," Vaccaro said. "I'm not going to lie to you, did we want Marvin Stone at camp? Yes. Why wouldn't we?"

Komara held put, however, and during the summer of 1998, both he and Stone attended the Nike Camp, Komara working as a counselor. The two later traveled to the Michael Jordan Flight School following a July of intensive AAU competition.

Senior year, at least on the court, was a dream season for Tree, the fruition of the potential he flashed as a boy. It started in November of 1998 when he signed a national letter of intent with the University of Kentucky. It continued through the winter, when he was not only named Alabama's Mr. Basketball, but helped lead Grissom to a state championship, beating city rival Butler High along the way.

More importantly, Stone qualified academically for his University of Kentucky scholarship. In March of 1999 he played in the prestigious McDonald's All American High School Basketball Game. Marvin Stone had proven himself worthy of being called Huntsville's finest player.

The city's fractured basketball community Stone left behind has also moved on—though nothing is quite the same since Tree.

Grissom is now a potential powerhouse, especially after Lasers coach William "Wig" Pearson admits he steered top area players to the school, including brothers Sherman and Chris White, who originally hailed from Florence, a small city sixty-seven miles west of Huntsville.

Meanwhile, Butler's Jack Doss says he's thinking about retiring from coaching soon.

"I think I've seen enough," he said.

Gilbreath, who had also considered getting out of a game he no longer felt proud of, changed his mind. He boasted about having a good young roster and looked forward to the city scene "settling down." He admitted, however, that the Alabama Aces summer 1999 travel schedule would be limited due to costs.

"We can't afford to go to Vegas unless someone comes along and gives us a bunch of money," Gilbreath said. "Airfare from Huntsville to Las Vegas is at least $300. That means for a team and a couple of coaches you are talking about $5,000 just to get there. We don't have that kind of money. We'll play in tournaments we can drive to."

With their Nike deal and bingo parlor money, the men who run the Alabama Lasers say they have no such concerns. Lasers president Flakes, an older, graying black man, raised concerns in Huntsville about the Lasers' tactics for assuring their future when he told the *Huntsville Times:* "We'll have to buy whatever it takes to fill the gaps."

Flakes, who by day is a special education teacher for Huntsville schools, continued, "Money talks. Anything good costs money. There's a difference in price between Cadillacs and Fords. Most people can drive Fords and Chevys. We want to be Cadillacs. That's our goal."

Indeed, Flakes has cast his buying eye past the Huntsville city limits and sees no reason why the Lasers can't recruit a kid from anywhere within the Lower Forty-eight. His 1999 team boasted Memphis, Tennessee, player Terrance Woods. It's just the beginning, Flakes promised.

"In a nutshell," he told the *Times,* "if you want a kid from West Hell and he lives in the projects and he can hoop it up, you have to do something—whatever is within the realm of reason—to make him part of the Lasers' program. Hopefully we can go international. I don't see why we can't be a national program.

"It takes a village to raise a child, and that's what we're going after. It's going to take this village. There will always be a 'Bama Lasers. Somebody will always be there to carry it on."

He says Komara's initial work with Nike will continue to

pay off as the Lasers develop into one of the shoe company's premier programs, worthy, he says, of a $100,000-a-year contract.

"I would be that optimistic that our program," Flakes said, "at some point, would take [its] place among the elite programs in the country."

But so as not to give the wrong idea that the Lasers are all about crass basketball glory, Flakes pointed out to the *Louisville Courier-Journal* that the team, which receives significant funding due to its nonprofit charity distinction, has actually given back to the community of Huntsville.

"Last year we bought ten winter coats for children out of the Lasers' funds," he bragged.

CHAPTER 6

Red, White, and Swoosh

To the casual viewer who happened to click over to CBS on Saturday, May 13, 1995, the "Basketball Hall of Fame Hoop Summit presented by Nike" that was being broadcast from the Springfield Civic Center in Massachusetts must have seemed like a brilliant idea.

Here was a collection of top American high school players, competing under the auspices of USA Basketball against a similar collection of international teenage stars. The game was designed to promote the Naismith Basketball Hall of Fame, which that weekend was set to enshrine seven new electees, including Kareem Abdul-Jabbar. It also highlighted how basketball, born early in the century right there in western Massachusetts, had become an international game. And it was created to promote peace and understanding among all nations. Heck, the foreign team even boasted one player from Bosnia and another from Croatia, which just doesn't happen every day.

But to some, that exhibition game, now called the Nike Hoop Summit, is a prime example of the commercialization and corruption of high school sports. By the time the game was held a fifth time during the weekend of the 1999 Final Four in St. Petersburg, Florida, it had been subject to a multimillion-dollar lawsuit as well as serious allegations about how a shoe company had managed to corrupt what was believed to be the serene world of USA Basketball and allowed the game's promoters to circumvent NCAA regulations. At the very least it is an example of how, in the billion-dollar business of high school/college basketball connections, networking and money is everything. And, not surprisingly, in this controversy, numerous questions are raised concerning a shoe company.

John Walsh thought he had come up with the perfect idea. The Chicago-based businessman with the incurable love of basketball figured in 1993 he had discovered a way to combine his talents with his passions. He wanted to get involved in amateur basketball. His idea was to run a high school basketball game each spring that pitted a team of the finest high school players in the United States against a team of the best of the rest of the world. Because he had been nosing around American youth basketball for years as a promoter and a would-be magazine publisher, and because he had strong international ties from his days in the military, he felt he'd be just the guy to put the game together.

"I called it the Father Liberty Game," Walsh said. "It would take place on Father's Day and celebrate the quest for worldwide liberty and peace. Today, when I look back on it, the whole event makes me sick." Walsh says this five years after he ran his first and only Father Liberty Game in Chicago and four years after he filed a lawsuit in United States District Court in Illinois against Nike and CBS, and accused those two, as well as the Basketball Hall of Fame,

USA Basketball, broadcaster Billy Packer, and former Big East commissioner David Gavitt of effectively stealing and profiting from his idea.

Walsh lost his suit, although parts of it are under appeal, mainly because he was unable to prove that Nike and CBS had prior knowledge of the Father Liberty Game when they planned the Nike Hoop Summit, and thus had stolen his idea. He says now that an independent guy like him has little chance of surviving in the world of basketball against a consortium of basketball heavyweights like the aforementioned. Walsh's assertion may be true, although it can be argued that competition is the heart of American capitalism. His complaints about the little guy getting squeezed out by big business are more appropriate for another time and place. But the story of the Nike Hoop Summit is an example of how in basketball today, no one, not the taxpayer-funded USA Basketball, the media, or the innocent player, is safe from getting dragged through the mud of the shoe wars.

Ever since Sonny Vaccaro founded his Dapper Dan Roundball Classic in the early 1970s in Pittsburgh, postseason national high school all-star games have been part of the spring landscape. It's a player's dream. An all-star game usually means a weekend trip somewhere for a couple days of playing basketball, hanging out with kids from around the country, and gaining some exposure by playing in a big arena, often in front of a national television audience. The most prestigious game in the country is now the McDonald's All American game, which takes place each March and rotates its game site around the country. Becoming a McDonald's All American is every prep player's ultimate goal. The title is a badge of honor they wear for the rest of their career. Other events, like Vaccaro's Magic's Roundball Classic in Detroit, the Capital Classic in Washington, and the Kentucky Derby Classic in Louisville, to name a few, also have strong tradition and appeal.

When Walsh thought about creating a new game, he knew the market for a U.S. all-star game was already over-crowded. But, he figured, there was room for an interna-tional all-star game, much like those he had seen take place in Europe during his military duty there. So in 1993, he began working to make it a reality. He found it was a strug-gle to both organize the game and line up the national and international teams. As if recruiting and corraling a team of stars from throughout the world and bringing them to the United States wasn't enough, there was the Byzantine world of U.S. state high school federations and their pecu-liar rules. But after countless hours of work and reels of red tape from state high school federations, he pulled it off. On June 18, 1994, Father's Day, the Father Liberty Game was held in Alumni Gym of the campus of DePaul Univer-sity.

Walsh had even secured sanctioning of the event from USA Basketball on the eve of the game and some compli-mentary shoes and gear from Nike. Because of the short no-tice given the event, attendance was sparse and television coverage nonexistent. "But we pulled it off," says Walsh. "Putting the first one on was impossible but we did it. We had so little advance publicity I had some of our players, Stephon Marbury, Felipe Lopez, everyone, handing out fly-ers on Michigan Avenue the day before the game, trying to drum up support."

Competition-wise, the game was an unqualified suc-cess. Walsh managed to lure nine future NBA players and a dozen soon-to-be college stars to the game, including Marbury, Lopez, Antoine Walker, Lorenzen Wright, Jhadi

White, Trajan Langdon, and international stars Todd Mac-Culloch and Boubacar Aw. "We had everybody," he boasts.

Walsh was excited about the prospects for the future. Sure, attendance was poor and Walsh said he lost more than $100,000, but he said getting people to visualize the event was the greatest hurdle. Now with one under his belt, he could work on improvements and the move toward profitability. But 1994 would be the final Father Liberty Game. The next fall during a board meeting of the Naismith Basketball Hall of Fame in Springfield, a plan was hatched to develop an exhibition basketball game which could not only raise money for the Hall, but provide an entertainment option to tie into the spring enshrinement weekend. The ensuing Nike Hoop Summit effectively ran Walsh and the Father Liberty Game out of business.

The Hall of Fame already ran two games at the Springfield Civic Center—a preseason exhibition NBA game and Thanksgiving weekend's Starter Tip-Off Classic, featuring two top college programs. But due to the then spring date of Enshrinement Weekend (it has since moved to the fall), both the NBA and NCAA were out of the question, since the college season would be over and the NBA playoffs would still be in progress. However, the board, according to court documents, decided that a high school all-star game might be appropriate. Board members David Gavitt, a former Providence College coach, founder and the first commissioner of the Big East Conference, and general manager of the Boston Celtics, and Billy Packer, a former Wake Forest player and top college basketball commentator for CBS, were delegated the task of putting the game together.

After some preliminary work and agreements, the Hoop Summit game was born, with the rights to the game owned by Packer and Gavitt. It was agreed they would pay the Hall of Fame $50,000 in proceeds from the game, according to court records.

Both Packer and Gavitt are well connected in the basketball world and savvy, successful businessmen. Packer used his relationships to secure a sponsorship deal with Nike, work a broadcast deal with CBS, and seek approval from the NCAA. Gavitt, meanwhile, worked his international contacts to arrange a team from, primarily, Europe and with USA Basketball to gain sanctioning. It was a solid, complete business deal. USA Basketball would supply the team, Nike would give money and handle game operations, the Hall of Fame offered credibility and CBS exposure.

The key, both Gavitt and Packer knew, was USA Basketball's involvement. The U.S. Team is officially the United States Junior National Select Team and the players are picked by a seven-member committee appointed by USA Basketball. It is as much a U.S. national team as the United States Olympic team.

That fact is paramount to the existence of the game. When Packer and Gavitt first decided to form the game they realized that getting American high school athletes to compete would be difficult without USA Basketball's help. NCAA regulations prohibit high school players from participating in more than two postseason all-star games. Since most top players will accept an invitation to the prestigious McDonald's All American game, making sure you can beat out the other proliferation of games would be a challenge.

A way around that, Packer and Gavitt realized, was to have the Hoop Classic receive a waiver from the NCAA by having the team not compete as an all-star team but an official national team sanctioned by USA Basketball. The NCAA does not count participation on official USA Basketball teams against its two all-star game limit.

"We were aware that there were high school all-star games during that period of time, but the problem was the two [game] limit," Gavitt said in a deposition. "Given the popularity of the McDonald's Classics already in place, being able to attract top players to play [would be difficult]. So we arrived at the fact that if it were a true national team, a national junior team, if USA Basketball could be interested in a game that involved a junior national team, then the players who played in those two McDonald's [or other] games would be eligible to play in this game. Because they'd be representing the national team, which would make it different and make it not an all-star game."

And that's what happened. USA Basketball became involved and, as part of the deal with Packer and Gavitt, according to court documents, would be paid $33,000 and reimbursed all team costs (training, housing, feeding, and so on of the players and coaches). "The $33,000 would go toward covering the expenses of committee meetings and things of that nature," Gavitt said in his deposition.

The NCAA granted the waiver, allowing the game to move forward, capable of pursuing the very best players in the nation. And it was a desirable package for the kids. Not only would they get to represent their country, but doing so during a third postseason game, shown nationally on CBS, would allow for added exposure and experience. Plus, because they were playing for a national team, they were allowed to keep USA Basketball–provided shoes and gear that the NCAA would require them to return if it was a traditional all-star game.

The key to everything was the sanctity of the selection.

It had to be a true Team USA. "In order to place in its present format, this game has to be a U.S.A. National team and, as such, it's going to be selected by the appropriate games committee of USA Basketball and not by a shoe company or a television entity or any other entity," Gavitt said in his deposition.

But since the heating up of the shoe wars in 1997, critics have howled that an outside entity is selecting the players. That outside entity is one of the game's sponsors: Nike.

Because of time constraints and the academic responsibilities of the high school athlete, the Junior National Select Team is one of only two teams (the elite national team, or Dream Team made up of NBA stars, is the other) sanctioned by USA Basketball which is not selected with the benefit of tryouts. It is handpicked by the USA Basketball Cadet and Youth Committee. "Logistically, because of school and the time of year, we can't do [tryouts]," says the committee's chair Rod Seaford.

And that selection process has raised concerns over the past few years as the players picked overwhelmingly have two common characteristics: They are American and they compete almost exclusively in the Nike grassroots basketball system, i.e. attending the Nike All-America Camp or playing for Nike-sponsored AAU teams.

"It's why the game is a sham," complained, not surprisingly, Sonny Vaccaro. "USA Basketball has let Nike come in and buy them out. This team, which is supposed to represent the United States, is instead picked by shoe affiliation and not ability. It doesn't represent the United States. It represents Nike."

The facts, to a degree, back up Vaccaro's allegations. Although USA Basketball insists the following is just a coincidence, there's plenty of fodder for critics. Here are the numbers:

The twelve-member 1999 team was overwhelmingly made up of Nike grassroots players. Only two of the players attended the adidas ABCD Camp. One of those, North Carolina's Jason Parker, played AAU ball in the Nike system for the Charlotte Royals, which, coincidentally, is organized by committee chair Rod Seaford. The other, Oregon's Michael Dunleavy, signed a national letter of intent with Duke, a program with close ties to USA Basketball. Even highly regarded adidas players such as Jonathan Bender, Carlos Boozer, Jr., and Dermarr Johnson were not selected.

In 1998, nine of the twelve members of the team attended the Nike Camp. Of the three who went to adidas, both Rashard Lewis and Tony Kitchings played traveling team ball under the Nike umbrella. The 1997 team boasted ten Nike Camp veterans against two from adidas' ABCD.

This took place during a time frame where the consensus opinion from independent recruiting gurus and talent scouts held that the adidas ABCD Camp had superior talent to the Nike Camp each year. To add to the controversy, there's this: Nike is not only the title sponsor of the game, but three of the members of the seven-member player selection committee run traveling teams that are outfitted and funded by Nike—Seaford's Charlotte Royals, Boo Williams's Boo Williams AAU, and Ron Crawford's Arkansas Wings. Seaford, a Charlotte, North Carolina, attorney, is also a member of the board of directors of the national Amateur Athletic Union, which also receives funding from Nike.

Adding to the conspiracy theory is the fact that Williams, Crawford, and St. Louis Eagles AAU coach Rich

Gray, also Nike-sponsored, have all served as assistant coaches for the USA team in the game. Then there is committee member John Farrell, who represents the high school federation on the board and is a former coach of San Diego Torrey Pines High School. Farrell, now a physical education teacher at San Diego's La Costa Canyon High School, has a long-standing business relationship with Nike, having run a Nike-sponsored summer AAU tournament in Las Vegas from 1984 until 1995. He now organizes the Nike-sponsored Best of the Summer AAU Tournament in San Diego. Nike provides not only sponsorship money but applies considerable pressure on its traveling teams to attend Farrell's tournament.

Ironically, it was Vaccaro who first brought Farrell into the Nike organization. "I started Johnny off at Nike in the mid-1980s," said Vaccaro. "He's been in business with Nike for years." Farrell did not return numerous calls from the authors.

Which means everyone from the game's organizers, Packer and Gavitt, to the majority of the talent selectors, to the coaches, to the majority of the players, has a sponsorship relationship with the swoosh. And that has created the perception that the USA Team is not made up of the best players the nation has to offer, but rather the best players Nike has to offer.

"I can see how that perception could come about, honestly, because there are three AAU members of this committee and we all have some type of sponsorship agreement with Nike," says Seaford.

So the important question arises, has Nike bought out the United States Junior National Team, a squad certified by USA Basketball, which receives taxpayer funds to exist?

"I can tell you categorically, where a kid has gone to camp, or who he may be affiliated with, has never been an issue or ever been discussed," Seaford said. "Now, obviously, you want to see the players you select. And I suspect if you are a Nike coach and you are going to Nike events, you are more likely to run across Nike players. That is true. It would make sense to believe that the guys you are familiar with are going to make an impression on you. I don't think we have ever picked a player that some member of the committee has not personally seen."

Outside of personal scouting, Seaford says the committee forms a master list based on player rankings in basketball magazines and recruiting newsletters. Committee members also ask around and seek the opinions of contacts throughout the country. Seaford says no one at Nike has any impact on their decisions. "I've never had anyone at Nike suggest a player or even nominate a player," Seaford said. "We've never had a conversation with Nike. One year I was on a Nike conference call [of AAU coaches] and I said what we were doing and if [they] wanted to make recommendations for players we'd be happy to hear from them. And I don't think I even got any nominations out of that."

Seaford says that comparing players who were picked against those who weren't by ability isn't necessarily fair, since, he says, the committee is not interested in selecting the twelve best players, but rather the best team. "Our charge is to win the game," he says. "To me, it's embarrassing to lose the game and we've lost twice."

And that criterion helps players who are familiar to the committee, Seaford says. "We try to place a very high premium on what we know about the kid personally, because to come in and become a basketball team in two, two and a half days is not easy. What we try to do is select the twelve players most likely to get a win, not the twelve best players. If we had our druthers we'd have a tryout, but because it occurs during the school year we don't have that luxury," Seaford said.

This charge of shoe tampering is taken seriously by USA Basketball, according to assistant executive director for public relations Craig Miller. Miller says he doubts the hierarchy of USA Basketball is influenced by Nike, but admits that few people at the Colorado Springs office are aware which grassroots program a player is in. "I'd be surprised if any of our committee members were preventing non–Nike Camp players from being invited to play for the USA team," Miller said. "I believe they want the USA to win and that they select the players who will give us the best chance to do so."

In court documents both Packer and Gavitt state that no one at Nike or CBS has ever asked them to select certain players.

Still, is such a high concentration of Nike players really just an honest coincidence? "We are going to look into it," said Miller. "When we first formed this committee our concern was balancing the interests of AAU and high school. That's why each group has representatives. Maybe what we need to look at is having Nike and adidas equally represented. We take our credibility on this very seriously and this concerns us."

Certainly the Nike Hoop Summit isn't the only game that comes under political, often shoe company, influence. The most obvious is Vaccaro's Magic's Roundball Classic, formerly the Dapper Dan, which Vaccaro makes no bones about being a de facto, adidas grassroots all-star game. Although its name sponsor is Magic Johnson, and nearly all proceeds from the game benefit Johnson's charities, the rosters are stacked almost exclusively with players from the adidas grassroots system. The coaches are from adidas high schools. The most prominent adidas AAU coaches come for the weekend regardless of whether they have a player in the game and some even use the weekend to recruit young prospects.

Darren Matsubara, of the adidas-sponsored Elite Basketball Organization, spent the 1998 Roundball entertaining DeShawn Stevenson, then a sophomore at Fresno (California) Washington High and one of the top five players in the class of 2000. In 1997, Joel Hopkins of the adidas prep school Mt. Zion Christian Academy in Durham, North Carolina, showed up with Marvin Stone, then a sophomore from Huntsville Grissom High, a Nike school.

"Pretty much," says Vaccaro, "you have to play at ABCD to be in the Roundball. But at least I admit it. I dare the rest of the games to do the same."

And there's more. ESPN and ABC broadcaster Dick Vitale is arguably the most influential voice in college basketball and speaks at both the Magic's game banquet and the ABCD Camp as part of his promotional contract with adidas. He also serves as color commentator of the Magic's game on ESPN2.

At the 1998 banquet, adidas' top pitchman, Kobe Bryant himself, in town for a Lakers game against the Detroit Pistons, came to the banquet and was treated like a rock star.

And the more savvy movers and shakers in the game are present also. Atlanta financial planner Bret Bearup, a player for Kentucky in the mid-1980s, who handles scores of professional athletes and entertainers, is a regular, making early contacts with players and their parents. Bearup, who says his financial company, ProTrust, pays adidas $5,000 to be a sponsor of the event, is a regular in the lobby bar of the local Marriott Hotel, buying anyone associated with the game—usually AAU coaches—drinks and cigars deep into the night.

At the 1999 game, Bearup paid for the meals of all the players and their families, according to Vaccaro. So happy was Vaccaro that in an after-dinner speech he not only praised Bearup's generosity, but presented him with his own Magic's Roundball jacket, which usually only the players receive. In a speech that had even the most grizzled college coaches rolling their eyes, Vaccaro claimed, "Bret doesn't do this because he wants anything, just because it's the right thing to do."

And he isn't the only one. As Magic's game veterans continually head directly to the pro ranks (the 1998 game had both Rashard Lewis and Al Harrington, 1999 included Jonathan Bender and Leon Smith), wise players agents and financial planners have made the event a must stop for the client procurement efforts.

The event is one of Vaccaro's centerpieces. The loyalty he provides is unforgettable to the kids. Unlike the Mc-Donald's All American game, Vaccaro provides round-trip transportation and lodging for not only the players but their families too. It's Sonny at his finest, hosting and hugging not only the nation's top players (and thus potential pitchmen), but their parents, their sisters, their aunts, their uncles, their advisors, and their coaches. He works all angles.

Vaccaro insists Raveling is jealous of the event's success and tries to undermine it by keeping the few Nike players Vaccaro invites away—a charge Raveling denies. As a way of helping the gate and generating local support, Vaccaro annually extends invitations to the top players from the state of Michigan, regardless of shoe affiliation. He says he usually hits a stone wall when it comes to the Nike players. He accuses Raveling of pushing them to play in the Capital Classic in Washington instead.

"Only three times have I had a kid turn me down," says Vaccaro. "Dane Fife in 1998. Shane Battier in 1997. Mike Chappell in 1996. All three Michigan kids who played at the Nike Camp. I mean Dane Fife and Battier? It [was] a sin that they didn't come here. To play in an abominable game called the Capital Classic, when Fife lives ten minutes from the Palace.

"That's strictly an attempt to hurt me. The shame of it is that it didn't hurt me. It hurt Magic Johnson. It hurt the fans. It didn't hurt the game, we went on fine."

More troubling, however, is the influence shoe company business deals have on the way America watches college basketball on television.

Although TV has long wrestled with the struggle of being courtside as an impartial member of the media while also being a vehicle for entertainment, the level of shoe company influence, and its inherent conflicts of interest, in the broadcast booths in the late 1990s is striking.

Consider Billy Packer. A self-described "walking conflict of interest" due to his dual role as media member and basketball promoter, his deal with Nike on the Hoop Summit alone raises questions about objectivity. Packer, according to court documents, is paid a minimum of $15,000 for his efforts to run the Hoop Summit. Some of that money comes from Nike.

In a March 1999 profile of Packer in *USA Today,* the newspaper said Packer was once asked by a class of college students about juggling his role as pitchman against his role as journalist. He responded: "We all have a price in life. There's some [dollar] number—maybe very high—that would make you go over and grab him and say 'You're mine tonight.' "

While he admirably refuses to discuss recruiting or high school basketball during broadcasts as CBS's top college color commentator, his off-camera comments to the print media on the subject can be telling.

In 1995, Packer caused a small outrage when he made an unfortunate comparison of Georgetown guard Allen Iverson to a monkey. Politically correct groups immediately cried racism and the storm of controversy could have ruined his career—much in the same manner as was former CBS National Football League commentator Jimmy "The Greek" Snyder's. However, in the immediate aftermath, two prominent black college basketball personalities—and friends from Nike—rushed to his defense and forgave him: George Raveling and John Thompson.

Those comments from two of the sport's most visible and outspoken black coaches soothed things over immediately. Packer survived with minimal damage to his reputation.

While the defense of Packer was justifiable and while CBS and Packer deny it, was it a coincidence that Raveling soon after became an in-studio host during the 1996 NCAA Tournament?

Or how about when *60 Minutes* broadcast a report questioning the role shoe companies, particularly Nike, play in high school sports, and Packer immediately leapt to the company's defense telling the Associated Press that the report was "shoddy journalism." Was that quid pro quo?

The most glaring conflict of interest is, obviously, Raveling himself. For two years he was an in-studio analyst on CBS, providing him with incredible exposure. At the same time he was head of Nike's grassroots basketball efforts, an advertiser of the broadcast. Was he ever loyal to one boss over the other?

Not surprisingly, Vaccaro thinks so. He admits to watching his old friend on television and wanting to kick his television set out of disgust.

"I and the people of America look to [the media] for conveying the truth," said Vaccaro. "And that's not necessarily the thing. CBS hires George Raveling and he's a recruiter of kids looking to put those kids into a corporate sponsor's coffers. Where is the journalistic integrity of this thing? This is so wrong. It is so wrong because Mr. and Mrs. America look at this thing and they see Mr. Raveling up there talking to Mr. [Pat] O'Brien.

"You can't serve two masters," Vaccaro continued. "You can't serve and work for Nike, who's a major buyer of time on your network. The guy is out recruiting kids to go play in the youth tournaments of this corporate sponsor that you are getting millions from."

Raveling parted ways with CBS in 1998, although the network refused to say why it no longer uses him as an in-studio host. He does, however, retain a major television presence by working since 1997 as the top color analyst on Fox Sports' Pac-10 games.

"George Raveling has as much right being on there as Chairman Mao," Vaccaro says. "He has no right being on there. He is everything [a journalist] is not supposed to be. Obviously a journalist is supposed to be unaffected by anything.

"But the height of hypocrisy in all sports, CBS in particular," Vaccaro said, "was the day they had George Raveling interview John Thompson on questions that needed to be asked. The gambling questions. John was brought into some gaming things in Vegas, and you had his best friend and Nike partner ask him the questions? Who can argue that is good journalism?"

The laughable interview occurred in 1996, after it came to light that Thompson, then head coach at Georgetown, had applied for a license in Nevada to be partial owner of slot machines at Las Vegas' McCarron International Airport. Because of the NCAA's staunch opposition to all forms of gambling—legal or illegal—the application caused national headlines.

Dispatching Raveling, then a paid consultant by Nike, to interview his longtime friend Thompson, then a member of Nike's board of directors, was tantamount to having an employee question his boss on national television under the guise of being an objective journalist. While CBS seemed to have no problem doing just that, it doesn't take the most media-savvy person to see a problem with Raveling tossing softball questions at Thompson.

Raveling, however, bristles at suggestions that he took it easy on Thompson and grows angry at anyone who questions his credentials or performance as a reporter, even implying that questioning his efforts might be racist.

"What does that have to do with anything?" says Raveling. "I asked him difficult [questions]."

Raveling may have thought he had asked difficult questions, but a review of videotape reveals that the most basic question of all—"John, is it appropriate for a college basketball coach to be involved in anything related with gambling?"—was never asked on air.

Raveling says that the reason people cite him as a potential conflict of interest is because of jealousy and the color of his skin.

"The most recent examples of people supposedly having conflict of interest have both been black people," Raveling said. "Len Emore [a registered player agent/broadcaster] and myself are the only two people that I know that have been questioned by the media as having conflicts of interest. No one says anything about Vitale. I could name you a lot of other people that have conflicts of interest. Billy Packer. Everybody has a conflict of interest. But the only people that have been attacked are two black people."

Even Vaccaro's objectivity can be questioned. He appears as a weekly guest on Southern California's all-sports-talk radio station XTRA, where he is identified as a basketball analyst, not an employee of adidas America. Likewise he makes frequent appearances on the CBS-TV affiliate in Los Angeles. "But I don't get paid," Vaccaro reasons. "I'm a guest. I'm just on. If I sign a contract with them, I wouldn't work for adidas. I wouldn't do that."

Raveling thinks the questioning of his ethics isn't fair. "I think there should be some balance there," he says. "Dick Vitale accepts money from adidas. ESPN's Robin Roberts accepts money from adidas, but [the media doesn't] say that that's a conflict of interest. And I find that interesting. You roast me and say I shouldn't be doing this, I shouldn't be doing that, but you won't do the same thing about other people that are doing it."

Raveling is correct, as both Vitale and Roberts receive money from adidas. Vitale speaks twice a year to the adidas grassroots basketball group.

"We pay him the same as any company would, we pay him through the *Washington Post*'s speakers bureau," said

Vaccaro. "It's different. You don't think he's been bought by IBM when he speaks for them, do you?"

That's a different subject, although even Vitale's most vocal critics don't think he's bought and paid for. This is despite the fact that his broadcasts often turn into an after-dinner speech chock-full of compliments to college coaches, players, administrators, journalists, even actors, baseball players, politicians, and anyone else that comes to mind. He even is quick to mention recruiting and high school players and coaches on the air.

Obviously, the possibility is there, but Vitale's effusive style, and his lack of intense involvement in the shoe wars, just doesn't portray a dark side.

But fairly or unfairly, when Raveling does the same during his broadcasts he makes skeptics wonder if he were to drop the name of a high school coach, might it be because it's the proper analysis or because he's trying to get one of the coach's players to the Nike Camp. Raveling's role as an active recruiter for the company subjects him to a higher level of scrutiny than a Vitale, who simply gives two motivational speeches.

Also a fair question is whether Vaccaro is truly concerned about the journalistic ethics of the American media or, rather, is just upset about the competitive advantage Raveling gets from all that television exposure.

"Let's pretend you are Mr. and Mrs. Smith and [your son] Joe is a real good ballplayer," Vaccaro says. "You're watching television—you don't know who I am. You have no idea about all this. But you look up there and you see Mr. Raveling. You think, 'My God, that's good. He knows people at CBS. They televise the game. Oh God! George Raveling called us.' See what I am saying. It is so bad. It's why I'll never win."

And with that, he's in agreement with John Walsh, founder of the Father Liberty Game. Without the proper connections, it's nearly impossible to win in the business of college athletics.

CHAPTER 7

Wesley Wilson

Up in the bucolic hills of central Massachusetts, where each fall the trees turn auburn and gold, sits the small town of Winchendon. It's classic New England, the common in the center, the creek running nearby, the woods grown thick as they stretch north over the nearby New Hampshire border.

It's the kind of scenic setting and quiet town a long way from the tough streets of Brooklyn, Los Angeles, or Chicago, a town where you would never imagine the sketchier elements of basketball to find a home. Winchendon doesn't even have its own high school—local kids attend a small regional school that has never produced a Division I scholarship player.

That all changed, though, when the local preparatory school—the Winchendon School—began thinking big a decade ago. The 170-student, sixty-year-old school resembles something out of the Robin Williams movie *Dead Poets Society,* a place where upper-crust Northeasterners send their sons to shore up academics or to find maturity.

In other parts of the nation students who have the desire

to improve the scope of their college opportunities attend junior colleges. But in New England, those with the means, many of whom are seeking a spot at an Ivy League or small private college, head off to schools such as Winchendon. The $26,500 per year price tag doesn't seem to be much of a deterrent.

But annually about twelve members of Winchendon's class are not your traditional New England prep school student. A decade ago, faced with dwindling enrollment, Winchendon embarked on an aggressive campaign to bolster its exposure and its student population through its athletics department.

It's a system used for decades by colleges seeking a national profile. Since the 1980s it has been used by a number of boarding schools and postgraduate institutions, the most notable being Virginia's tiny and distant Oak Hill Academy. There Oak Hill coach Steve Smith has built a national high school powerhouse, attracting future NBA stars such as Rod Strickland and Ron Mercer to the hundred-person town of Mouth of Wilson, deep in the Iron Mountains of southwest Virginia. Smith's successful basketball program has turned the school's financial fortunes around, setting the stage for other schools to follow suit.

Taking Oak Hill's cue, Winchendon assembled a basketball and hockey team in the late 1980s, offering high school graduates a chance to qualify academically for college and showcase their game to Division I recruiters. Winchendon offers no scholarships, but does have an extensive financial aid system.

In the spring of 1996 with the basketball program in full swing, Winchendon hired a new coach, Mike Byrnes, a Canton, Massachusetts, native and former reserve on John Calipari's early University of Massachusetts teams. In the early 1990s he was the successful head coach of Hargrave Military Academy, a boarding school in Danville, Virginia, and then spent the 1996 season as a volunteer coach on UMass' Final Four team.

Having worked at Hargrave, Byrnes had seen his share of recruiting headaches. Finding players for an NCAA Division I school is difficult enough, but getting kids from around the country to come to a high school can be mind-numbing.

To start, no one grows up dreaming of playing in prep school. There is a natural resistance to even being recruited, which means most kids put off the decision until the last minute. Second, very few kids heading off to prep school have previously seen their name printed on the honor role, so trying to decipher transcripts where the only time one of the first three letters of the alphabet appear is in gym class can be exhausting.

Then there are few, if any, rules in the world of prep school. Unlike at the college level there are no letters of intent to bind a student to a school. Kids routinely commit to more than one school and, even after classes start in September, often skip town for a better offer.

That's one of the advantages, Oak Hill's Smith says, of living in a distant locale.

"Once they get here, I pretty much know I've got them," he says. "You can't catch a subway out of here."

And finally, you can't help but stereotype the kids you are dealing with. Most players who hail from a solid family, are good citizens, and take care of their grades are never going to come in contact with Byrnes or Smith. While both coaches have good kids who enrolled because they sought exposure to college coaches, the majority of the top players have, as it is known in the business, "a history."

Byrnes had experienced all of those headaches and he thought he had seen just about everything trying to convince kids at the end of the basketball playing rope to come to a military school on the Virginia–North Carolina border. Everything, he says, until he shakes his head and recalls what happened to his prize recruit for the class of 1999.

"Strangest thing I've ever seen," he says. "I never thought I'd have to worry about losing recruits over what kind of shoe they wear."

But he would. Because at Winchendon players wear adidas and Byrnes's star recruit, Wesley Wilson, wears Nike. And what Byrnes would learn is that in 1999, recruits don't care so much about your academics, your dorms, or your schedule of opponents, as much as they, and the people around them, seem to care about what they'll wear on their feet.

Growing up in Vallejo, California, a city of 100,000 in California's Bay Area, Wesley Wilson admits he wasn't much of a player. But by the time he was sixteen and a sophomore at Vallejo High, he was nearly 6-foot-10 and despite rough edges to his game, he was in hot demand along the California AAU circuit. Since then, Wilson's is the story of the modern high school basketball star working through a system where another perk, another team, another school, a scholarship to Georgetown awaits because the demand never cools.

From the day he was first discovered as a tall kid who could run as well as a guard, he's been courted and coddled from coast to coast, jetted overseas courtesy of Nike, and been offered opportunities at the nation's finest schools despite an aversion to classwork. And although his grades have never been much, Wesley Wilson isn't dumb. He knows exactly what multinational shoe companies, smarmy AAU coaches, prep schools, and college coaches want from him: the same thing they've wanted from him since he was sixteen. Just play ball.

"I wasn't even that good back then, but they saw the potential, I guess," says Wilson. "I was tall and I could run without tripping over my feet."

Wilson played at the time for a Los Angeles–based traveling basketball team called Sports Express, which is coached by Miles Gonzalez. Although Sports Express was routinely one of the nation's most talented and prominent clubs, in 1995, they had no shoe affiliation.

That would change the year George Raveling got his job at Nike. He called Gonzalez and invited him to dinner. The two had known each other since Raveling tried to recruit one of Gonzalez's players—Kenyon Johnson—to Southern California in the early 1990s. Johnson went to Cal, but Raveling and Gonzalez stayed tight.

By the time dinner ended that night in Los Angeles, Sports Express was suddenly a Nike team, agreeing to a deal where the shoe company provided $15,000 in sponsorship money as well as shoes, gear, and bags for the players, Gonzalez says. It's an average deal by Nike standards, but Gonzalez was grateful. In exchange for the company's loyalty, he makes no bones about steering his players to the Nike All-America Camp and has a tremendous sense of loyalty to the swoosh and Raveling.

"I do try to help bring certain top kids to the All-America camp," Gonzalez says. "Those are the people that donate to my program. I try to bring the players [to camp] to give them that exposure. I don't see anything wrong with that."

Wilson was flattered by the offer to play with Sports Express, but as he burst onto the scene as a sophomore, he began realizing Gonzalez wasn't the only one interested. He was routinely approached by AAU teams throughout the state, he says, looking for him to leave Gonzalez.

"In between games there would be people approaching me, saying play with my team. Just trying to steal players," Wilson says. "There were always people calling me on the phone trying to get me to play basketball for their team. 'I'll give you this, I'll give you that.' Shoes and stuff. Clothes. My phone rings all the time, even now."

Like most young players, he was initially amazed at the urgency AAU coaches placed on getting players, not to mention the suddenly high demand he was in. It calloused him quickly. "It's 'Play for this team, we're about to go to Georgia. Play for this team, go to L.A. Play for this team.' All the time. Every day there are two or three that try to talk to you, get you to travel with them. They don't consider it taking you away. They just say, 'Come play this one tournament with me. Can I get your number, call you up sometime. We'll have shoes and we'll have the gear when you get there.' "

Ignoring the offers, Wilson stayed true to Gonzalez and Vallejo. And by the middle of his senior year Wilson was 6-11, strong and vastly improved. Although scouting services still ranked him as low as a top one hundred player, it was clear Wilson was about to become a serious force. He was reaching his potential on the court.

The problem was grades. Books never interested him like shooting baskets did, and as a result Wilson was way behind academically. It was obvious his senior year that he would struggle to earn his high school diploma, let alone qualify academically to earn a Division I scholarship. He began thinking about junior college until Gonzalez thought that a year at prep school might be perfect for him. By sending him away, particularly back East, Wilson could spend one year honing his game and shoring up his transcript. When he was done he'd still have four years of NCAA eligibility remaining.

So in late December of 1997, Gonzalez decided to find a school for Wilson.

"I've never done this before, as far as dealing with prep schools," Gonzalez says. "I was starting to get worried and I didn't want Wesley to get left out. I'm like, I gotta call around, and Winchendon is the first school that I talked to."

At the time, Gonzalez said, he had no idea Winchendon had a deal with adidas. Byrnes says the company provides his team free shoes, but nothing else, not even warm-up gear, and no monetary compensation.

"Hey, I'm grateful for what we got," Byrnes said. "I have a lot of inner-city kids who wouldn't be able to afford those shoes. I'm thankful for what Sonny [Vaccaro] gives me."

Gonzalez says he called Raveling and asked his opinion on where Wilson should go to school but, partly because of Raveling's busy schedule and partly because Wilson was not considered an elite player, it was months before the two talked at length about the player.

And by that time Wilson had called Byrnes himself.

"The kid called me one day in my office after practice and said, 'I'm not going to qualify. Tell me about your school,' " Byrnes said. "We talked for about forty-five minutes. I had heard of him. This was late January. He faxed me his transcript. I went through it, told him what he had to do. I spoke to his mother. He said, 'I'm coming.' "

The transcript would be an issue. One college coach who recruited Wilson calls his transcript "the second worst I've ever seen in my career. It was a joke. No way he was getting eligible." Byrnes told Wilson that in order to make it he would have to spend three semesters at Winchendon. That meant coming to central Massachusetts in June of 1998 and attending summer school before playing during the 1998–99 school year.

"He needed six core classes," said Byrnes. "That meant if he got two done in the summer and four during the school year he had a shot to make it. I was the first coach to break it down for him like that."

That made sense to Wilson, so he verbally committed to Winchendon and admits he told Byrnes he'd be there for summer school. He also says he had a high opinion of Byrnes and his straightforward manner.

"I liked him," Wilson said. "I liked his personality. I liked everything about him. We just clicked when we were on the phone. In the beginning we talked maybe once every two weeks, then it was like once a week, sometimes twice a week."

That changed in April of 1998 when Wilson accompanied Sports Express to Nike's major spring event, the Boo Williams Classic in Hampton, Virginia.

Wilson was phenomenal, running the court, using his powerful frame to score inside, and blocking shots at will. He became the talk of the tournament. His stock soared with college recruiters. And everything began to change.

"I started not hearing from the kid as much," Byrnes said. "So I called Miles, and I said, 'What's going on?' "

"He said Wesley played really well at the Boo Williams

tournament. Apparently some Nike representatives saw him and said they wanted him to come to the Nike Camp. Miles said Wesley has to go to Nike Camp.

"I said if he comes here, he can't. He needs like six core classes. The only way I can take him is if he comes to summer school. Miles said he has to go to Nike Camp.

"People [began] telling me, 'You're not getting him [Wilson].' I'd say, 'What are you talking about? I talk to him three, four times a week. He told me last night he's coming.' A lot of college coaches said after the way he played at Boo Williams, he's not going to an adidas school."

Byrnes decided to call Gonzalez and separate rumor from fact.

"Miles said, if Wesley goes to the Winchendon School, I can never deal with your program again," Byrnes said. "It totally floored me. He said, 'You're an adidas school, I'm a Nike program. He can't go to your school.' Miles told me it was out of his hands. I felt like it wasn't his call. A higher power was making that call."

Gonzalez does not deny that shoe affiliation became an important factor in Wilson's decision. But as spring rolled on, Wilson said he was still interested in Winchendon.

"I talked to Wesley," Byrnes said. "He said, 'Can I wear Nikes in layup lines and adidas in games?' I told him you can wear slippers if you want to. It's not about that. Like I care. He said, 'I'm catching flak from people who said you're an adidas school.' He said, 'Are you going to make me go to a certain college? I don't want to be forced to go anywhere.' I was like, 'I don't care where you go, I'm not like that.' "

Wilson says he asked about wearing Nikes in layup lines just to get Byrnes's reaction.

"I just wanted to see if he cared," Wilson says. "And he was like, 'I don't care whether you wear adidas or Nike.'"

Eventually, however, Byrnes says he realized others did care what shoe Wilson would be wearing. "The mother finally told me one day he won't be going to Winchendon School," Byrnes said.

Wilson attended the Nike Camp in Indianapolis in July of 1998 and was one of the camp's best performers, cementing himself as one of the nation's top twenty players. He also made a trip to France and played for a select group of Nike all-stars. He attended no summer school.

He did, however, commit to a scholarship offer at Georgetown University, one of the nation's finest academic institutions, which, at the time, was being coached by John Thompson, a member of Nike's board of directors.

By fall, Wilson was enrolled not at Winchendon, but at Maine Central Institute, a Nike-sponsored school and one of the country's most powerful prep programs. Like Winchendon and Oak Hill, MCI has made the small town it occupies, Pittsfield, Maine, a haven for college recruiters. During the three-week period each September that the NCAA allocates for coaches to visit recruits in their homes, these towns become overrun with college coaches attempting to proselytize recruits to their school.

With as many as a dozen Division I prospects on each team, it's not unusual for 250 coaches to roll through town each September. They crowd into the tiny coffee shops, sitting shoulder to shoulder at the counter in Armani suits. They line their rental cars up in the school parking lot and overwhelm the place with a different type of tourist than the usual outdoorsmen and foliage seekers the area is used to.

"When the coaches fly into Bangor and rent cars," says then MCI coach Max Good, "at the rent-a-car desk they say, 'Oh, you must be going down to MCI.' There are so many of them, they know."

Coaches from the most prominent schools, the ones that own their own planes, can even crowd the local airport. Oak Hill's Steve Smith recalls a day in the early 1990s when he drove University of Kentucky coach Rick Pitino back to a small airstrip in Sparta, North Carolina, about twenty minutes from Mouth of Wilson, where Learjets can land.

Just before Pitino was about to board the Kentucky plane, a jet owned by the University of Indiana touched down and Hoosiers coach Bob Knight emerged.

"He and Rick start talking and Bobby points to the UK jet and says, 'You call this a plane? Look at the size of my plane. It's much bigger than yours,' " Smith said.

In the case of placing Wesley Wilson at MCI, Gonzalez swears George Raveling never mentioned MCI's Nike affiliation to him when he suggested MCI, but admits he thought of it himself. He does say Raveling praised Good as a coach, as did the coaching staffs at Georgetown and Michigan, both Nike schools recruiting Wilson. Good said he first heard of Wilson from Michigan coach Brian Ellerbe.

That, however, is not unusual. Good is considered one of the finest coaches at the high school level in the country. From 1980 to 1988 Good was the head coach of Eastern Kentucky University. He has since made certain that Maine, despite rarely producing a high-level basketball player, has one of the premier high school programs in the country.

Good's recruiting pitch is a simple one. He is popular with players because he runs his program, particularly practices, like a college coach, helping prepare them for the future. College coaches love him because he rarely interferes in recruiting and, although his team wears Nike, he is not considered a Raveling stooge.

"Max is one of the few guys in the country that's never looking for anything," said one prominent coach.

"No, I'd die first," Good said. "In fact, a couple of people have asked me about going back to college with a kid. And I let them know very quickly that I'd never go back to a college where one of my kids went. I'm not looking to go to college anyway, I've been there and this is very rewarding for me. I can make a living on my own. I don't need somebody else to do that. To me, that's totally demeaning to make a living off of a kid's back. I wouldn't feel right about that."

Although Good has since returned to the college level as an assistant at UNLV, that mentality served him well during his days at MCI.

In addition to landing Wilson, as well as top Nike player Caron Butler of Wisconsin, Good also added Maryland's Dermarr Johnson to his 1998–99 roster. Johnson not only played for the adidas-sponsored Kensington (Maryland) Newport School (although it's now with Nike) and the adidas flagship program Team Assault, of Washington, D.C., but is extremely close with Sonny Vaccaro.

"Unlike my competitor," Vaccaro said, "I want guys like Dermarr to go where it is best for them. I want him to be happy, not worry about what shoe he's wearing there at MCI."

Johnson, like Wilson, is in his fifth year of high school. Considered the number one player in the country since his sophomore year, the smooth 6-9 Johnson had struggled for more on-court intensity his junior year. A change of scenery was deemed necessary.

And like Wilson, Johnson listened to the AAU coach, the adidas-sponsored Curtis Malone, whom he lived with his junior year of high school. Malone said Johnson needed Good's top-notch coaching and motivation. Team Assault also featured top five prospect Keith Bogans, a skilled 6-4 shooting guard headed for the University of Kentucky, who, Malone felt, had better fundamentals because he learned the game from Hyattsville (Maryland) DeMatha High coach Morgan Wooten, a legend of the high school ranks.

"You watch Dermarr and Keith mess around in the gym and Keith can't do any of the things Dermarr does," Malone said. "But on the court Keith knows the game. He knows how to play. That's because he's gotten great coaching from Morgan Wooten at DeMatha. Dermarr needs that."

For his part, Chris Chaney, Johnson's coach at the Newport School, also approved of the move.

"Dermarr needs a father figure and I think I'm more of a big brother," said the twenty-nine-year-old Chaney. "He needs to be pushed. I love the kid and I just want what's best for him."

Good is just the man to lower the hammer. The Gardiner, Maine, native is tough on his players, breaking them down before rebuilding them. He's stern, sometimes nasty, and always means business. Four times in his ten years at MCI he broke his hand punching a blackboard.

And it worked. His teams were 270-30 over the last decade. And more important, of the sixty players who came to MCI needing to academically qualify for college, fifty-five made it.

"The 270 wins and thirty losses isn't nearly as important to me as fifty-five of sixty kids qualifying," he says. "We never brag on our kids. I find [stuff] they can't do and tell them. We spend a lot of time here telling them how good they aren't. We don't tell them how good they are. They've already gotten enough of that."

So driven is Good, he says he won't accept any trophy from a tournament unless it's the championship one. He stuns tournament directors when he discreetly ships back runner-up trophies with a note saying thanks but no thanks.

"I think that's what's wrong with our society," he says. "Goddamn, we're giving trophies now to a losing team."

Not surprisingly, he patterns his program after the most disciplined college ones. "If a kid comes here I think he can go to Temple or Indiana and make the adjustment," Good said. "I don't think there is much of an adjustment. Dermarr visited Cincinnati and he said I was much worse than Bob Huggins. I take that as a compliment."

Although you would imagine losing Dermarr Johnson, one of the top players in the nation, would be devastating to Chaney and Newport, in prep basketball the top programs just reload.

Chaney sprung back, merely restocking the team at his $12,000-a-year private school in suburban Washington, D.C. He is at a disadvantage to the boarding schools such as Oak Hill and MCI because the Newport School has no dorms. If a player comes out of the area, he helps find sponsors that might want to house him, but mainly he relies on local kids.

Upon losing Johnson, however, he did switch shoe companies, leaving adidas after three years to take a sponsorship deal for Newport with Nike.

"Adidas was great," says Chaney. "They did a great job and I liked being with them but I'm very happy to be with Nike now. I'm not as into the shoe stuff as other people but I think Nike is the best company and I wanted to establish relationships with a company I hope to be with for the rest of my life.

"I had just heard a lot of rumors when I was with adidas," Chaney continued. "You hear Sonny may retire soon. I want to be with the same company for as long as I'm coaching and I hope that's Nike."

And Nike had the kind of contacts that could help.

"A lot of the AAU teams we deal with are Nike," Chaney said. "Plus Georgetown is right here and I've always been close to Georgetown. One of our players [Victor Samnick] is going to Georgetown and Lou [Bullock, whom Chaney coached at Laurel (Maryland) Baptist] is at Michigan and they're both Nike schools. It just made sense."

And it didn't kill him with adidas-affiliated programs. Chaney worked the adidas ABCD Camp each of the past three summers. Last July on his camp team he coached Donnell Harvey, a top five prospect in the class of 1999 from rural Georgia. Harvey played AAU ball for the adidas-sponsored Atlanta Celtics and coach Wallace Prather.

"After each of the games Wallace and I talked and we established a good relationship," Chaney said.

That paid off when Prather mentioned that one of his younger players, 6-2 point guard Jamison Brewer, of East Point, Georgia, was in need of a new school for his senior season. Chaney found a local sponsor family for Brewer to live with, the kid moved north, and Brewer starred for Newport during the 1998–99 season.

Everybody was a winner in the deal, though the adidas-loyal Brewer and the now Nike-clad Chaney had to sit down and have a preseason talk about appropriate apparel. "We had a meeting when he came here," says Chaney. "He's been an adidas man his whole life. He's got so much adidas stuff it's unbelievable. Every jacket. Every shirt. He's like, 'Can I wear this on the court?'

"I was like, 'Anything to do with Newport you have to wear Nike. We are 100 percent Nike.' I told him off the court he could wear whatever he wants, I have no control over that, but not on the court."

Chaney sympathizes. After three years of collecting complimentary adidas gear, his closet is full of three-stripe clothes and shoes. He has to watch what he slips on.

"It's gotten so bad that when I pack for a trip I have to look at each T-shirt, each sweatshirt, and make sure it's not adidas. I have to make sure I only pack Nike stuff. I have to be careful myself. The whole shoe stuff complicates things, but that's the way it is."

Max Good says he has yet to have a kid pull together the courage to come to him and say that he won't wear the Nikes MCI provides. Which is probably fortunate for the kid. For the record, he says they'll either wear the Nikes he gives them or they'll wear street clothes and end up off the team.

"I wouldn't let a kid do that," Good said of wearing another brand. "I feel this strongly: If Nike is going to do that for our program and it saves us a considerable amount of money, then you wear them."

He says he receives free shoes and gear but no money

from Nike. He's been with the company since the mid-1980s when Vaccaro approached him at Eastern Kentucky.

"Sonny Vaccaro started me at Nike my first year as a head coach," Good said. "He gave me a hundred pairs of shoes free, which I couldn't believe."

Gonzalez, Wilson's AAU coach back in California, says while there was no outward pressure to attend a Nike-affiliated school, it did weigh on his decision to push Wilson there.

"I knew it was a Nike school," he said. "I know the business."

And he reminded his young player.

"These people helped me when nobody else would," Gonzalez says of Nike. "I just said [to Wilson] they've always been good to us and they've always helped us and I believe in them. I believe what they're doing is right and I believe they're trying to help him to get to that level he wants to go to."

Even if that means skipping summer school, which might make him ineligible at Georgetown?

"I said, if Nike wants you to go to MCI, there's nothing wrong with it," Gonzalez said. "It's like a friend giving you advice that you trust. I feel that Nike is my friend. I feel George is my friend."

You can imagine Byrnes didn't think Raveling was his friend when he not only lost his big recruit but had to face Wesley Wilson on the court three times during the 1998–99 season. Fortunately for Byrnes, Winchendon won two of those contests.

"I see Wesley at the game and I wish him well," Byrnes said. "There's no bad blood. Max runs a good program up there and Wesley is a good kid. I wish the best for him."

Which doesn't mean it didn't leave Byrnes shaking his head.

"It's the most blatant situation I've dealt with, ever," he said. "You read different articles about the so-called sneaker wars, but when it trickled down to me this year, I was surprised. This sneaker thing is such a big deal now, you always know it's out there, but until you deal with it, listen to the kid tell you he wants to wear Nikes in the layup lines, you can't believe it.

"It just amazes me it's gotten to the high school level and below. And people wonder why kids are leaving college early or they don't go to college. The kids' mind-set is totally different now."

But it's more than that. Maine Central does not offer scholarships to its basketball stars, which means the players, or their handlers, need to find the necessary funds to foot the bill. And that's where influence is important. How a teenager of limited means comes up with tens of thousands of dollars to pay for tuition and room and board is an issue no one wants to discuss. Financial aid assumes some of the costs, but rarely all of it. Which means sponsors need to be found and that's where having a strong relationship with shoe executives can get you more than a new pair of Jordans.

If you listen to Wilson discuss his views on high school basketball, you can understand Byrnes's concern over the mind-set of the modern player. Wilson admits that if the shoe deals were reversed and Winchendon wore Nikes, he'd probably be in Massachusetts not Maine. When asked the deciding factor on why he enrolled at MCI and not Winchendon, he's blunt: "Probably because it was a Nike school," he says. "It seemed like all of a sudden when it was found out that I was going to a school that was sponsored by adidas, it seemed like maybe some more universities and some other prep schools got my number, and they started calling me, and so my attention wasn't focused on Winchendon anymore. I kept saying I was going to Winchendon, but that was kind of dumb, because that was the first school I talked to.

"Max Good called me back and I started talking to him too. He was like, don't just listen to what I'm saying, listen to other people who know something about me. He was like, what schools are you talking to? I said Georgetown. He's like, I know John Thompson. I talked to an assistant coach [at Georgetown] and he's like, yeah, that's a real good school. I trusted Georgetown. At Michigan, Brian Ellerbe called, he recommended MCI. Some other schools called that I can't remember."

Although he was happy to get Wilson, Good doesn't like to hear that a kid chose his school because of his shoe deal. "Well, I feel very badly [about that]," Good said. "That isn't why I want him here."

And he is quick to point out he runs a program where the kids wear Nike shoes, but it is not a "Nike program."

"Dermarr Johnson wears adidas but he's here," Good said. "I think the biggest compliment we've gotten here is that there are some prep schools which are adidas and yet Dermarr Johnson is here. They know what he needs the most, regardless of what kind of friggin' shoes he wears. So that's a big compliment despite the fact that, obviously, he shouldn't be [affiliated with adidas], but all these high-level kids are affiliated with somebody."

And Wilson is one of them.

"Personally, I wear Nikes," he says. "Nike is, to me, the better shoe. Not because colleges might give them to you but because I just wear it, maybe because Michael Jordan wears it. Because MCI wears Nike, it's like mentally you like Nikes better so you go to the school that wears Nike. And the other prep school, Winchendon, they wear adidas. You don't really wear adidas all the time. So you go to the school that wears your type of shoe."

Wilson says he fully understands what sneaker companies are trying to do and although he might look like a pawn in a multinational chess game, he says it's him doing the playing.

"You've got to learn to use them [shoe companies] just as much as they use you," he says. "I've been all over the United States. That is something I wouldn't have done without these traveling teams. I've been to Europe [two trips to Paris on a Nike all-star team]. That was a great experience.

"They're just looking for the next Michael Jordan, and they want him to wear their shoes," he continues. "It's all about mucho dinero. It's all about the money. And I understand that. That's what it's all about. They're looking for the next best player, the next superstar. That's why they give you all this stuff. It's all about money."

To say Wilson's values have been shaped in a capitalistic society is an understatement. In a game where talent is a commodity and your body is all you have, his views on academics are understandable. The kid has been recruited, pushed, and told what to do with his career and his schooling by people interested in him first and foremost because of his ability to put a ball through an iron rim. And that's one reason why an articulate kid has such a shoddy transcript.

"You're told by every single person, get that education, boy," he says. "That education is the key. It don't really click. I mean I can tell you this now, but it don't click in. 'Cause all you think about is the money. You want to go to the league, you want to make some money. My point is [when people talk about the virtues of college] I always come at them with what do people go to school for? [What do they] get an education for? So they can make money."

And his opinion on amateur basketball? He says he learned all he needs to know about the game from shoe companies and summer basketball.

"It teaches you that when you play, you're supposed to get something," he says. "When you go to the tournaments, that's the first thing coaches hear: 'Where's my stuff at?'

"The best teams are gonna be with the person that's giving away the most stuff. That's what the recruiting is all about. If you win a tournament, you're gonna be fitted. Sometimes they might just give you a little something in the beginning of the summer. But if you don't win, then don't expect too much."

Despite having already attended high school for four years, and despite still needing to pass six basic core classes to earn a Georgetown education valued at about $120,000 in tuition but worth so much more, Wilson skipped summer school. Instead he played ball for Nike. And of all the experiences he had during the summer of 1998—the guest speakers at Nike Camp, the academic classes, the AAU tournaments, even the trip to Paris on the Nike all-star team—what was his most vivid, horizon-broadening memory? How he realized that the Nike Camp was really nothing more than a giant meat market.

"At these camps, they count you like numbers and tell you, 'One, two, three, four, five, over there. One, two, three, four, five, go over to that court.'

"Then they got the college coaches over there, looking

at you like they're owners. 'Look at his teeth. Are his teeth good?' You just feel like cattle. That messed with my mind. I didn't like that feeling. It makes you feel like you're cattle, like you're the best athlete, the best horse. That's what you feel like."

For a kid who was once surprised anyone would want him to play basketball, he's had quite an education before he even got to college.

CHAPTER 8

Mt. Zion

I t was springtime in Daytona Beach, Florida, a time and a place which conjures images of college kids cruising Atlantic Avenue in search of a party. Joel Hopkins wasn't looking for a good time when he rolled into Daytona Beach in March of 1998. He was looking for players. He had spent the afternoon in Orlando, recruiting an Edgewater High junior named Marquis Daniels. It had gone well, Hopkins had convinced Daniels to pack his bags, kiss his family goodbye, and head off to Hopkins's high school/basketball factory, Mt. Zion Christian Academy in Durham, North Carolina.

And now, with one already in the fold, Hopkins with his chief Florida scout and close friend Alvis Smith alongside, was barreling up I-4 with Daytona Beach and a 6-4 shooting guard named Tony Bobbitt on his mind.

The Sunshine State, particularly this swath of central Florida, had been a gold mine for Hopkins, what with Smith, one of adidas' top bird dogs and a personal friend of Sonny Vaccaro's, making the rounds from the Atlantic to the Gulf. Smith had proven himself adept at two things over the past few years—finding talent and angering high school coaches. Hopkins coveted the first skill and didn't seem to care about the second. He needed players to keep Mt. Zion a national power for a couple reasons. One, basketball gave his tiny and young boarding school an identity. It also gave it much of its funding.

For Joel Hopkins, a self-proclaimed basketball savior with an admitted sinful past as a drug abuser, a couple of angry high school coaches weren't going to stop him from making sure he wasn't long on identity and rich with funds.

Of course, the gold mine of all gold mines that Smith delivered to Hopkins was 6-foot-9 Tracy McGrady, who the scout found tucked away in Auburndale, a tiny town that sits halfway between Orlando and Tampa, during the spring of 1996. McGrady was a stud of a talent, but a complete unknown in national basketball circles following his junior year of high school. Auburndale High wasn't just small, it wasn't very good and Smith used those points to convince the young forward to give up on his school, transfer to Mt. Zion and attend Vaccaro's ABCD Camp that July in Teaneck, New Jersey. That turn of events so discouraged veteran Auburndale coach Ty Willis that he retired from the game.

"One of my best friends told me about Alvis and told me he can get me an in with adidas," says McGrady today. "So I was like, 'Cool.' So I talked to this dude [Smith] and he told me he worked for adidas and wanted me to be part of the family."

Exposure would prove to no longer be a problem. McGrady was immediately the talk of the nation, a long, strong athlete who could run the court and drain the three. After his performance at the 1996 adidas ABCD Camp, the nation's recruiting gurus were in a lather. "He's the biggest summer sleeper since Shaquille O'Neal," panted *HoopScoop*'s Clark Francis, quickly ranking him the number one senior in the country. It was the same ranking Bob Gibbons, Van Coleman, and the rest of the nation's talent scouts would grant McGrady.

"I was one of the top players that came out of camp," McGrady said. "When I came, I was unknown at the time. The man at camp was Lamar Odom. [But soon] I was ranked number one. That's when the relationship with adidas really started getting closer with Sonny and everything."

And that was enough for college coaches to pounce on Mt. Zion, trying to make up for lost time. Kentucky, Michigan, North Carolina, UCLA, to name a few. But McGrady was destined for Mt. Zion first and gave Hopkins the most important recruit of his young program's life. Not only did McGrady give him immediate credibility on the national prep circuit but he provided the ultimate, almost religious-sounding, recruiting pitch—once unknown, McGrady was now found. And just as wonderfully the national media quickly followed, lining up to write and film glowing accounts of the Mt. Zion program and how an admitted former drug abuser like Hopkins could find God and then dedicate his life to saving the nation's wretched basketball-playing souls in the name of the Lord.

ESPN filmed an entire hour of *Scholastic Sports America* from Mt. Zion. HBO sent Frank DeFord to Durham for a piece. *Sports Illustrated* spent four pages on McGrady and Hopkins, the accompanying photo spread featuring at least one adidas logo in each frame.

By spring, the McGrady college sweepstakes was over, but Hopkins and Smith were about to truly cash in. The most memorable campus tour for McGrady wasn't a college, but

rather a shoe company. Tracy was heading for the 1997
NBA draft, following closely in the footsteps of ABCD
Camp's 1995 star, Kobe Bryant, and choosing to be too cool
for school. He went ninth, to the low-profile Toronto Raptors, which didn't deter Nike and adidas from getting into a
heated bidding war for the right to put shoes on his feet.

Although, due to the Mt. Zion connection, you would
think McGrady was a lock for adidas, he said he gave strong
consideration to Nike even before he toured their facilities
in Beaverton, Oregon. "I think when I declared myself for
the NBA, I wanted to sign with Nike," McGrady said. "The
funny thing about it is, I visited [the] Nike campus and I
never visited [the] adidas campus. A young guy coming out
of high school and getting into this new era where Nike got
Michael Jordan and Penny Hardaway, they take you to this
campus and they show you all these guys' pictures and their
shoes and how they make the shoes and everything like that.
A young guy is like, 'Dang! I want to be there. I want to be
a part of that family.' "

McGrady said he even got a tour of the NikeTown store
where he was told to help himself to the merchandise. "Yo!
Whatever I wanted," McGrady said. "I went in there and
went shopping. I got so much stuff, man."

Showing his impressionable age, McGrady, who was
about to become a multimillionaire, says he almost chose
Nike over adidas because of a mere thousand-dollar shopping spree. "I was ready to make the decision in the store,
but I was like, 'Hold up,' " McGrady said. "I stopped myself. I was like, 'I can't do this. Me and Sonny are very close
and adidas, we're like family. So I can't go [with Nike].
Kobe's with them, Jermaine's with them. Antoine's with
them.' I was like, 'They got the young guys, so I just want to

be a part of them.' My relationship with adidas and Sonny was so close, that's why I didn't go with Nike."

By the time that was done, McGrady had landed a six-year, $12 million endorsement deal with adidas that put the basketball world on its ear. Maybe more startlingly, McGrady donated $300,000 to the Mt. Zion Christian Redemption Church, which enjoys the benefits of nonprofit, tax-free status, and then cut in both Hopkins and Smith on his new-found shoe fortune.

"That's part of Tracy's contract," Vaccaro said. "When we gave Tracy a contract we gave him X dollars. He said, 'Take Y dollars off of me and give it to Joel and Alvis.'" Y dollars is, Vaccaro says, an approximate split of $300,000 annually. Which means adidas pays both Hopkins and Smith approximately $150,000 in each of the six years of McGrady's contract, which runs through 2004. Which also means scout and coach will, by the time the deal is done, have made almost a million each off of McGrady's senior year of high school.

"The check came from adidas and not Tracy directly in an effort to save Tracy on taxes," Vaccaro explained. "There was no stipulation in Tracy's contract that said adidas had to pay that money to Mt. Zion. That was Tracy's choice."

But the contract does stipulate payment to Hopkins and Smith, Vaccaro said. McGrady says he felt indebted to both the scout who "discovered" him and the coach who "coached" him for introducing him to adidas. "I felt like they gave me a second chance," McGrady said. "They didn't have to let me in their school. Coach Hopkins didn't have to let me play for his basketball team."

Regardless of whose choice it was, no one's life has been the same since. Hopkins and Smith were now wealthier than either had ever imagined this basketball game could make them. And with a steady flow of money coming through well into the next decade, they knew now was no time to let up looking for the next gold mine. But they were not alone.

The McGrady deal changed the game of prep basketball. As details of McGrady's deal and Smith's and Hopkins's windfall flew through the nation's prep ranks, the country realized that there was now big money at stake in amateur basketball. Where once you might be able to sell a player to a cheating college for tens of thousands in dirty money, a shoe company could legitimize you with hundreds of thousands in above-the-table greenbacks.

The multinational apparel companies had just raised the bar on the selling price of a blue-chip athlete.

As Hopkins and Smith pulled up in front of Tony Bobbitt's home on Lewis Drive in Daytona Beach, they were making a random grasp at some talent. They were just showing up, unannounced and unexpected, hoping that Hopkins's persuasive arguments could get the all-state guard on a plane to North Carolina.

It was a classic Hopkins maneuver: swoop in, make your pitch to the family, and whisk the kid out of town before too much thought can be paid to the pros and cons of life at Mt. Zion. It's why to high school coaches in central Florida there is no more frightening nor sickening sight than Hopkins and Smith whispering to your star player. And why some Florida coaches have dubbed Hopkins "Coach Midnight" because of his history of recruiting a player when everyone else was asleep.

"How they work is they take a kid in the middle of the night," says Auburndale High coach David Saltman, who didn't work at the school when McGrady left but did see his best player in 1998–99, Theron "T" Smith, leave for Mt. Zion for three days. That ended when Smith says he called and begged Saltman to drive to North Carolina and get him. Smith says that although he got to spend a couple of nights with McGrady at a nearby condo and McGrady bought some clothes for him, he never felt comfortable there. Thus he asked Saltman to bring him home. The coach did just that, roaring alone up I-95 for fourteen straight hours before snagging Smith and turning back. "Sunset, the kid is there. Sunrise, the kid is gone," Saltman continued. "And you're going, 'Where the hell did the kid go?' And Mt. Zion says it's doing kids favors. With T. he left without even packing a bag. Didn't even take a toothbrush. He was just gone.

"What [high school coaches] do is we don't trust a single soul," Saltman said. "Our kids, we don't let them out of our sight. Your kid might be here today, gone tomorrow. And you may have done everything possible for that kid. But kids today want instant gratification. And a school like Mt. Zion says, 'I'll give you clothes, I'll give you shoes, you'll be flying around the country. You're the next Tracy McGrady. You've got to get out of your town. No one knows where it is. Everyone knows where Mt. Zion is. No one knew who Tracy McGrady was but look what happened to him!' "

Tonight Hopkins was going to try to make that same pitch to Bobbitt. Hopkins had approached the smooth guard the summer before at the adidas ABCD Camp in Teaneck. Hopkins told Bobbitt he admired his game and just wanted to get to know him. They talked briefly. There were a few subsequent phone calls over the next ten months, but not much. "He used to call and ask how life was," says Bobbitt.

Smith, the Florida scout, however, knew Bobbitt well. But neither coach nor scout had called ahead of time and told Bobbitt they were coming. They just walked up to the house and rang the bell. "He didn't call, he just showed up," said Bobbitt. "I was just sitting in my house watching TV. I wasn't expecting him. I barely knew him."

That didn't stop Hopkins from making his presentation. Nattily attired, he sat in the Bobbitts' living room and said Mt. Zion was the best place for Tony to spend his senior year. He said the exposure he would get would improve his stock with college coaches and raise his ranking in national recruiting magazines. He said he could provide superior coaching. He said the academics at Mt. Zion were better than Bobbitt's current school, Daytona Beach Mainland. He said it was so obvious that Mt. Zion was the place to go, that Tony ought to get in the car with him and Alvis and drive to Orlando Airport immediately. If he wanted to sleep on it, they'd return early the next morning and take him off to North Carolina.

"It was unreal," Bobbitt said. "They spoke to my father and me and they were asking me if I wanted to go to Mt. Zion. And I just said, 'No thanks.' They wanted me to go right then. They were going to come back the next morning if I had my mind made up. Then they said they'd give me a week but they still wanted to come back the next morning. But I didn't want to go. I'm at a good program where I am at. I'm not saying that they are bad, but I'm okay."

The only thing Bobbitt says Hopkins didn't mention was the strict religious convictions Hopkins often claims his school adheres to. "That's the thing he didn't do," Bobbitt said.

After being rebuffed, Bobbitt says Hopkins told him Mt. Zion had something Mainland High couldn't offer, the key to him securing NCAA freshman eligibility. "He said he'd take care of me," Bobbitt said. "That my test scores would be taken care of. Stuff like that. Me and my dad, after they left, we were like 'naaaah.' We couldn't believe it. Like it was the wrong thing to do."

Repeated attempts by the authors to reach Hopkins for comment on Bobbitt's allegations were unsuccessful.

Bobbitt, who as of September 1999 had not passed his ACT standardized test on his own, said that promise had no effect on him. The two things that made Mt. Zion unappealing to him were Hopkins disparaging his coach at Mainland, Charles Brinkenhofer, and Bobbitt's belief that if he went to Mt. Zion he would not have complete control over choosing the college he wanted to attend. "They said a few things about Coach Brinks," Bobbitt said. "And, the way I look at it, you can't criticize a good coach and Coach Brinks is a damn good coach. That's what turned me against him when he went bad against Coach Brinks."

As for the other players who went there, Bobbitt feels bad for them. "The way I look at it, those guys probably didn't have grades," he said. "Then, I don't think you even get to pick your college after you leave Mt. Zion."

Bobbitt says that while Hopkins didn't offer him any money to go there he did make it known that the player shouldn't worry about the costs of traveling home. "He said he [would make] sure I'd be able to come home anytime I wanted," Bobbitt said.

And, Bobbitt says, some kids are sucked into it by parents who believe what Hopkins tells them. "Some parents will listen," Bobbitt said. "Once they get you, they got you and there isn't nothing you can do about it." Bobbitt's father, John Albright, didn't appreciate Hopkins's pitch. After a little while, Hopkins and Smith departed. "He didn't like them at all," said Bobbitt. "He didn't agree [with them]."

For once, central Florida hadn't been so kind to Hopkins.

The Mt. Zion recruitment of Jamario Moon, a 6-foot-7 small forward from rural Coosa County, Alabama, went a little differently, but the teenager's experience at the school was bizarre in its own right. Moon said he first heard from Joel Hopkins when the Mt. Zion coach called him up in late May of 1998 and told him about his school. He quickly invited Moon up for a visit. The player asked if he could bring his mother, Ruby Thomas, and grandmother Delphine Thomas along too.

Moon says he had never heard of Mt. Zion until then and wasn't looking to transfer from Coosa Central High School. He just wanted to go on a trip and knew his mother and grandmother would love the chance to travel. "I figured I'd take a free trip to North Carolina," said Moon.

For the family of limited means it was a nice trip. All three flew from Birmingham to Raleigh, where Hopkins met them and put them up in his stately home in the wooded outskirts of Durham. Not far, say some who know the area, from where Duke coach Mike Krzyzewski lives. "And it was nice," says Ruby Thomas, the mother. "Me and my mom stayed there. Oooh yeah. Very nice. I enjoyed it. It was right in the country where it needs to be. It's pretty. It's really nice. I enjoyed myself." She also liked Hopkins and his family. "The time I knew him, he and his wife were real nice," Ruby says. "I even got to play with their babies."

After a few days mother and grandmother returned home and Moon stayed, even though he says he was ready to leave right then. Hopkins's sales pitch had some appeal, but Moon was skeptical. He says Hopkins continually brought up Mc-

Grady, telling Moon that he would be Mt. Zion's next player to go directly to the NBA. "He said he got [a lot of] money when Tracy McGrady went pro," Moon said. "He said he was going to do that with me. He wanted me to go [to the NBA] from high school. I wanted to go from high school but not like that."

And if the NBA didn't work out immediately, Moon says Hopkins assured him his academic transcript would be in line to receive a scholarship. "They said I didn't have to worry about academics," Moon said. "You had to go to class but you didn't have to worry about no grades."

It being early summer, Moon says in the month he was there he never attended a class at Mt. Zion, so he has no idea if that recruiting pitch would have come to fruition. But he didn't want to find out. "That didn't sound right," Moon said.

Moon says he was ready to head home just after his initial visit, but his mother and grandmother had left the day before and he had no way back. He says he told Hopkins he wanted to return to Alabama but the coach wouldn't let him. He said that the players stay in a three-story brick house in "the roughest part of town" and are locked in day and night so no one can leave. "They told me I was just coming up there to see how it was and then they were going to let me come back home," Moon said. "But then they tried to get me to stay up there. They fixed up an old house and put all the players [there]. We'd barely ever see Joel, they had assistant coaches watching us. Then they had us in lockdown. Night. Daytime too. All day."

How serious a lockdown? "I told him I wanted to come home," Moon says. "He said no." Ultimately Moon left Mt. Zion, returned to Alabama, and signed a national letter of intent with Mississippi State. Poor grades, however, sent him to junior college.

Before leaving, Moon said to pass the time the players would play basketball on a court in the yard or hang out and sleep. Due to its religious mission, Mt. Zion prohibits the playing of rap music and Moon says he and his bunkmate, Chicago native Steven Hunter, who also left the school after a month, got in trouble for sneaking in a CD player. There was also mandatory morning mass and players weren't allowed out of sight of the assistant coaches. Players were also not allowed to use the telephone to call home, nor to receive calls. "They don't want you to do nothing," Moon claims. "They just want to control you."

His greatest act of rebellion, he says, was using the phone when no one was looking and sneaking off the property to hit the McDonald's on the corner.

Moon has heard the media accounts of how Hopkins says he takes wayward youths and, as a service to the Lord, reforms them. He's heard Hopkins explain why winning basketball games is important because, "Jesus Christ wasn't a loser." He's heard all the "God Bless You"s and "Praise Jesus"es which Hopkins routinely says when recruiting parents and have made him famous among college basketball coaches who often mock him as "Preacher Joel."

Yet not everyone shares Moon's experience. Some former players say Mt. Zion played a positive role in their lives. Corey Hightower, for example, a 1998 graduate of the school, credits Mt. Zion with turning him around. The year the Flint, Michigan, native graduated, he told one newspaper, "If it wasn't for Mt. Zion and the school's connections, I'd be running the streets in Michigan, like I used to. This has given me a chance to have a future." Hightower went on to become a star in junior college basketball. McGrady also credited the school: "Mt. Zion really helped me to get the discipline I need."

Personally, Moon says, he doesn't have a checkered past and didn't need reforming. Listening to rap music, by his estimation, is hardly a mortal sin.

Concern with Mt. Zion is not limited to recruiting techniques. It's not always a pleasure to have Mt. Zion at your tournament either. The Christian Warriors, Mt. Zion's nickname, have a reputation on court for bad sportsmanship and off court for all types of mischief. Mt. Zion is frequently involved in bench-clearing brawls, having gotten into it in recent years with teams from around the country. "The last five times I've seen them play," said one major East Coast college assistant, "there has been a fight."

Which are nothing, witnesses say, to the wild December 1998 off-court, late-night donnybrook during the Reebok Las Vegas Invitational when a half dozen Mt. Zion players squared off with a similar-sized group from Compton (California) Dominguez High at the McDonald's inside the Excalibur Hotel on the Las Vegas Strip. In that fight, witnesses say, innocent McDonald's patrons had to abandon their Big Macs and flee the room when members of each team began throwing the restaurant's heavy metal chairs at each other.

"It was nuts," said one high school coach who was also in the restaurant that night. "One of those old-time bar brawls." It didn't subside until casino security and the Las Vegas police arrived. Since Mt. Zion is a heavily sponsored adidas team and Dominguez is an equally funded Nike flagship school, the battle could be declared a true shoe war. Repeated calls to Dominguez High coach Russell Otis for comment were not returned.

That, of course, is just one story. Ask college coaches

around the country to name the recruiting situation causing the most concern and Mt. Zion almost immediately comes up. Because Mt. Zion does not belong to the North Carolina High School Sports Association, it does not need to comply with its regulations. But many coaches, so concerned about Mt. Zion's recruiting tactics, simply do not associate with the school.

One coach in the Atlantic Coast Conference, which Mt. Zion sits in the heart of, says there has been discussion of creating a handshake agreement between league schools that no program will recruit any Mt. Zion players. None of the league's nine schools has signed a Mt. Zion player since 1997.

Unlike most high schools, coaches say requests for the academic transcripts of players are often denied or ignored. Phone calls, even from prominent head coaches, often go unanswered or unreturned. Phone calls to recruits are limited, if permitted at all. And recruiting mail is not always delivered.

According to sources at the University of Cincinnati, when the Bearcats began recruiting center Donald Little in 1996–97, the basketball staff sent the Mt. Zion junior dozens of recruiting letters. When Little transferred to the Winchendon School in Massachusetts for his senior campaign, 1997–98, they found out he had never received any of the letters. Little says the only school he thought was recruiting him was Virginia Commonwealth, because those were the only letters he received. The player signed a letter of intent with UC in 1998 and the Bearcats no longer recruit the school.

Other schools cite academic concerns in their decision not to recruit the school. "We don't recruit Mt. Zion because we are concerned with the academic standards there," said

North Carolina State assistant Larry Harris, whose program is just down the road in Raleigh. "In a couple of instances, things have gone wrong and we just don't recruit any of their players. We feel it is best for the NC State program to have nothing to do with that school."

Said a Big East head coach: "At some point everyone knows Mt. Zion is going down in flames. The best thing to do is stay away completely. We don't want any association with the school which might somehow get us in trouble. We have nothing to do with them."

Not surprisingly, the man who helped give Mt. Zion major exposure nationally and the money to continue running its program hears more than his share of these stories. Sonny Vaccaro says he's fielded complaints from a number of college coaches about Mt. Zion's tactics. They wonder how he can be associated with them. "Yes, I hear that," Vaccaro says. "I hear that a lot."

Vaccaro is clearly both wary and weary of Hopkins, but claims he won't dump the school without substantial proof. And, because of his contract with Hopkins, which requires adidas to pay him approximately nearly $150,000 each year through 2004, his hands are somewhat tied.

"I called Joel up and told him, 'The first time that anything happens that you actually are convicted of, you're gone,' " says Vaccaro. "I'm not going to dump a guy on allegations, there are so many allegations. I've screamed at him nine thousand times. I hear he gets money back from [colleges]. [I tell him], 'Anytime, if it is found [to be true], you lose your money [from us].' In his agreement with adidas, even with Tracy, if he ever gets convicted of anything illegal like that, he loses a lot of money."

Vaccaro knows the heavy suspicion of Mt. Zion throughout the basketball world is damaging him. "In my mind that's a black eye for adidas," said David Saltman, the coach at Auburndale. "If they were really into helping these kids they wouldn't be in cahoots with Mt. Zion Christian Academy. They would remove themselves from that situation and go on like it didn't happen. Not continue to help them out. It isn't going to end until the shoe companies back away from this high school situation."

But Vaccaro is not too concerned about Florida high school coaches. "What they have is a fear of Alvis," Vaccaro said. "But Tracy ended up with like fifty million or so dollars, so it's not like it was a failure." And, Vaccaro argues, until the NCAA comes in or a college coach is willing to go on the record in the media, all charges against Hopkins and Mt. Zion, no matter how detailed, are still just charges. "He's never been caught with anything that violates any rules," says Vaccaro.

In fact, Vaccaro dares college coaches to catch Hopkins. "What I want them [college coaches] to do is put a tape recorder on one day and get him," said Vaccaro. "I really do."

As for stories such as Bobbitt's, where the player claims Hopkins said he didn't have to worry about a standardized test score, or Moon's, where school wasn't going to be a problem? "If that was proven, if there were tests taken there that were illegal, he'd be gone. But I don't know," said Vaccaro. "I don't know what's true."

And would just an offer be enough? "I'm sure that happened," Vaccaro said of the offers. "But since he never actually did it, how can you convict him? The crime never actually was committed."

American College Testing of Iowa City says Mt. Zion is a testing site twice a year, once in the fall, once in the spring.

The company says that they have never investigated any allegations of test fraud at the school.

However, in 1998, the NCAA Clearinghouse challenged the standardized test results of Mt. Zion's star player of 1998, power forward Travis Robinson, ruling him ineligible to receive a Division I scholarship. Robinson had originally signed a national letter of intent with the University of Missouri during the fall of 1997, part of an impressive recruiting class by then Tigers coach Norm Stewart. The group also included Fort Lauderdale guards Keyon Dooling and Clarence Gilbert, who both had close ties to Alvis Smith.

Robinson never enrolled at Mizzou, however. He begged out of the agreement in July of 1998 because, school officials say, he claimed Columbia, Missouri, was too far away from his family, which is scattered throughout the Southeast. Apparently lacking an awareness of geography, Robinson promptly attempted to enroll at Fresno State University in California.

That summer, Fresno State officials say, the NCAA challenged Robinson's test score, citing various improprieties. The NCAA told Robinson he would have to sit out the 1998–99 season as a Proposition 48 nonqualifier, or retake the ACT and prove his score was legitimate. Robinson, Fresno State says, refused to retake the ACT, instead opting to arbitrate with the NCAA and argue his innocence. The arbitration lasted the entire 1998–99 season, costing Robinson his freshman season anyway. The Association and the player had still not reached a decision as this book went to press.

While stories like Robinson's could work against Hopkins's recruiting pitches, it has not stopped high school coaches around the South from worrying about when and where Hopkins will pop up next. "You don't want to see [Hopkins] in your town," says Travis Jones, head coach of Orlando Edgewater High School. Jones lost his star player, Marquis Daniels, to Mt. Zion on the same recruiting trip where Bobbitt said no to Hopkins. "I was pretty close with my player, but they came in and told him he was going to be the next Tracy McGrady and they did it all in the name of the Lord. I mean, when you're seventeen, all you want to do is get to the league. The kids believe it. And all of a sudden, the kid was gone.

"I went away for the weekend and when I came home on Sunday night there was a call from a local sportswriter asking me if I knew that Marquis was at Mt. Zion. I was like, 'No way. I just saw him Friday afternoon.'"

It was Coach Midnight at his best.

CHAPTER 9

Be like 'Mique

For a while there, one of the most painful moments of George Raveling's life was when the media would ask him about Nike's search for the next Michael Jordan. The former coach's eyes would roll as frustration surged in him. He hated the question, from its implications to its lack of originality, but he always had a stock answer at the tip of his tongue. "We already found him," Raveling would blurt out. "He plays golf."

Indeed, for a couple of months during the spring of 1997, it appeared that Nike had found its next pitchman-savior. Tiger Woods was the hottest athlete in America after his historic and thrilling victory at the Masters, and throughout Nike's Beaverton campus there were hoots and hollers of excitement as marketers began calculating an ensuing golf boom and the swoosh's role in it. From private meetings in Beaverton to huge media spreads, everyone concluded that the cool, handsome, articulate twenty-one-year-old was not only going to change the American sporting world—if not the world at large—but was about to cause a windfall for Nike. To some, of course, that could turn a stomach. "Tiger

Woods burning bright. Selling shoes for Philip Knight," mocked writer Charles P. Pierce in *GQ*.

But despite the jokes Nike appeared to have hit the jackpot with its $40 million sponsorship deal with the Tiger, whose swoosh-splashed figure dominated the increasingly popular weekend golf telecasts.

Sonny Vaccaro watched the 1997 Masters also. Says he cheered for Tiger like the rest of America. He also says he was unfazed by his rival's sponsorship deal with Woods. "Tiger Woods is not going to sell shoes to kids in the neighborhoods of L.A.," said Vaccaro. "He does not sell to the inner-city kids of the world. Tiger is Tiger. He's selling golf clubs and golf shirts. He's not selling basketball shoes and running shoes. And Nike needs that."

Indeed, Woods's success as a pitchman has been solid, but hardly off the charts, says Nike. And Vaccaro's initial read on the subject turned true. The need for a pitchman capable of moving large quantities of high-priced, high-profit, high-fashion shoes and apparel is still out there. Nike built an empire selling to kids interested in what looks cool. And, Tiger or no Tiger, the stuffy game of golf could never set a national fashion trend. Which meant the next Michael Jordan was, potentially, still out there. Although, some would argue, the next Michael is actually a woman.

Deep in the eastern Tennessee Smokys, in a town which must sell more gallons of bright orange paint per capita than any other place in the world, is where the most marketable, and possibly finest, women's basketball player in the world called home for most of the last four years. Chamique Holdsclaw, the University of Tennessee's wondrously talented 6-2 forward, has been the star of the most popular and promoted women's basketball team of all time since she arrived in Knoxville, from a Queens, New York, housing project in the fall of 1995. Proving to be more than just a colorful name and a New York City prep legend from Middle Village Christ the King High School, Holdsclaw graduated in 1999 as a four-time All-America, a three-time national champion, and a cultural icon to a generation of young American girls who have suddenly gone mad over hoops.

"Everyone wants to be like Chamique," says Jennifer Thomas, a 1999 high school All-America from Detroit Country Day, who is now a freshman at North Carolina. "Everyone is like, I want to be 6-2 and handle the rock." To girl athletes around the country, especially the surging number of basketball players, everyone wants to be like 'Mique. Not Mike.

Not surprisingly, she became the potential endorser extraordinaire for the shoe companies which hoped to outfit her, celebrate her, and ride her to improved profit margins as she embarked on a career in the high-profile Women's National Basketball Association. And she also represented the possible future of women's basketball. Where the potential of big-money professional careers and eight-figure shoe deals could lead the simpler women's game down the same dangerous roads the men's currently travels. "When you put money into the mix, people change," says Connecticut's Geno Auriemma. "I don't care what business you are in. Things change. And that's what we face in women's basketball. There's money now and more coming."

The basketball tale of Chamique Holdsclaw is more *Hoop Dreams* or *He Got Game* than that of most women's basketball stars. In a game that, at least at the college level, is still heavily reliant on the suburban, often white athlete, Holdsclaw's ascent from the hardscrabble streets of Queens, through the all-boy games she infiltrated on the playgrounds near her housing project, through the Catholic high school and off to the big, national university is traditionally more male than female. Holdsclaw was raised by her grandmother in an apartment near Astoria Park. Her parents were nonfactors in her life, and as a way of entertaining herself the athletic young girl used to beg her way into the boys' games on the local blacktop. There she learned the cross-over dribbles, the spin moves, and the toughness that you can only acquire when there are a hundred boys and one girl playing all day. She also developed the killer instincts of a champion under the winners-stay, losers-walk culture of the crowded playground.

"If you lose, you might not get to play again the entire day," said Holdsclaw. "So you made sure you won."

But her game is more than street. She learned the fundamentals from Vincent Cannizzaro, the hugely successful coach of Christ the King High School in the Middle Village section of Queens, the same high school boys' star Lamar Odom attended for three years. There she helped lead Christ the King to four New York state championships and was a two-time *Parade* All-America. When it was finally time for Holdsclaw to choose a college she didn't lack for more than a hundred or so suitors.

Connecticut, fresh off a magical 35-0 season in 1995, was a natural fit, just a few hours up the road from her beloved New York City and dear grandmother. The Huskies, coached by the telegenic and charismatic Geno Auriemma, boasted a passionate fan base, top-notch facilities, and a ton of media exposure. But so too did Tennessee's Pat Summitt, who also had at her disposal a reputation as the finest women's basketball coach in the history of the game—she was dubbed, a few years later by *Sports Illustrated,* in reference to UCLA's John Wooden, "The Wizard of Knoxville."

And when Summitt, and her tenacious recruiter Mickie DeMoss, want a recruit, they rarely don't get their wish.

Holdsclaw, of course, chose Tennessee, in part because the school had a separate athletics department for women, but mainly because the coach everyone calls Pat had convinced her that to be great, truly great, she needed to be pushed and hounded every day for four years. And Pat was the perfect person to do it. The result has been legendary. In her first year Holdsclaw helped Tennessee to a national championship and became just the third women's player ever to be named Kodak All-America as a freshman. Summitt immediately declared that Holdsclaw had the potential to be the greatest player she had ever been associated with, strong words from a coach who through the years had been associated with nearly every great the game has ever known.

Years two and three found the same results, not to mention consensus national player of the year as a junior. Following that year, she became the only college player on the 1998 U.S. National Select Team, where she more than held her own against the game's professional stars. And by the time Holdsclaw returned from her native New York to Knoxville for her senior campaign she was widely regarded as the greatest college player ever. And already—still just a collegian—the finest women's player in the world. Certainly some of the older American pros, including the sensational Cynthia Cooper, two-time WNBA most valuable player with the Houston Comets, and flashy point guard Dawn Staley of the now-defunct American Basketball League, could argue they might be better players. But they couldn't argue they were more famous.

Holdsclaw came to women's basketball at the perfect time. National interest in the game soared during the mid-1990s as grassroots participation grew and fans became turned off by what they perceived to be greedy, misbehaved NBA players. Meanwhile, men's college basketball was annually losing its best and most identifiable players to the NBA at younger and younger ages, leaving women's basketball in the market for a star.

Holdsclaw was it. At 6-foot-2, strong but quick, she had the total package of skills that all players could relate to. Unlike another media-hyped star of the 1990s, UConn's Rebecca Lobo, she projected a far cooler, hipper persona to the kids of America. And she could make plays the other women, like Lobo, couldn't. She sometimes brought the ball up, could shoot very well, and was a killer on the break. And she played the game, if not above the rim, at least at it. In the 1997 National Championship Game, where the Lady Vols would beat Old Dominion, Holdsclaw converted an alley-oop pass in breathtaking fashion (she didn't dunk it, but did athletically lay it in) that was shown over and over during ESPN's heavily watched broadcast of the game.

She was a star. But a star with fundamentals. She had killer instincts. But she had a nice smile—albeit full of dental braces—and was understated and polite with the media. She wore No. 23, not because she wanted to be the female Michael Jordan but "because of Psalm 23: 'The Lord is my shepherd, I shall not want.'" Try finding an NBA star doing that.

She was nice enough for the Christian right to like. But she could play well enough that she became the first woman to ever grace the cover of influential *Slam* magazine, the New York–based hoop publication that brings heavy credibility to the ballers of America's cities. Earning that honor—she wore a No. 23 New York Knicks jersey for the shoot—was a serious sign of respect, especially from a mag-

Jonathan Bender went from tiny Picayune, Mississippi, to fifth pick overall in the 1999 NBA draft, thanks largely to his play on the adidas-sponsored New Orleans Jazz AAU team. (*PHOTO by A. Scott Kurtz*)

Fresno's DeShawn Stevenson, a top player in the Class of 2000, was one of many stars of the adidas-sponsosred Elite Basketball Organization (EBO). (*PHOTO by A. Scott Kurtz*)

Juneau, Alaska's, Carlos Boozer, Jr., helped bring the EBO and its coach, Darren Matsubara, into the big time. (*PHOTO by A. Scott Kurtz*)

After more than three decades in college coaching, George Raveling (*center*) now recruits for and runs Nike's grassroots basketball system. (*PHOTO by A. Scott Kurtz*)

D.C. Assault, an adidas traveling flagship team, at the company's 1998 Big Time Tournament in Las Vegas.
(*PHOTO by A. Scott Kurtz*)

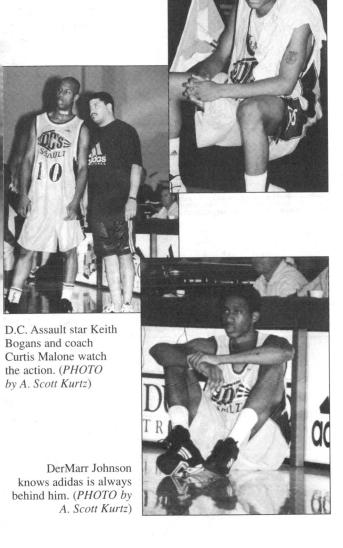

Val Brown of D.C. Assault has his dream tattooed on his left bicep. (*PHOTO by A. Scott Kurtz*)

D.C. Assault star Keith Bogans and coach Curtis Malone watch the action. (*PHOTO by A. Scott Kurtz*)

DerMarr Johnson knows adidas is always behind him. (*PHOTO by A. Scott Kurtz*)

Chris Grier, coach of the high-powered adidas-sponsored Michigan Mustangs, and three of his star players. (*PHOTO by A. Scott Kurtz*)

San Bernardino, California's, Tyson Chandler was featured on *60 Minutes* when he began commuting an hour each way to attend the Nike-sponsored Compton Dominguez High School. (*PHOTO by Rick Notter*)

Using star power to attract kids is nothing new. Which is why Hollywood stars such as Sinbad are common guests at the Nike All-America Camp. (*PHOTO by Rick Notter*)

Indiana's Bob Knight (*left*) and Louisville's Denny Crum watch
the talent at the Nike All-America Camp.
(*PHOTO by Rick Notter*)

The Kansas City
basketball scene
would never be the
same after Jaron
Rush. (*PHOTO by
Rick Notter*)

Dana and David Pump flank DerMarr Johnson at their Best of the Summer Invitational Tournament in Dominguez Hills, California. (*PHOTO by A. Scott Kurtz*)

For years John Thompson served as both head coach of Georgetown and a member of Nike's board of directors. (*PHOTO by A. Scott Kurtz*)

After dominating the Florida high school hoops scene, Frank Martin and his Miami Senior High program ran into trouble for using ineligible players. (*PHOTO by A. Scott Kurtz*)

Proving it's the world's game, Nike brought 7-foot-5 Yao Ming from Shanghai, China, to its 1998 All-America Camp. (*PHOTO by Rick Notter*)

Dane Fife and Corey Maggette battle during the 1998 Nike All-America Camp. (*PHOTO by Rick Notter*)

Marvin Stone's prep years in Huntsville, Alabama, included stints with three high school teams and two AAU teams, not to mention one Ford Explorer and accusations of wrongdoing. (*PHOTO by Rick Notter*)

By attending the Nike All-America Camp Casey Sanders, according to his coach at Tampa Prep, earned his school a sponsorship contract with the swoosh. (*PHOTO by Rick Notter*) azine that likes to make fun of Lobo-types. And on the playground, respect is everything.

Simply put, she had it all. And everyone from shoe executives to WNBA types knew it. "We think Chamique will be a star in our league," said WNBA Commissioner Val Ackerman before Holdsclaw's senior season. At the time, Ackerman thought her league would be faced with a 1999 bidding war for Holdsclaw with the rival American Basketball League. The ABL, however, folded during its 1998–99 season. "She has the kind of ability which brings fans out to the arena, creates a lot of excitement, and brings people to women's basketball. I think she represents the future of the sport. She has a real star quality."

A quality not lost on companies seeking a potential endorser. Shoe companies learned the power of the women's market during the mid-1980s aerobics craze when Reebok briefly surpassed Nike as the world's biggest apparel company by marketing colorful shoes to women. Not since has Nike understimated the purchasing power of female athletes.

"It's about selling product," said Mike Flynn, director of the Blue Star girls' basketball camps, one of the original such camps for girls. "That's the greatness of Jordan. He transcends color. What makes Jordan sell is his game and his smile and his persona. That's what sports demands. It doesn't demand pure athletic ability. But damn if you got it with the others. He's got the color for the city and the smile for the suburbs. And God bless him. He crosses the lines. All the lines. He's a marketer's dream. And Holdsclaw has some of that."

Just one reason shoe companies began to drool.

One of the selling points of women's basketball, one of the reasons more Americans, men included, are turning to the game, is its sense of purity. There is less taunting, prancing, and trash talking on the court. In its place is increased team play. Academic casualties are rare. The players are hardly ever thrown off the team for drug abuse, violence, or insubordination. The pro leagues, albeit young, showcase players who appear to be motivated more out of a love for the game than a love of their paycheck. It harkens back to a simpler time when men's basketball was more about layups than lockouts, coach chokings, and Allen Iverson.

And so the courting of Chamique for a shoe deal had an eerie similarity to the wooing of Michael Jordan. Holdsclaw had no street agents, no AAU coaches who had latched on to her at age twelve, looking for a payout. She had no agent until her senior season ended and the NCAA said it was okay. The controlling Summitt made sure everyone steered clear until then. She had no preconceived brand loyalty. No closet full of skeletons. She would choose a company in the same above-the-board manner Jordan did, mainly because it offered the best business plan.

"We think Chamique wants to wear adidas," said Jon Dillon, an adidas representative who handles the company's contract with the University of Tennessee. "But we know she is going to make her decision based on what is the best business deal for her. And that's good."

Adidas felt good about its position in the Holdsclaw derby because she had been wearing its shoes since she arrived in Knoxville. The school had signed an all-sport endorsement contract with adidas in 1995, mainly because the company wanted a piece of the million-dollar business that the sales of UT merchandise has become. That is largely because of Tennessee's hugely popular football program, which on fall Saturdays packs over 100,000 Orange-clad fans in Neyland Stadium on the banks of the Tennessee

River. And adidas' investment in UT was a good one. Not only did the Volunteers win the 1998 National Championship, but during the previous four years they starred at quarterback the likable Peyton Manning, who signed an endorsement contract with adidas before being selected number one by the Indianapolis Colts in the 1998 National Football League draft. But as a bonus came Summitt's powerful program, which captured three consecutive national championships from 1996 to 1998 and became the nation's college basketball team, usurping UConn in popularity polls. And that also gave adidas the feet of Holdsclaw and running mate Tamika Catchings, a brilliant talent who is two years Holdsclaw's junior and also has a shot at being a four-time All-America.

Adidas had done well in choosing its sponsorship deals. The 1998 title game between Tennessee and La Tech found both teams adidas sponsored, as was North Carolina State, another Final Four team. The year before, Notre Dame, another adidas all-sport school, made the Final Four along with the Lady Vols. Although its role in women's basketball was limited—a few high school and traveling team sponsorships—adidas realizes the potential in the women's market. "There are a lot of shoes to be sold to the girls," said Vaccaro. Vaccaro says this despite having little to do with distaff hoops, which may be why adidas trails Nike in that game. "I'll never be involved in girls' AAU," he said. "That day will never come."

Even without Vaccaro's help, adidas hoped Holdsclaw would follow Manning's lead and sign with them. That hope, however, took a hit in February of 1998 when, in a *Sports Illustrated* story about Summitt, one of the accompanying photos showed a number of the Lady Vols, Holdsclaw included, wearing Nikes following a practice session. It was not only the loss of countless dollars in subliminal advertising, but a personal embarrassment in the shoe war. Not surprisingly, the people at Nike found the photo amusing, passing it along at meetings back in Beaverton.

Robert Herb, adidas' director of college sports marketing, admits he was shocked and angered at the sight. The company immediately inquired about it with Tennessee officials and were told that the Lady Vols found the Nikes to be both more comfortable and of higher quality. "We were mad but what we were really mad at was that our product wasn't good enough for them," admits adidas' Herb. "We immediately flew a team of designers down there to find out how we could improve the product and do a better job serving Tennessee. And we did. If you look at what they wear this year, in games and in practice, it's adidas."

Buoyed by the hope that Holdsclaw agreed with Herb's claims of newfound quality, adidas began designing prototypes of "The Holdsclaw" before the 1998–99 campaign even began.

But Nike was not to be deterred. The swoosh is the dominant shoe in the women's basketball market and the *SI* picture fed rumors that it is the brand that Holdsclaw truly prefers. (Like Jordan wearing Converse because he had to at the University of North Carolina, Holdsclaw may also have no affinity for the three stripes.) Nike also had current endorsement deals with some of the biggest names in women's basketball, including Sheryl Swoopes, Cynthia Cooper, and Dawn Staley. It was also a major promoter of the WNBA and NCAA basketball. After adidas dominated the 1998 Final Four, Nike teams rebounded in 1999, with three programs (Purdue, Duke, and Georgia) making the Final Four, with Purdue edging Duke in the championship game.

Plus, unlike adidas, whose girls' grassroots system is

small and scattered, Nike has been active in youth basketball for years. It ran its first girls All-America Camp in 1994. That event has now expanded so much that it runs just a week and a half after the boys' event in the same Indianapolis basketball facility—the National Institute for Fitness and Sport on the campus of Indiana University–Purdue University Indianapolis (IUPUI). If it wasn't for the ponytails and below-the-rim action, an observer would be hard pressed to tell the difference. In women's basketball Nike is everywhere.

"Eighty-five percent of the females wearing basketball shoes are wearing Nike," says Flynn. "You look at the top players and they are wearing Nike. And Nike has a camp. So there is a certain cachet to be involved with Nike because a lot of the top programs are with Nike."

For Phoenix Mountain Point High's Nicole Powell, one of the finest players in the class of 2000, it's more than cachet. She is rarely seen without at least one swoosh (shoes, shirts, even earrings) on her person. "I love Nike," she said. "I love it. I love my earring, my bandana, my socks. They are comfortable, they look good. I like them."

That, she says, is for a variety of reasons, most notably style, comfort, and Nike's stable of promoters, which run from Michael Jordan to Dawn Staley. "I love the Bulls," Powell said. "I love Jordan. I'd buy all of his shoes if I could. Obviously you are going to see the shoes the best players wear. They have the commercials. You see them play in them and stuff like that. And you say, 'Those are really cool. I'm going to get those.' But once you go to the store and look around, you are going to look for the best-looking shoes. But usually they are wearing the best-looking shoes. That's why I like Nike."

Nike's market dominance in girl's basketball just sort of

sweeps you in, says Cedar Rapids (Iowa) Kennedy High's Anne O'Neill, another top player in the class of 2000. "The WNBA girls wear it," said O'Neill. "A lot of teams around here wear them too. High school and college. Everywhere you look there's Nike. You just want to wear them too. I mean, everything is big [with Nike]. Everything is huge. You've just got to be like everyone else."

Reebok, meanwhile, was set to make its own pitch and was relying on its stature as a legitimate competitor to Nike in the women's market. Although its grassroots system is not as far-reaching, nor as heavily financed as Nike's, Reebok does run its own All-America Camp each July in Chicago, funds numerous AAU teams, and sponsors a number of high-profile college programs. And so the race for Holdsclaw was on. A race with stakes bigger than had ever been contested in women's basketball. Which was what made some around women's basketball a little nervous.

Mike Flynn says he'd know if there were any street agents in women's basketball for one simple reason: "I was in this business when there wasn't a street. I remember the farms and the dirt roads."

Flynn founded his Philadelphia Belle's AAU team in the late 1970s and won his first national AAU championship in 1979. Realizing the need for improved summer competition for girls, he founded the Blue Star Camp in 1981 and held it for a week in the Poconos. It was all very part-time. "There was no money here," says Flynn, who worked full-time as a writer and editor for the *Philadelphia Bulletin* and later the *Philadelphia Daily News.* "It took six years before we even broke even on the camp. I was into it because it was a hobby. It was my free time. I had a job and this was my hobby. Girls' basketball."

At the time, it was an unusual hobby and one Flynn says he never could have expected to emerge into this. He remembers the early days of the modern era of the sport, the Immaculata College games at Madison Square Garden in the early 1980s and the old AIAW championship tournaments. He vividly describes the day he watched a California kid, then just a high school sophomore, almost dunk a ball in summer play. She turned out to be Cheryl Miller. "I was there for all of it," says Flynn. "I remember going to watch Rhonda Windum, who was general manager of the [WNBA's Los Angeles] Sparks, play at the city championship in the Bronx and I think there were fifty people in the gym. There was just no interest, no following. But I was there because I loved it."

Two decades later he is one of the most powerful people in girls' youth basketball. His scouting service—Blue Star Index—is subscribed to by nearly every college program in the country. His Philadelphia Belle's still boasts major talent annually. His developmental camp, held each July in Terre Haute, Indiana, which features the best fourteen- to sixteen-year-old players in the world, is a must stop on the summer recruiting circuit. Moreover his contacts around the globe make him an insiders' insider. His frequent trips to Europe and beyond give him a grasp of international talent. His close friendships with his players and their families make him a source for recruiting information. No assistant coach in the game worth his or her paycheck doesn't know Flynn's toll-free pager number. Blue Star and women's basketball is now his full-time job.

But he isn't Sonny Vaccaro.

He works for no one. Only himself. He professes no interest in influencing the game and instead still considers himself an unabashed fan. He loves promoting the game, watching the young players, and seeing old friends. He has few business deals outside of his camp and it's difficult to find a college coach who will say a bad word about him. Even off the record. He appears to have no ulterior motives, except to run his camp and enjoy the burgeoning game he helped build. Flynn doesn't overly concern himself with which shoe company will sign Holdsclaw or how the recruiting derby for one of the Belle's top class of 1999 players—say Long Island's Nicole Kazmarski—is going. But he is a little worried about the future of girls' youth basketball, especially as the professional game brings six-figure contracts and huge shoe money.

On a crisp July day inside a gym on the campus of Indiana State University, as he watches his campers, the best and brightest young players in the game, run through drills, he knows things are currently good. But will money change women's basketball? "You see [the street agents] in the men's game," he says. "I've been to the Nike Camp. I was at the Euro Nike Camp the last two years. I went just to see it. One of the things we talk about is what is it like in the men's game and can that happen here? There are no Kansas City–type teams. There are no Myron Piggie–type teams. If you get coaches on the side they'll say I think this one is shaky or that one is shaky. But it's not to the Myron Piggie, Kansas City 76ers level.

"I don't see the street people yet, but I can see it coming. Probably five years down the road or once there are million-dollar contracts in the women's game. Then you'll see people counting money from the beginning. And I think that's the big thing. Once the huge pro contracts and the shoe money came, and the shoe companies went after the young kids, the men's game was hurt. Once the money's there, they'll come. [But] it's not there now. And there's no street. But it is coming.

"Maybe there is some street person, some rec guy that says, 'Hey, I could get a bunch of these girls together. I saw this girl, she was ten, she was great. I'm going to get them together and I'm going to ride this coattail for a while.' That's what they do on the men's side. But not yet on the women's."

To date, shoe companies have provided mostly positive influences. But signs of trouble are there. In numerous media accounts college recruits have mentioned the importance of a university's shoe affiliation in the decision-making process. In a January 1998 *Sports Illustrated* article on girls' recruiting, Lewiston (Pennsylvania) High's Krista Gingrich created a buzz among women's college coaches when she reasoned that a college with a Nike sponsorship was more desirable than an adidas or Reebok school because Nike signifies "a first-rate program." She wound up signing with Duke, a Nike school, after considering Penn State (Nike) and Notre Dame (adidas).

To reason that the comments of one teenager don't signal a trend in how colleges recruit, consider that in the same article Dayton's Tamika Williams said she once received a recruiting letter from veteran Virginia coach Debbie Ryan, who signed it: "Have a Nike day, and come to UVa!" Current high school players read that article also but think shoe contracts are a bad reason to choose a college.

"If I were deciding between two schools which were really even, and it was one or the other, then maybe [shoe affiliation would play a role]," says Nicole Powell. "But location and the chance for your family to see you play are more important than shoes. You know, college is going to give you good shoes. They are not going to give you crap."

But the girls understand why shoe companies are sponsoring youth sports. Although they say they'd like to believe that it is truly to promote the sport, common sense tells them it's business. "I read in *SI* and [watched] on ESPN and you know the boys go to all these tournaments and Kobe Bryant, he always had adidas, so that's why he signed with adidas," says Powell. "It's called the 'Nike' Camp. They are going to give you shoes and uniforms. They are trying to get people when they are young, but they are just doing business.

"It hasn't reached the [boys'] level yet," Powell continued, "but eventually it will. Just as it gets larger and it gets more and more popular. They know [you will] go with a company that was with you all the way."

Take the case of fourteen-year-old Baton Rouge, Louisiana, native Seimone Augustus, who appeared on the cover of the spring 1999 issue of *Sports Illustrated for Women* under the heading "The Next Michael." The supremely talented 6-foot-1 Augustus has such a following in Louisiana that the magazine reported that one day she purchased a pair of $5 drugstore sneakers ("about the ugliest shoes I've ever seen," said her mother, Kim) and within days middle school girls throughout Baton Rouge were wearing them. "I couldn't believe it," Kim told *SI for Women*. "Those shoes were ugly!"

"I wonder sometimes what we have created here," says UConn's Geno Auriemma. "Is this going to become like the men's game? I have friends in the men's game, I know what they go through. I know what the assistant coaches on the men's side have to go through, what they have to deal with. Can you imagine having to deal with those people, the AAU types on the men's side? The ones there for the money. And then I think, 'Am I going to have to deal with this?' Is the money going to change this? The summer recruiting, the

AAU coaches, the people with their hand out. I'm starting to see it. It used to be people who just liked the game. Now, the way some people talk to you, [it is] like they want something. I don't know. I don't know. If it does change, if it gets to be like that, I hope I'm out of here by then."

Concord, New Hampshire's, Becky Bonner, another top player in the class of 2000, has seen both the boys' and girls' sides of things. Her brother, Matt, was a top fifty recruit in the class of 1999 and signed a national letter of intent with Florida, but not before heavy courtship from Duke, Kansas, and Connecticut. She says choosing a shoe company summer camp was almost as stressful for Matt as picking a college.

"He got tons of pressure from both," Becky says. "He chose adidas. They sponsor his high school and AAU team. And they sponsor mine. We have to be nice to them. Normally, Concord High is not going to have a shoe affiliation. I mean, what's Concord High School? We know what's up. They do it because they hope he'll be adidas. I've gone to Nike Camp. I don't think there is an adidas women's camp, so I don't have to worry about that."

She says she doesn't blame the companies and says the free shoes, the wining and dining, and use as a corporate billboard doesn't affect her. "I don't know if I get the shoes because of me or because of [my brother]," Bonner continued. "I don't care. But I wonder if it is because of my play or because of his play. I can't really tell. But there are girls' teams sponsored by shoe companies. And you can imagine why. You go to Nike Camp [and] you stay at the best hotels, get the best treatment. You are a king or a queen. They show you all these videos of their people. Adidas is the same thing."

Bonner says she does realize that because she comes

from a middle-class family—father is a postman, mother a grade school teacher—and not an impoverished one, material goods hold less sway with her. "It's just material," she said. "It doesn't affect me. But if I weren't as educated as I am? If I wasn't as confident to say no and to stand up to whomever? I don't know. I guess maybe I would go with them [if they offered an endorsement contract as a pro]. If I didn't have anything else. If I can't afford a pair of sneakers, I'll take a free pair."

Bonner illustrates a fundamental difference between the current status of boys' and girls' basketball. Race and economics. Women's basketball is still a game very reliant on the middle-class, suburban player, most of whom are white. Because youth sports are better organized and funded in the suburbs, girls living there have more opportunities to play. In the city, boys play because it is part of the culture. Girls are less likely to get female-only playground games going, which means a girl who wants to learn the game on her own, without the structure of rec league, must be the strong-willed, Holdsclaw type.

That makes women's basketball a game where Connecticut can have a predominantly white suburban team—including its top two stars, Rebecca Lobo and Jennifer Rizzotti—and enjoy an undefeated, national championship year. Even the Huskies' top black player, Nykesha Sales, grew up in a suburban environment in Connecticut. At Flynn's 1998 Blue Star camp, which boasts many of the top one hundred fourteen- to sixteen-year-olds in the world, nearly 75 percent of the players were white and a mere 15 percent hailed from the nation's largest cities. Meanwhile, in men's college basketball, the game is predominantly black, even at the perceived preppy programs, schools such as Duke, whose 1999 team featured only one white in its top twelve players, although many of those players had suburban backgrounds.

"Right now, the women's game is played all over and I think you'll see, I don't want to sound racist, if you're going to sell a product you're going to sell more to the white community than the black community," said Flynn. "Because in the black community, girls' sports is not that big of a deal because, if you're playing basketball, you might as well be a boy. You're a social outcast. But for a suburban girl it's encouraged. It's part of the group thing. It's part of the team thing."

The question now is how are things changing? The 1984 signing of Michael Jordan by Nike was one of the most significant events in men's basketball, a day that changed nearly every facet of the game. As money poured into basketball, and trickled down to youth basketball, the scene for a kid growing up these days is the polar opposite of what Jordan experienced.

Almost to a person, you can't find anyone in basketball who thinks today's culture for boys' basketball is preferable to the old one. With the money came the opportunists.

Women's basketball faces the same crossroads today. Will Holdsclaw's signing send girls' basketball the way of boys'? Will unsavory coaches look to latch on to potential meal tickets? Or will the game maintain the image and culture that its proponents cite as its best quality?

"It may be getting too commercialized," said Carolyn Peck, coach of Purdue in 1998–99 and now of the WNBA's Orlando franchise. "We don't want the quality of the education an athlete gets to be overshadowed. Women's basketball has always done a good job of being about student-athletes. As money comes into the game, you might get players with a different goal. I think we need to keep it from getting to the level of the men. I think the more opportunities that kids have to play basketball is great. But [shoe-sponsored teams and camps] have to be used for a purpose. Use it to develop basketball players, not for a company to market what they want to promote. It has to help young people."

In the spring of 1999, Holdsclaw signed a multiyear deal with Nike that her agent boasted was "the wealthiest ever for a women's basketball player."

Nike hopes she will sell products like Michael Jordan.

Women's basketball purists like Mike Flynn just hope she doesn't signal the future commercialization of the sport, like the signing of the original Jordan did.

CHAPTER 10

Recruiting Rush

The day things truly got out of control, Glenda Rush figures, was one fall day in 1995 when her seventeen-year-old son, Jaron, pulled up in front of their South Kansas City home in a new 1995 GEO Tracker. The car was magnificent, sharp and sleek-looking, with a polished black exterior and not even a hundred miles on the odometer. It retailed for about $17,000. Where he got it was what made Glenda Rush nervous.

"He came in and I asked him, 'Where did you get that from?' " she says. "He said someone had bought it for him. That's all he said."

That someone, Mrs. Rush suspected and later confirmed, was Tom Grant, a forty-six-year-old millionaire Kansas City businessman, major booster to the University of Kansas, and the man who not only owned and help fund the Nike-sponsored AAU team Jaron played for but just loved doting on Glenda's oldest son.

This was the same Grant, Glenda knew, who had be-friended Jaron at age eleven, when a youth coach introduced the two. At the time Jaron was just a skinny basketball prodigy, but Grant took particular interest in him and over the next few years paid his tuition to attend an exclusive Kansas City private school, had the teenager over to his stately Shawnee Mission, Kansas, home for dinner, and dropped lavish gifts on the youngster, including a cash allowance, clothes, and vacations to places as grandiose as the Cayman Islands and to Chicago to meet the ultimate member of the swoosh stable, Michael Jordan. The car was just the latest in a long line of benefits.

"It's the wildest thing I've ever seen," said Glenda Rush. "I've just never seen anything like this recruiting stuff."

And she hadn't seen anything yet.

By the time Jaron Rush enrolled at UCLA in the fall of 1998, some two and a half years later, the All America small forward would be the center of an amazing saga of youth basketball gone bad. It was a story rife with an ex-convict coach, allegations of illegal recruiting, gunplay, tens of thousands of dollars of Nike's money, the rise and fall of a prominent AAU team, and a foul recruiting odor that would find its way to the previously believed to be straight and narrow world of Kansas Jayhawks basketball under Roy Williams.

Of all the stories in the big-ego, big-money, high-stakes modern world of AAU basketball, where well-heeled boosters and unsavory street presences, funded by huge sums of shoe company dollars, yield considerable influence over where the nation's top young players attend college, Kansas City was one of the most out-of-control.

Because just when Glenda Rush couldn't imagine what could come next, everything did. Within weeks of showing up with the GEO Tracker, Jaron's coach on Grant's Children's Mercy Hospital 76ers became Myron Piggie. The burly thirty-six-year-old Kansas City native who sports a number of gold teeth was a novice AAU coach, but Grant hired him to run his high-powered summer team on the recommendation of Jaron Rush and Korleone Young, a top player out of Wichita, who happened to be Piggie's second cousin, once removed.

Although Piggie wasn't well known in summer basketball circles, he had been a familiar person to the Kansas City police department. Piggie's record included arrests for drug trafficking and assaulting a federal agent, not to mention being shot and wounded in 1989 by Kansas City police officers during an early morning gunfight outside a local bar.

In his two-year run with the 76ers, Piggie would bring opportunism within summer basketball to new levels. He worked a deal with Nike to deliver top K.C. area players to its All-America Camp, in exchange for, as he would tell friends, $50,000 annually in funds that Nike says was supposed to help offset travel and operational costs of the 76ers. However, he used that money personally, never sharing it with Grant, who says he had no idea Nike was sending money to the 76ers. Later, in violation of his contract with Nike, he would sell complimentary shoes the company sent him for $100 a pop in the gymnasium of Kansas City's Pembroke Hills High School, the same tony prep school attended by Jaron and his younger brother, Kareem, also a top prospect—each boy's $10,000 annual tuition paid for by Grant.

Although Piggie denied most allegations, he couldn't shake the memory or the cashed checks of a dozen people who bought pairs of Nikes from him one winter day in 1997. Piggie arrived that day at the gym of the plush Wornell Campus of Pembroke Hills with a large box of Nikes. As the school's varsity and junior varsity players crowded around, Piggie offered a one-time deal. One hundred dollars per pair, a "cut-rate price," he bragged. He sold twenty pairs of the shoes, which he later admitted he had received complimentary from Nike. By selling the shoes Piggie was in direct violation of Nike's "travel Team Contract," which strictly forbids such profiteering.

(The shoe sale, which violates state federation rules, caused the Missouri High School Athletics Association to investigate the incident. In the end the MHSAA suspended no Pembroke Hills players.)

"And they were cheap," Stephen Dunson, the father of Pembroke Hills junior Shawn Dunson, told *Basketball Times* in the fall of 1997. "They weren't even Jordans. You probably could have bought them for $80 at the Foot Locker."

Dunson would later regret being quoted on the record. Two days after the issue of *Basketball Times* detailing Piggie's sales job hit the streets, Dunson was lying in bed with his wife in the south Kansas City home he had lived in peacefully for twenty-one years. Shawn was standing in his parents' doorway and all three were conversing when they heard a car slow outside before gunshots rang out. The Dunsons' home was peppered with bullets from a 9-mm gun— one shell smashing their bedroom window before winding up on the bedroom floor, five more slamming into the house, and three hitting the family van in the driveway. No one was injured.

"Twenty-one years and I've never had anything like that happen," said the elder Dunson.

Kansas City police were called and investigated but never found a suspect. At the time of the shooting Piggie was on a flight from Kansas City to Portland to attend a meeting for Nike-sponsored summer coaches, high school coaches, and company officials at the Nike campus in Beavertown.

Although police never got anywhere with the investigation, Dunson has his suspicions about it.

"You don't get your windows shot in by accident," he said.

As bizarre as that incident was, what shocked most people in Kansas City was how a prominent businessman such as Tom Grant II and a seemingly clean college coach such as Roy Williams could get caught up in such a sordid mess.

Grant, now forty-nine, is a distinguished, graying graduate of Kansas who inherited a fortune from his namesake grandfather and made another through profitable business deals of his own. His grandfather, the original Tom Grant, founded the Businessman's Assurance, an insurance company, in 1909, which Grant sold to European investors in the early 1990s. Since then he purchased majority ownership in Lab One, the world's number one blood testing company, which controls a hefty share of that expanding market. He lives in a large, lavish home in the upscale Kansas City suburb of Shawnee Mission and his worth is estimated in the eight-figures.

Grant has stayed in close contact with his alma mater by becoming one of the school's most generous donors, including regularly contributing to the athletics department's Williams Education Fund. His eldest two sons both attend KU and he has season tickets to both Jayhawk football and basketball games. His seats at Allen Fieldhouse are so prime that, according to one person who has used them, "you could see the shine off Dick Vitale's head."

In the late 1980s, Grant says he was first approached about donating a few dollars to a local boys' club basketball team and he agreed. One thing led to another and in 1990 he founded his own team called the Businessman's Assurance 76ers.

It was then that Grant was introduced one afternoon to Jaron Rush. Grant had shown up at practice to see how the troops were doing when local youth coach John Walker says he called Rush over and had him work out for Grant. As Rush became a star for Grant's twelve-and-under team, he began paying close attention to the young prospect.

When at age fourteen Rush was struggling academically in the Kansas City public school system, Grant offered to place him and his younger brother, Kareem, at Pembroke Hills. Jaron would have to repeat eighth grade, Kareem would enter seventh, and Grant would handle both tuitions ($10,000 per year).

Grant says that he regularly pays the tuition of needy students, including nonathletes, at Pembroke Hills. He estimates that over the past decade he has spent nearly $800,000 on tuition. But while his philanthropy was wide-ranging, it was clear that Jaron was becoming his all-time favorite.

Glenda Rush says she was wary but went along because she knew Pembroke Hills would be good for her sons.

"When Jaron first started, I didn't have a clue about what was going on," she said. "I didn't even know what AAU stood for. I didn't even know anyone in our family could play basketball well."

Jaron couldn't just play well, he could play it the best. As he sprouted, his coordination only improved. His national reputation was burgeoning, aided by playing for Grant's traveling team, which crisscrossed the country. As an eighth grader he was named the number one player nationally in his class by *HoopScoop* magazine.

As a junior he was 6-foot-7 and had developed into a talented wing player, strong, fast, and smart with the ball. He had a lethally quick first step, and when teamed with Korleone Young, a powerful 6-7 forward, the duo was unstoppable.

And the 76ers became the hottest AAU team in the country. With Grant flying the team to tournaments on chartered planes and Nike lavishing on the players the latest shoes, uniforms, and warmups, the 76ers were the team everyone wanted to play for. And no one wanted to play against.

Rival coaches, more than a little jealous, sneered at the 76ers' excess, nicknaming the group "Team Cash and Carry" and wondering aloud if the team was over the salary cap.

It was during those days that Rush began spending considerable time at Grant's home. Grant arranged tutors to help with schoolwork, set curfews for Jaron, and fed him dinner regularly.

"He basically spent a lot of time at my home since he was eleven years old," Grant said. "I've tried to help the young man in terms of parental influence. I've tutored him. I've stayed up nights trying to keep him off the streets. Basically, I've treated him as if he was my own son."

Part of that relationship, Grant admits, included providing Rush spending money, sometimes as much as $300 a week, new clothes, and other gifts. One spring day in 1996, Jaron walked through Glenda Rush's door, smiled at his unsuspecting mother, and showed off a new set of braces.

"He just came in here with them on," recalls Glenda Rush, who works as a sales clerk at a local lumber company. "What could I say? I mean, I can't afford none of that. I can't say nothing. They were on."

Jaron also began vacationing with the Grants, taking trips with Tom, his wife, and his three sons all around the country. One time they went to Chicago on Grant's private plane to attend a Chicago Bulls game. There Rush was able to meet his hero, Michael Jordan. For a normal Kansas City kid, gaining a private audience with Jordan wouldn't be easy. But Jordan is not only the hero of Nike basketball, but he also played at North Carolina under then Tar Heel assistant coach Roy Williams. Rush, cementing his ties with Nike, would later work as a paid instructor at the Jordan Flight School, an instructional camp held in Santa Barbara, California.

Rush was an experienced traveler by then. He had also made repeated trips with the Grants to the Cayman Islands.

"He's gone down to the Cayman Islands with us, been on trips with us to Chicago, been all over the place," said Grant.

And during his junior year he rolled home in the Geo Tracker.

"I assumed Mr. Grant gave it to him because I know I didn't buy it," said Glenda Rush, who at the time drove a 1989 Dodge Dynasty. "I didn't think it was his place to buy him that car, but it was too late to even give it back. I didn't appreciate it though."

In fact, Grant didn't buy the car for Rush but rather leased it, ironically, from a car dealership in Overland Park, Kansas, just down the road from NCAA headquarters.

"The car is in my name," said Grant then. "I lease the car and let him use it. I let him use the car, I didn't give it to him. I basically told him that if his grades were good enough and he made the honor roll, I would help him with a car. That's kind of what I do with my own kids. If the kids were making good grades, then I helped them out with some transportation."

Grant defends his generosity with Rush, saying he helped many local kids. He has done more for Rush, he says, but not because of his basketball abilities.

"Can I see that it can be portrayed in a negative light? Yeah, I can see that," Grant said then. "But I have done a lot positive for the young man, and not just financially. I mean in terms of time spent with him."

"Why does Mr. Grant do all this?" asked Glenda Rush the fall of Jaron's senior season. "I want to say KU, but if you talk to him he says he doesn't care where he goes. I don't know though. Why would he do all of that stuff for Jaron? Which is why I say I don't understand what his motives were behind this."

Grant emphatically denied that he was pushing Rush to any school.

"I am a fan of KU, yes, but honestly in terms of where he goes to school, I don't care if the young man goes to the University of Kansas," Grant said during the fall of 1997. "You know, the University of Kansas has a pretty successful basketball program. I don't think they need Tom Grant to help them. I am just interested in Jaron Rush."

To keep things on the level, Grant says, he disclosed every dollar he spent on Rush in a letter to the NCAA where he admitted being a booster of KU athletics. That prompted the NCAA to begin a file on the case, which would ultimately determine where Rush would end up.

"[In 1996] I sent a letter to the NCAA and basically said here are the types of things I've done for this young man," Grant said. "It said I am an alumni of the University of Kansas and I know they are trying to recruit this kid."

Grant even discussed the situation with KU coach Roy Williams, whom he says he speaks to regularly. The closeness of their relationship, Williams says, is overstated by Grant—"I barely ever speak with the guy," Williams said.

"I told [Williams] up front that if you ever recruit this young man, I'm sorry if I am an alumnus of Kansas, but I am more interested in helping this young man than I am as far as the University of Kansas basketball efforts," said Grant.

Williams knew that suspicion was rising around the country and even brought up possible NCAA violations with the Rush family during his home visit in September of 1997. Sitting in the 59th Street home of Janette Jacobs, Glenda's mother, he told the Rush family not to worry about Grant costing Jaron his eligibility.

"He talked about it," Glenda Rush said. "He mentioned that there was nothing against [NCAA rules] because Tom Grant has done [everything] because he is a friend of the family."

Did Glenda consider Tom Grant a friend of the family?

"Well, that's what he said he was. A friend of our family."

In fact, Glenda Rush was concerned her son had been influenced. She encouraged Jaron to listen intently to the other coaches who came through Kansas City to recruit him, including John Thompson of Georgetown, Tubby Smith of Kentucky, and Kelvin Sampson of Oklahoma. She insisted that no one would push her son to a school.

"When Jaron first started going over there, that's all anyone was saying, that he was a booster for KU," she said. "I was totally against it. I didn't want him going to KU if Tom Grant was behind it. I wanted him to go where he wanted to go, not because someone was telling him he needs to go there."

That feeling held true on the eve of the one-week national signing period in mid-November. Like many of the nation's top players, Jaron Rush was tired of the recruiting process and wanted to sign his national letter of intent. He said he wanted to sign with Kansas.

Upon receiving confirmation that Rush was verbally

committed, there was a celebration in the KU basketball offices in Allen Fieldhouse in Lawrence. High-fives and pats on the back were exchanged as Williams and his staff eagerly awaited the signed letter from the future McDonald's All American they had deemed a major recruiting priority. But it wouldn't come.

The national letter of intent was created by the Collegiate Commissioner's Association (CCA) in the 1950s as a way of curbing aggressive recruiting. By signing the letter a player becomes the de facto property of a school and the letter prohibits other NCAA schools from recruiting him. It allows coaches to relax during the summer, knowing the kids they had recruited in the spring would arrive on campus in September.

Because of the document's legal nature and very binding language, the CCA, which still oversees the letter, decided it would be best if it required recruits under the age of eighteen to have a parent or guardian co-sign the letter of intent. Recruits eighteen and over were considered adults and could sign on their own.

As of the November signing period in November 1997, Jaron Rush was seventeen. For his letter to be binding, Glenda would have to co-sign.

And she refused.

"I felt he needed more time to think about it," she said at the time. "Why rush? If he still wants to go to KU next spring, then he'll be old enough to sign on his own and he can go to KU. I just want him making his own decision."

Kansas was stonewalled. The November signing period lasts one week, and during that period Jaron pleaded with his mother to change her mind. One night that week, during a Pembroke Hills basketball game, Tom Grant and his wife, also a Kansas alum, approached Glenda and discussed the situation. Mrs. Rush held firm and when the period ended, Rush's recruitment was on hold.

Everything was fine until January.

During the fall, the NCAA had director of enforcement Carl Hicks look into Grant's role as a Kansas booster, especially his supplying Rush with the Geo Tracker, the money, the gifts, the clothes, the vacations, and the lodging. The association commonly refers to such gifts as "extra benefits" and could place a school on probation for violating its rules.

Kansas, however, could not be punished with probation or any other infractions penalty, since Rush was technically not a signed recruit but, thanks to Glenda Rush, just a prospect.

The NCAA could, according to Hicks, rule that the extra benefits Grant provided Rush gave the Jayhawks an unfair recruiting advantage. If so, the NCAA could prohibit Rush from signing with Kansas, but allow him to go anywhere else he wanted.

Because Rush never signed with KU, the case was not considered a major penalty case, Hicks says. That means the NCAA does not make its findings and conclusions on the case public and Hicks would not comment on the judgment. He did say, however, that the NCAA sent its judgment to Kansas on February 9, 1998.

The next day, coincidentally, Rush, who was still orally committed to KU, was quoted in the *Kansas City Star* complaining about Williams's substitution patterns. "Roy subs too much for me, but I still might want to go there," Rush told the *Star*.

He was criticized immediately by KU fans and that afternoon called into KMBZ-Radio to defend himself. He said he was quoted accurately but that he was misinterpreted.

But the next day, February 11, at his weekly press conference, the quote was brought up to Williams, who suddenly had a different take on the young man whom he had been recruiting closely for five years and whose verbal commitment just two months before he had rejoiced in winning.

"The NCAA rules [are] that you cannot comment on recruiting of individual prospects other than to confirm or deny you are recruiting them," Williams said, slowly but deliberately. "I'm denying. We are not recruiting [him]." Asked whether that decision was still open to change, Williams said, "I've heard it sometimes said that it takes an act of God to change something. This is a lot stronger than that."

Rush was taken aback. "It was a shock to me when he said they were no longer going to recruit me."

And to everyone. Williams's performance was quickly hailed around the country by newspaper columnists and television pundits as a coach finally standing up to the demanding modern player. Rush was suddenly cast in a negative light, his reputation as a hoop punk cemented with one press conference. The story is repeated to this day and will likely stick with Rush until his college days are over.

Meanwhile Williams was loudly applauded by KU fans and the national media for standing by his principle of team play. Even if it cost him a McDonald's All American.

Yet the move never made sense to some rival Big Twelve coaches, who among themselves discussed and doubted that a quote about substitution patterns was what really cost Jaron Rush his scholarship slot at Kansas. Wouldn't it be easier to believe, they argued, that after five years of recruitment, including scores of unofficial campus visits, Rush and Williams had built up a relationship where the coach might call the recruit up and ask him to explain himself? After seven years under the wing of booster Tom Grant, hadn't

Rush become close enough to the program that he would be given some leeway? Particularly since the very afternoon his comments went public, he immediately went into damage control? Wouldn't any coach, particularly one who is quoted as often as Williams, know that people, particularly those who are not media savvy, are sometimes quoted out of context and at least give enough credence to Rush's explanation to call the player and ask, "What's up?"

Does it really seem likely Williams would turn his back on a player of that magnitude, a player he desperately sought, because of one quote? Without ever asking for an explanation?

Not likely.

What did happen, according to a source very close to the investigation of the recruitment of Jaron Rush, was the NCAA told Kansas that by virtue of Tom Grant's largesse, it had gained an unfair recruiting advantage and could no longer recruit Jaron Rush. Kansas spokesman Dean Buchan denies this.

Although Association rules prohibit not only Hicks, who now works for the Southeastern Conference, but anyone at the NCAA from commenting publicly about the case, a source inside the NCAA says Kansas was informed of the NCAA ruling by fax on February 9, 1998.

"Roy is clever, he knows what he's doing," said the source.

Moreover, the basketball news Web site, *College Hoops Insider,* reported the week following Williams's public comments that sources on the KU basketball staff confirmed the NCAA's decision prevented the Jayhawks from offering a scholarship.

Regardless of why, in the fallout of the Kansas-Rush breakup a number of things occurred.

Rush committed and eventually signed with his second choice, UCLA, who had continued to recruit him despite his verbal commitment to Kansas.

"Jaron never told us to stop," said UCLA coach Steve Lavin, who had landed another Kansas City product, guard Earl Watson, the previous season despite Watson's verbally committing to Iowa State. "We just kept working him."

In Westwood, Rush would become part of one of the most highly acclaimed recruiting classes of all time at UCLA. His classmates—Matt Barnes and Ray Young of California, Dan Gadzuric of Holland via a Massachusetts prep school, and Jerome Moiso of France—would give Lavin a talented, albeit young, squad to compete with.

More interestingly, almost immediately following Rush's commitment to UCLA, he stopped driving Tom Grant's GEO Tracker, which instead took up lodging in Grant's driveway and the two began spending less time together. That didn't mean Rush was without transportation, however. CNN/*SI*'s Sonya Steptoe reported that Jaron was now driving a white sports utility vehicle.

"All I know is it's not mine," said Grant, mirroring the comments of Glenda Rush.

Grant himself had been through the wringer. He swears his initial interest in youth basketball was innocent and he isn't sure how everything got so out of control.

All he knows now is that his foray into the modern world of shoe-company-sponsored AAU basketball left his reputation damaged. Stories in national magazines, in Kansas newspapers, and on local television had given him the kind of attention he says he was not looking for.

"Obviously I'm not used to this kind of publicity," Grant said.

So bad was the local publicity that Children's Mercy

Hospital, which Grant had regularly donated money to and in past years had made his players volunteer at, convened a board meeting in 1997 and decided it no longer wanted its name associated with the team. "Once we became aware of what this was about, that this was high stakes, competitive basketball, our board decided it didn't want any part of this," said CMH spokesman Tom McCormally. "They felt it wasn't beneficial to the hospital to be associated with this type of behavior."

Meanwhile Grant fired Piggie as his coach. He had supplied Piggie with what he describes as a "small stipend, less than $10,000 a year" to coach but was upset Piggie had withheld Nike funds and was shocked by the extent of his criminal background.

"I knew he came from the street, he's a tough guy," Grant said. "He was coaching one of the teams because he knew Jaron when [Jaron] was younger and some of the other kids in the program, including his son [Myron Piggie, Jr.]. He was up front with me and told me that he had, at one time, had some problems with the law. I believe it was drug activity. I said, 'Is that all behind you?' And he said, 'Yes.'

"I was led to believe it was all when he was a younger man—[Piggie was twenty-nine at his last arrest]," Grant continued. "Everyone is entitled to a mistake. In fact, I thought he could talk to some of the kids about making a mistake and [the consequences]."

Still, Piggie was fired and Grant replaced him with Lafayette Norwood, a former assistant coach at Kansas, who had been working with some younger teams. Grant also said he was scaling back on the 76ers' aspirations.

"If the kids want to play, I'll fund it," Grant said. "It's good for the kids. But we are only going to have local players."

Piggie, meanwhile, tried to stay in the AAU business. That's not a surprise, since he hadn't held a full-time job since 1991, when he says he worked as a janitor for the Kansas City school system and had a family to support.

"It's an all-year job," Piggie said of being a summer coach. "We make sure they do well academic-wise. We look at other kids, kinda keep promoting the program."

Now Piggie felt he could step out on his own. He founded the Piggie Foundation, a not-for-profit organization that would allow him to use donations to his program tax-free. And he continued to work with Nike to recruit Kansas City players to its camp.

Piggie said there was big money in that business. He says in July 1997, the summer before the senior seasons of Korleone Young and Jaron Rush, Sonny Vaccaro came to his home in Kansas City and offered $25,000 to Piggie if he delivered Young to the adidas ABCD Camp. Piggie says he refused. Vaccaro refutes that story and says Piggie turned it around.

"Two nights before the start of the ABCD Camp, Myron Piggie calls me and says he will deliver Korleone Young to ABCD if I can guarantee him a Tracy McGrady–type deal for Korleone next spring," Vaccaro said. "I laughed at him. He was trying to sell Nike out. I'm not getting into a deal with a guy who is backstabbing someone else. Anyway, I didn't give Tracy that [$12 million] deal because he was just anybody. Every NBA guy I talk to thinks he'll be a star.

"As for me going to his house, that's not true. I've never even met the guy, let alone go to his house. I don't even know what he looks like."

Young went to Nike Camp and by fall had left Kansas altogether, transferring from Wichita East High School to Hargrave Military Academy in Chatham, Virginia. Not only did Hargrave change its shoe affiliations over the summer—from Reebok to Nike—but Myron Piggie, Jr., a 5-10 point guard considered moderately talented at best, went to Hargrave also.

Colleges remained hot for Korleone however. At 6-7 with good touch inside, he reminded some scouts of former Cincinnati power forward Danny Fortson or Arkansas star Corliss Williamson. UNLV went so far as to offer Myron Junior a spot in its recruiting class in hopes he'd bring his second cousin along. It would never happen. Young's academic situation remained sketchy and instead of trying to work himself eligible, Young declared himself eligible for the 1998 NBA draft, following prep phenoms such as Bryant or McGrady. Unfortunately for Young, the NBA didn't think he was another Bryant or McGrady. He was drafted in the mid–second round by the Detroit Pistons, where he saw minimal playing time. Instead he spent much of the 1999 season on the team's injured reserve list.

Moreover, Piggie's dream of landing a "McGrady-like deal" fell through. Nike offered only a minimal package, reported to be less than $25,000 total, and the NBA lockout meant Young was not earning a check for all of 1998. The Piggie Foundation, without what was expected to be its best donor, Korleone Young, saw its funds dry up. During the summer of 1998 Piggie's team didn't travel much, even dropping out of a June tournament in Des Moines, Iowa, because he couldn't afford the entrance fee, according to one of Piggie's coaches.

"He fooled a whole community," said John Walker, who worked with Piggie that summer. "He told everyone he had all this money and everybody committed to us but he fooled us."

Suddenly Kansas City wasn't so hot anymore. Jaron

Rush headed west, Kareem wound up at Missouri, KU's arch rival, Grant was embarrassed, Young was in a netherworld, and Piggie was broke. KC AAU ball had gone bust.

Jaron Rush was off to UCLA, but it appeared Kansas would suffer little because it had added one of the prized recruits of 1996 to take his spot on the floor. The recruit, Lester Earl, was one of the hottest players in the country when he chose Louisiana State over Kansas and UNLV.

While some coaches might have given up, the Kansas staff didn't. Dale Brown, then coach at LSU, started to sense something was wrong when Earl, during the Maui Invitational in November 1996, stayed after practice to chat with Kansas coaches. Brown said a coach and a Kansas booster pulled Earl aside, keeping the player so long he nearly missed the team bus.

A few weeks later, Earl, despondent over his poor play with the Tigers, skipped practice and was suspended from the team by Brown. While Earl returned to the Tigers after asking Brown's forgiveness, the player also begged his former AAU coach, Thad Foucher, to call Roy Williams about a possible transfer. According to Foucher, Williams—who had sent Earl a Christmas card signed by the entire Kansas team—called back on December 20, 1996, and said he'd love to have Earl and planned to discuss the prospect with his team.

One Kansas coach even called Earl during halftime of a televised Jayhawks game on January 6, 1997—all this while Earl was still on scholarship at LSU, an act which runs in violation of NCAA statutes. Then, after being booted from the LSU team altogether, Earl took a road trip to Kansas and showed up on national television sitting behind the Jayhawks bench.

Once at Kansas, Earl made a deal with NCAA investigators to level charges against LSU's staff in exchange for a return of his eligibility. Eventually, LSU was placed on probation because a booster had given Earl $5,000, but none of Earl's charges against the coaching staff held up.

"What happened here is a crime," Brown said. "Lester Earl took money [at LSU] in violation of the rules, but working with the Kansas staff found a way to get his eligibility back. Someone needs to expose Roy Williams for the phony he is. He worked the system to get a player even though that player was on scholarship elsewhere."

After Brown went public with his complaints about Williams, a spokesman for the University of Kansas told the *New Orleans Times-Picayune* that the coach denied all wrongdoing. Kansas fielded no further questions on the issue.

Ironically, what Kansas got was the shell of a former All-America—and trouble, to boot. Earl injured his knee shortly after showing up in Kansas and never regained the aggressiveness that marked his high school and LSU days. What he did gain was a lot of attention for the 1997 GMC Yukon he was sporting when he came back to the Kansas campus. The Yukon is registered to Baton Rouge fireman Tosh Johnson, who said he lent the vehicle to Earl, even though Johnson himself kept driving a late 1970s Ford pickup back and forth to work.

Though all sides deny it, suspicion ran high that the truck was from rap star/sports agent Master P, who lives in Baton Rouge and befriended Earl there. Master P did acknowledge that he and Earl hang out together in Baton Rouge and Los Angeles, where P has a home in Beverly Hills. Their hanging out is a possible violation of NCAA rules because Master P founded No Limit Sports, which represents NBA stars Derek Anderson and Ron Mercer as well as Heisman Tro-

phy winner Ricky Williams. P said he sold his portion of the
agency in 1998, months after Roy Williams received reports
of the agent and his player running around Los Angeles together.

"You have to admit it is kind of funny that Kansas
worked so hard to get Lester Earl and stirred up so much in
the process only to have him sit at the end of the bench," one
LSU athletic staffer said. "Sometimes you better watch what
you ask for."

Not that Williams seemed concerned. The telegenic, connected former Dean Smith assistant saw virtually no damage
to his reputation despite his difficult-to-defend actions in the
Rush scandal. Although fellow coaches began casting an increasingly wary eye on him, and discussing the situation behind his back, powered by a strong media image Williams
moved on like nothing had happened.

He was the only one who escaped unscathed.

CHAPTER 11

"Buy Your Own Goddamn Shoes"

Elvert Perry wouldn't know Jim Delany if he bumped into him on E Street in San Bernardino, California. And Delany has never been on E Street. And that's just part of the problem.

Delany is fifty-one, white, and the commissioner of the Big Ten Conference, a job that commands a six-figure salary. He's North Carolina educated (BA 1970, Law School 1973), a former attorney in the North Carolina Justice Department, and one of the most powerful insiders in basketball. He counts Tar Heels types such as Dean Smith, Roy Williams, Eddie Fogler, and Bill Guthridge as friends.

Perry is 37, black, and counselor at the Cicero Hope Boys Club in San Bernardino, where he says he makes only $8.50 an hour despite having a degree in psychology from Cal State San Bernardino. As a way of helping local kids, he runs the Inland Valley Basketball traveling team, which receives shoes, gear, bags, and about $5,000 a year from adidas. He says his greatest fear is getting caught in a drug crossfire. Among the loud fraternity of AAU coaches, the loquacious Perry is the most opinionated and outspoken.

They are linked by basketball, but just barely. Perry and Delany are at the opposite ends of the hoop food chain and represent the remarkable racial, social, and economic diversity of the game of basketball.

And not surprisingly, their opinions on shoe company involvement in AAU basketball are night and day.

"The apparel companies' involvement in youth summer basketball is problematic," says Delany. "There is no question that the practices of traveling team basketball can set up an environment that blurs the lines of acceptability. There is a possibility that this could really damage and corrupt the game. It is a problem that is four or five years old, but has gotten real bad in the last two years."

"If they feel this way about Nike and adidas," Perry suggests, "why don't they do this? Take the shoe company out of it and buy their own goddamn shoes. Stop blaming the shoe companies, stop blaming AAU coaches, and put the blame where it lies. College basketball is a business. The NCAA, almighty God, got $1.2 billion from CBS. I don't see them giving back shit. So don't sit up there, talking about, well, this AAU coach and that AAU coach."

To illustrate the point, Perry likes to point to the hypocrisy of, among other schools, Delany's alma mater, North Carolina, which has a $7.1 million endorsement deal with Nike.

"And I don't see Bill Guthridge giving back that damn check," says Perry. "I don't see Roy Williams giving back that check. Nobody giving up no paychecks. That's crazy. That's crazy, man. Ain't nobody giving up no paychecks. But they say we should. I'm lucky if I get five grand and equipment. Maybe two grand, sneakers and bags. And they're making millions. It's sickening, man."

Delany and Perry are just one example of the hurdles college basketball faces in attempting to regulate summer basketball, let alone have an intelligent conversation about it. And at the heart of it is two sides who have almost no common ground, speak different languages, and basically don't care if the other side exists.

It's just one reason shoe companies and summer basketball appear like an unsolvable problem. All while the future of basketball hangs in the balance. Delany looks at college basketball from an interesting angle. He's a former player for Dean Smith at UNC, where his teammate and roommate was Eddie Fogler, now head coach of South Carolina. As conference commissioner he works closely with Big Ten coaches. His background as attorney for the North Carolina Justice Department and a four-year stint in the 1970s as a NCAA enforcement representative gives him experience in dealing with the sordid stuff and the judgment to smell a rat. From 1979 to 1989 the New Jersey native was commissioner of the Ohio Valley Conference before taking over as the head man in what is probably the most powerful athletic league in college sports.

He's seen the good, the bad, and the ugly of college basketball and is as wired into the game as any administrator in the country. And it is those contacts—hearing the coaches complain about the state of summer hoops not only at official meetings but over rounds of golf at the unofficial Carolina basketball alumni weekend in Pinehurst, North Carolina—that caused him to step to the forefront of the battle to reclaim the summer.

In 1997, he decided to begin to do something about it. He set up an informal committee—which included such other notable NCAA heavyweights as Kentucky athletic director C.M. Newton, Virginia AD Terry Holland, and former Big East commissioner Dave Gavitt—to discuss the situation.

He isn't naive. He gives credence to arguments such as Perry's and realizes that the NCAA can be accused of hypocrisy. He bemoans low graduation rates, worries about increased commercialism and the soaring compensation packages for coaches. He favors ideas such as freshman ineligibility. He says he is searching for a better way, but also a simpler way.

"I think I'm in a unique position to speak out," Delany says. "I have become concerned about the health of the game. I think parts of the game are as healthy as they have ever been, but I also think there are parts of the game that raise suspicion and serious concern about the fate and future state of the game. What I thought needed to be done was to raise the issues and try to be constructive about it."

And it has worked. Since Delany began leading the cause, college administrators and coaches have spoken out about what they view as the evils of summer basketball. Coaches have penned mission statements, including "An Alternative Approach to Recruiting in Division I Men's Basketball," which hopes to "shift the recruiting opportunities away from the summer and into the academic year." The National Association of Basketball Coaches convened its board of directors and created a proposed recruiting model because, as the document states: "Head and assistant coaches are dissatisfied with the present recruiting model and are calling for change. A dramatic increase over the past few years in the number of summer, fall, and spring camps/tournaments has resulted in higher recruiting costs, strained family relationships for college coaches due to the lengthy recruiting trips, and reduced influence of college and high school coaches in the recruiting of prospective student-athletes."

It recommends that the NCAA work with USA Basketball to run summer camps and tournaments in an effort to "reduce influences in the recruiting process" and "dissuade influential alumni from the ownership of 'summer' teams." Although opinions differ from coach to coach, there is almost universal agreement that the current system of shoe-company-sponsored AAU teams and camps is bad for the game. Many complain that the culture of top players jetting around the country and, indeed, the world, being provided expensive clothes for free, and being coddled by summer team coaches and shoe executives creates immature kids with distorted perceptions of the real world.

There was a time not too long ago when high school and traveling team basketball was long on amateurism. High schools were made up of players from the school district and travel teams rarely recruited across town. Both groups rarely played teams from outside their home state. Purchasing shoes and clothing was, invariably, left to the individual player. Young players may have had an affinity, but never an affiliation, with a particular brand of shoe.

"The board of the NABC doesn't think [summer basketball is] good because it sends the wrong signals to what is right as far as living everyday life," says Purdue coach Gene Keady, a member of the board. "We don't think it's good. You have to earn your way. You don't get things given to you. If you get things given to you, you never appreciate them.

"By the same token," Keady continued, "the good part is, those kids are taken out of these bad element areas and they have a chance for life. There's a two-edge sword."

But Keady thinks getting the easy travel, the early fame, and the free goodies for playing basketball actually hinders a player's development. In their search for the next Michael Jordan, Keady says, shoe companies are actually shooting

hemselves in the foot by stunting the development of star
players. It takes much more than talent, he argues, to make
t in the NBA.

"Jordan got cut as a sophomore," Keady says. "Kids like
hat usually are very hungry. They develop this desire to be
he best because something happened to them in eighth
rade or they got cut or they weren't playing. They're dri-
en. They're driven people like Michael is.

"The best thing about Michael is that he's a better person
han a player. That's what's great about him. I talk to kids at
amp and I say, 'Michael Jordan is tremendous and we all
ove him because he is so entertaining to watch. But your
reams shouldn't be a Michael Jordan. Your dreams should
e a Steve Kerr because that's possible.' He worked this
ame. You shoot a hundred free throws a day. You shoot two
undred three-pointers after you run five miles. That sort of
hing is possible for a player that is not of super talent."

But Keady realizes few dream of being like Steve.

"That's our biggest problem," he said. "The players we
et [at Purdue] think they're going to be NBA players so
hey don't go to class, they don't study hard, and they don't
ave the right values in life. So you end up spending two
ears de-recruiting them to get them on the right channel
nd in the right focus. Our job now is more mind managing.
They just don't have the right values about what it takes."

Keady thinks instead of playing so much AAU basket-
all, a player would be better served getting a job and buy-
ng his own shoes.

"Work eight hours at a Saturday job," Keady said. "You
ave to be on time, work four hours, get an hour off for
unch, and work another four hours. You're off at five."

But it's becoming increasingly difficult to find a profes-
ional basketball player who has ever held a real job, even a

part-time one. Even stars with good images, such as Detroit Pistons forward Grant Hill, admits he's never worked a real job in his life.

"No," says Hill, a little sheepishly. "In my free time, I played basketball. Summers, weekends, every chance I had. I suppose that's not the best way to develop values but that's how it is these days."

And it will continue to be so.

"They're not going to do that anymore," said Keady. "That's a pipe dream."

The pipe dream to Elvert Perry is that Gene Keady and the rest of the establishment are going to leave grassroots basketball alone and look in the mirror. In no uncertain terms he scoffs at Keady's and Delany's view of the world. He bristles at people telling him that he and other AAU coaches are inadequate role models.

"I'm telling you, it's unfair how they label us," says Perry. "There's a lot of good AAU coaches in this business."

He says he knows where it's coming from though. Across the race line. Perry's theory is that older coaches, athletic directors, and conference commissioners like dealing with high school coaches because they are mostly white. AAU coaches, however, are mostly black. He says there's been cheating in college basketball for as long as anyone can remember, but no one ever formed committees and proposed eliminating the white high school coaches.

"I'll say it on the record," says Perry. "When the white guys were in control and they had it, it was cool. But the minute we get involved with our own kids, it's a problem. Every time black people are involved with their own kids, there's something wrong with it. And I don't understand that.

"They are saying that me and other guys are not qualified

to teach our own kids something," Perry said. "I don't understand that, man. Every time blacks are involved in something, we're the bad guy and that's ridiculous. Every time we're involved with our own kids, why must we be the villain? That's some sad shit, man.

"I know personally I would give my heart and soul to kids if I had to," Perry continued. "And you know, even some of them going back East to the prep school, I'll help pay for their bills by getting an extra job, working extra hours. I ain't going to see no high school coach do that. They ain't gonna go down there in the 'hood. Damn sure [they] ain't going to go in the 'hood. They don't know how to go in the 'hood. But I got to go there."

That said, Perry admits there are abuses in AAU ball. He isn't afraid to call out what he says is the purchasing of some Southern California players. His team is usually pretty good, but by no means a high-powered AAU entity. He says that is because his adidas-sponsored team will not recruit players, like some area Nike teams.

He mentions 7-foot Tyson Chandler, one of the top players in the class of 2001, who lives in San Bernardino, and gained a measure of national fame when *60 Minutes* featured him in a 1997 piece about the sneaker wars entitled, "There's No Business Like Shoe Business."

As an eighth grader, Chandler signed up with the Nike-sponsored Southern California All-Stars, coached by Nike-paid consultant Pat Barrett. That summer, he transferred from his local high school in San Bernardino to Nike-sponsored Compton Dominguez High, some fifty miles away, and began making an hour commute each way to school.

"Some teams will do whatever it takes to get the kids," Perry said. "If you have a kid that's a great thirteen-year-old, they'll definitely go after him and steal him. I call it the

African slave trade. It's here we go again, buying young black men. It's a shame it's gotten so ugly, but it is whatever it takes.

"Is it a car payment? Is it paying for a mother's car? Is it paying for a mother's hair to be done? Whatever it takes.

"You know, you got some people here that are going to try and win at all costs," Perry continued. "And to do that, they're going to solicit players. I'm not going to do that. I ain't buying nothing. Either you want to play for me or you don't. And if you don't, then the hell with you. That's how I look at it. If you want to be down, then we can be down. But [I'm] not about buying."

And there are more horror stories.

During the summer and fall of 1997, there was no more coveted high school athlete in the country than Hampton (Virginia) two-sport star Ronald Curry. A stud option quarterback and defensive back in football and quick point guard in basketball, he was hotly pursued for each sport by Virginia, North Carolina, and Florida State, each of whom saw Curry as someone who could lead its athletic teams to both the Bowl Championship Series and the Final Four.

"He'd just be a wonderful addition to the University of Virginia," said a member of the Cavaliers' basketball staff at the time.

That addition became expected during a September Thursday night football game at Virginia, when, live on ESPN, Curry's verbal commitment to UVa was announced. As word of Curry's decision rippled through the crowd at Scott Stadium in Charlottesville, fans began chanting his name and cheering.

But by December, Curry had reneged on his commitment to Virginia (although he said he was still considering the Cavs), and his high school football coach, Mike Smith, caused a stir when he told the media he was concerned that Nike representatives were trying to change his mind. Virginia football and men's basketball are sponsored by Reebok. North Carolina and Florida State are Nike schools.

Curry had played basketball in the Nike grassroots system, starring at the 1997 Nike All-America Camp (where a crew from NFL Films tailed him) and for the Nike-sponsored Boo Williams AAU team, which is coached by Hampton Roads native Boo Williams, a longtime associate of Raveling and Nike board of directors member John Thompson.

Although Smith's allegations were never substantiated, they were powerful. "I have no doubt they're doing it right now," Smith told the *St. Petersburg Times* in the spring of 1998, as Curry weighed his college choices. "Their representatives, you know, I don't know how high-level they are. I think it's wrong for a child to have to deal with that."

Curry wound up signing with UNC and although there are no sustainable allegations that shoes played a part in it, eyebrows were raised. And on subsequent visits to Charlottesville for football and basketball games, Curry has been lustily booed by fans who once celebrated him.

And that's why the hypocrisy can swing both ways. Comments like these from the front lines of the recruiting wars rightfully make Delany shudder all the way back at Big Ten headquarters in Chicago. It's what shook college hoops to the core and created the entire concern over summer basketball.

But Perry maintains you can't throw the baby out with the bathwater and for every bad AAU coach, or sketchy shoe deal, there are ten good people.

"There's some bad high school coaches out there," said Perry. "There's bad schoolteachers. You pick up the paper, there's schoolteachers molesting kids. That don't mean all schoolteachers are bad. You got priests molesting little boys. That don't mean all priests are bad. Stop making us the scapegoat. That's bullshit.

"Let me explain something to you, there is no power game here," he says. "We all are about the kids. Every time you turn around, they want to do something to make us look like the villains and that's bullshit. I'm not a villain, man. I don't make millions. That's how I look at it. So that's how I feel, man. I'm just tired of seeing, every time I pick up the paper, that we're the flesh peddlers. We're this. We're that.

"Has anybody ever talked to an AAU guy? Does anybody know an AAU guy? Most of us don't make no money, man. I don't make a damn quarter. I wish I did. I don't make shit. I don't even know what that is to make money."

He isn't alone in defending the summer system.

"I tell people I hate all college coaches," said Darren Matsubara, who runs the adidas-sponsored Elite Basketball Organization out of Fresno, California. "The college coaches say they hate all AAU coaches, so I say I hate all college coaches.

"There's a difference between people," Matsubara continued. "If the NCAA finds a college coach cheating does that mean Mike Krzyzewski is? Of course not. It's the same with AAU guys."

Tennis Young, who coaches the adidas-sponsored Huntington Park Warriors out of Philadelphia, says he hates being lumped in with some of the seedier AAU coaches.

"Every profession has some bad people in it," Young said. "You have some doctors who are just horrible, they don't seem to ruin it for all the doctors out there. You have some bad judges, bad lawyers, bad schoolteachers, and

omehow they don't get lumped in together and told they are
ll bad.

"But in our thing, we should be shut down completely
because there are a couple of unscrupulous guys out there."

He also points out what Sonny Vaccaro likes to say. For
he most part, college coaches complain that AAU coaches
ell their players to certain schools. Which, Vaccaro points
out, means someone is buying.

"The day college coaches stop cheating," Vaccaro said,
"AAU coaches stop cheating."

That's not necessarily true, of course, since the pot of
gold a shoe company can give a kid is overwhelmingly more
than a college will pay for a player, but it has some merit.
And it's another angle to the hypocrisy.

"And this is really the bad thing to me," says Young.
"The people [AAU coaches] are taking the money from the
college coaches. The exact same college coaches who are
aying shut them down. If the college coaches don't spread
he money around there's no money for anybody to take.
've never heard them say let's shut down the college
coaches."

The image of the AAU coach is so bad, some coaches say
hey don't bring up their side job at cocktail parties or when
hey meet new people.

"I tell people I coach an AAU team on the weekends and
hey look at me funny," says Bob Pryor, who runs the Nike-
ponsored Bloomington Red out of Bloomington, Indiana.
"They think I must be making all this money from all these
ources. Make? Coaching costs me money. Our resources
don't cover expenses."

And some college coaches are sympathetic. Some claim
AAU coaches are no worse than high school coaches, while
many realize the hypocritical position they are in. They dis-

like the current shoe-company-funded system, but they, as Perry points out, aren't returning any checks.

"The shoe stuff is crazy, the influence they have is crazy, but who am I to criticize?" said Mississippi State head coach Rick Stansbury. "I've got a deal with Nike."

Even Delany agrees.

"From the perspective of the conflict of interest that occurs as a result of heavy institutional and coach involvement with apparel companies, and apparel companies' involvement in youth basketball, it's problematic," he said.

Most realize publicly criticizing the people who may be able to dictate where a recruit attends college is unwise.

"It's one of those things where you don't want to say anything negative because that AAU coach may turn against you," says Purdue's Keady. "You won't get his player."

Other coaches see some benefit to the wild summer AAU scene, where a tournament such as the adidas Big Time can have nearly two hundred teams (over two thousand players) competing in it.

"I've been recruiting for a long time," said Syracuse coach Jim Boeheim. "And I remember the old days. Today [at the Big Time] I saw a player from Florida in the morning, one from New Jersey after that, and one from California after that. Twenty years ago to do that I would have had to get on a plane in Syracuse and fly to Florida, fly to New Jersey, fly to California. This is so much easier. The player from California, I didn't think he was good enough. In the past I would have gone all the way to California to decide a player isn't good enough. What a waste of time."

Perry is quick to point out that criticism of AAU coaches taking shoe money doesn't make sense because few AAU coaches make the kind of money the majority of college coaches do.

"Name me a rich AAU coach," he says. "Name me one. You can't, can you? Now name a couple of millionaire college coaches. Coaches making the fat check. All right, then, name me some assistants. Where can you be in this world as an assistant making $100,000? Recruiting. That's crazy, man. What they need to do is leave the summer alone. 'Cause the NCAA can't tell me, and they shouldn't be able to tell our kids what to do. That's crazy. They made all this money off of us. Now you done made all that money, you going to tell us what to do?"

Money and race, says Perry, are what this is all about. AAU coaches do need to be more honest, he says, but having a school president or a conference commissioner who takes so much from shoe companies tell him he can't is ludicrous, he argues.

"Let me tell you something right now," Perry says. "College coaches are going to cheat because regardless, college basketball is a business. Let's all understand that. If you don't win, you are fired. Let's cut off the bullshit. You don't win, you are fired. So you gotta win."

He also scoffs at the suggestion that AAU basketball is going anywhere. The coach-player relationships are too close, he argues. High school coaches have no interest in dealing with kids during the off-season; most he knows, he says, roll the balls out in the fall and lock them back up after the season. Not AAU guys.

"I mean every day we have to deal with them," he says. "Kids call you at two in the morning, 'Coach, I'm in jail.' They call you, 'Coach, I'm hungry.' 'I ain't got no shoes.' You don't see any high school coach there. He's home with his family.

"I'm close to the kids because I understand the kids," he says. "If I'm dealing with a black kid or a white kid, and most of the time I'm dealing with black kids, I'm going to know the kid. I'm from that environment.

"Look, I'd rather see the kids going to these events than the dope dealer, then have them out there robbing you. You know what I'm saying?

"Oh, yeah, I give a kid a pair of shoes. I'd rather he get them from me than sticking you up. Because if he don't get them [from me], he's gonna get them one way or the other, brother. I'll tell you that, man. He's going to, legal or illegal. That's the rule of the jungle, man."

Perry cites an example. He says one summer one of his players had fallen into the lucrative local narcotics trade because he needed the money. Perry knew that if it didn't end, college basketball would be out of the question.

"When I went out to the gym, whenever I went to his crib, I knew the kid was selling drugs," Perry said. "So I had to go to the man who was giving it. And I had to go to ask him, out of respect because that's his domain, to let my kid go."

Did he do it?

"Yeah, he let him go."

You went to the drug dealer's home?

"I went to the dealer's house. And you got to know them."

What'd he say when you walked in?

"I knew them. I just said, 'Let my man go, 'cause he's got a future.' "

What did he say?

"He said that was cool."

And the kid stopped dealing?

"No question. He's doing fine now. That's the name of the game."

There are other, less eye-popping examples of the good side of summer basketball. In lieu of cash repayment for jetting around the country playing ball in July, coach Rich Gray makes the members of his Nike-sponsored St. Louis Eagles volunteer at the local children's hospital in August.

"You have to teach the kids that giving back is important," said Gray. "They wind up getting more out of it than they put in."

Others cite mentoring and educational support programs. But it's easy to wonder if nonqualified students with plenty of basketball ability wouldn't be better served just staying home in July and attending summer school.

And for college coaches, the bad easily outweighs the good. No, not every team has a criminal behind the bench, but clearly coaches who have been recruiting for years find the present system and the AAU coaches undesirable.

"The summer period never used to bother me," said Xavier's Skip Prosser. "But now, by the end of the summer I'm usually completely fed up."

"The problem with some AAU coaches," said a Big Twelve coach, "is they have no shame. Everything is for sale and nothing is for free. It's outrageous. I mean, I've been in this business quite a few years, but the last couple have become nuts. I just don't enjoy the summer."

And even coaches who won't weigh in with an opinion admit the recruiting game has changed.

"When I first started out it was really more or less you were dealing with the parents, the high school coach, and that was about it," said Texas coach Rick Barnes. "Obviously you tried to get to know most of the people around the situation but most of it was around the school, the teachers, the guidance counselor, and most of it was done right there on campus.

"You tried to get to know who it was that was going to be pivotal in making the decision," Barnes continued. "But now you've got to deal with so many different factors and because you have a limited amount of days you don't feel like you get to know who's doing what.

"And when you go in, often, your first couple trips there or as you start getting involved in the recruiting, you've got to figure out who it is you are dealing with there. Is it the high school coach? Is it the AAU coach?

"And so it is different. There's just so many more people involved. I remember during the summer you always made an effort to go by the high school and see the people there, and you try to do that now but it seems like this time of year you're just going from camp to camp to camp.

"I don't know if we are recruiting as much as we are trying to just keep up with each other in terms of seeing how many good players you can get involved with," Barnes said. "But it is definitely a different ball game."

No more different than Elvert Perry and Jim Delany.

CHAPTER 12

The Summer Season

With his right hand draped over the steering wheel, left hand holding the cell phone he's talking into, Curtis Malone turns his fifteen-person minivan onto Rodeo Drive in Beverly Hills like he was pulling onto Minnesota Avenue back in southeastern Washington, D.C.

How he can conduct a phone conversation right now is beyond comprehension. Blaring from the minivan's speakers and pulsating out the windows is a Tupac Shakur tape playing to the delight of the twelve members of the D.C. Assault AAU team that Malone coaches and is driving around L.A. on a sightseeing tour.

And right now on a clear July night in 1998, Beverly Hills is about to meet inner-city Washington. Heads turn on Rodeo as Tupac rattles the windows of the Bentleys, shakes the doors of the designer stores, and disturbs the ears of the plastic surgery survivors walking the capital of American consumer excess. This is an AAU cultural exchange program, a ridiculous culture clash that befits the state of the summer game. On an off night of the Best of the Summer AAU Tournament held on the campus of Cal

State–Dominiguez Hills, Malone has loaded up his AAU team and promised a tour to help them remember L.A. There was a walk along Ventura Beach, a drive through UCLA, and now a look around Beverly Hills.

"Hey," shouts Malone over Tupac, "I'm trying to find O.J.'s house."

"Well, I think we're close," shouts someone from the back of the van. "I think I just saw a bloody glove."

The van erupts in laughter as Malone drives north onto the tree-lined streets housing the posh residences of those living the good life. The kids oohh and ahhh at the his and hers Mercedes in the driveways, the multiple swimming pools, and the palatial digs rising up from behind thick gates and brick walls.

"See," shouts Malone, "this is what you guys have to work for. You have to go to school for. So you can have stuff like this. And I'll say this, if you guys knew your schoolbooks like you know your Tupac, you'd have no trouble."

The van groans.

Coaches of traveling basketball teams will tell you scenes like this play out every day. They call it expanding horizons, giving city kids something to dream about, reinforcing values, or simply letting people see the sights.

Americans of all socioeconomic classes like driving through Beverly Hills, spying for celebrities and dreaming of owning multiple Mercedes. So do city kids. Malone, thirty, isn't what you'd normally consider a teacher. A former ballplayer in Metro D.C., he now wears a mustache, is almost always outfitted in adidas apparel, and talks on his cell phone nonstop. Because of his close ties to youth basketball in his hometown, he has built his Team Assault AAU program into one of the most powerful and closely watched in the country.

In the summer of 1998 he had two of the nation's top five players on his squad, 6-9 Dermarr Johnson and 6-5 Keith Bogans, not to mention six other seniors who would sign Division I scholarships. His team was the team of the summer. A brash, confident, talented squad. Needless to say his cell phone rang incessantly as college coaches called looking for a recruiting edge.

A teacher, no. A coach, maybe. But in AAU ball he's both. The criticism that this, thirteen black men driving around Beverly Hills, is somehow wrong, is what causes some summer coaches to cry foul. In the game of college basketball, where the vast majority of players are black but coaches and athletic directors are white, there's a culture war waiting to happen. And not surprisingly it can run along the race line.

A look inside a team like this, however, shows all the angles of AAU ball—the positives, the negatives, and the reality that falls somewhere in between. This team is heavily sponsored—about $15,000 per year, plus clothes, shoes, and athletic gear—by adidas. They'll spend three straight weeks together on the road, including a week in Las Vegas and this one in L.A. They'll play an aggressive style of basketball, a city style, one that their number one sponsor, adidas, loves and rival coaches hate. They wonder if their name, D.C. Assault, shouldn't also include "and battery."

They'll do so with a group of players who are all good enough for Division I scholarships but also need serious work in the classroom before they can qualify for them. And, needless to say, three thousand miles from summer school, there isn't a textbook to be found. Most of these players are from broken homes, lack parental guidance, and come from the hard, drug-infested neighborhoods of the nation's capital. One of the team's best players, Johnson, lives with Malone. If a conflict needed a home, it could come here.

But they are also about sightseeing, safe summer nights, and the kind of camaraderie and leadership skills that develop from athletics. They are about teenagers being teenagers, making fun of O.J. while the summer melts away.

So is this good for basketball or bad?

Depends on whom you ask. Right now as Beverly Hills is treated to a drive-by Tupac concert, and the poof-haired host/ aspiring actor at Spago has fear flash through his eyes as the van rolls by, you can only think that they are, at the very least, entertaining.

It's trite to present the benefits of keeping city kids out of the city for a summer, out of harm's way, out broadening their horizons. It is also, sometimes, true. Every kid in this van could tell a serious horror story or three about life in D.C. and they can all talk about how nice a few weeks away can be.

"But the thing is," says forward Derrick Payne, "when you go back everybody is doing the same thing. Nothing changes. I went away to Mt. Zion [prep school] this year and when I came back I was like, 'has anything changed?' The same guys are still dealing drugs and the shootings are still going on. Everything is the same. D.C. is crazy. I don't miss it."

But while it is fine to say that the kids are away from the violence and the narcotics trade of their Washington neighborhoods, it isn't why they are here. AAU basketball isn't really about gaining life experiences or hanging out on Venice Beach or the Vegas Strip. It's about basketball. While these side trips are nice, in truth, most of the kids in the van would be just as happy back in the hotel sleeping, watching

TV, or playing cards. They'd even be happier, teenage boys being teenage boys, if there were any girls living near their Hampton Inn in Carson. Although Malone is quite pleased with the hotel's isolated location.

"One less headache," he says. "Keeping an eye on these guys in Vegas was not easy."

Other than that, all anyone on Team Assault wants to do is win this tournament, the team's final entry of the summer. They are still bitter about losing in the quarterfinals of the prestigious adidas-sponsored Big Time Tournament in Las Vegas the previous week. As defending champions, and boasting the superstar duo of Johnson and Bogans, they expected better. They fared worse.

So now they are focused on redeeming themselves here in Southern California so they can return to D.C. as champions.

They have twelve very promising prospects on the team and even with Bogans, a wondrous shooting guard, back in Maryland attending summer school, no one here lacks for confidence.

"We'll win it," says guard Al Miller. "No doubt about it."

Malone helped start this team five years ago. A former high school and college player (Potomac State) he returned to his hometown in Maryland—the same neighborhood that produced Sugar Ray Leonard—in his early twenties and began working at the Columbia Park Rec Center. He had been a good player, but had a bad attitude as a teen, he admits. He always thought he knew more than the coach, thought school wasn't priority number one.

"I was a guy who didn't want to listen, I was a spoiled guy," he says.

Things started simply enough in Columbia Park. He coached some youth recreation leagues and worked out with kids on the side before he and his close friend Troy Weaver decided to start a traveling team for all the young talent in the area.

The first year Malone and Weaver were sponsored by Reebok, which had a shoe called the Assault. Hence, Team Assault. The name stuck in 1995 when they secured a Nike sponsorship and played in a handful of tournaments. Then, with Johnson and Bogans finishing up their freshman year of high school, adidas came in and offered a three-year contract, providing shoes, uniforms, gear, and money. With all the young talent in the program Team Assault became an immediate summer powerhouse.

When Weaver left in 1996 to join coach Ralph Willard's staff at Pittsburgh, Malone had assistants Mike Brown, Damon Handon, and others step up. Since then Team Assault has won a number of national tournaments and secured a big reputation across the country and, more importantly, on the playgrounds of the nation's capital.

"Team Assault is a big deal back home," says guard Val Brown. "Everyone from around the way wants to play here. It's like the Dream Team of D.C."

Which is just one reason adidas loves this team so much. Malone's hotel room in Carson is like an adidas locker, with shoes and gear stacked up. They are a walking three-stripe advertisement, just the kind of credibility Sonny Vaccaro knows no amount of television commercials can buy in D.C.

And, indeed, Assault can play.

All twelve players, Malone believes, will one day receive Division I scholarships. Although they lack a big man, Assault is extremely athletic, better shooters than you'd imagine, and talented up and down the roster.

In line with their name—they aren't the quietest group you've ever come across—their game is a city game, their persona a city persona. They aren't so interested in just beating an opponent as humiliating one. Why, for example, take an easy layup when you can alley-oop it off the backboard to a teammate who can slam-dunk it so hard it spikes off a defender's head? The highest compliment paid all week was after one player converted a particularly violent dunk on an opponent's cranium and the bench shouted, "Damn nigga, you busted that brotha's ass right in front of his dip [girlfriend]!"

Team Assault likes to bump after baskets, talk trash, perform all sorts of trick dribbles and street moves, and lock guys up on defense. All macho playground stuff.

Basically, they are a product of their environment. They are hell to play and the type of team that if you don't know them, you might hate them. But if you do know them, all that menacing and prancing on the court is just a show of toughness for a group of normal kids. It's actually comical.

One day this week Team Assault arrived at the gym to discover they were about to play Team Nebraska. It took about one second before the guys started in on the cracks about cornhuskers, farm boys, and country hicks.

"It's a unique team," says forward Dermarr Johnson with a smile. "They are very proud of where they are from. And they let everyone know that."

The tough, physical style of play is just a way to represent D.C.—a place where only tough people survive. And these are tough kids.

"Most of my guys don't come from the best situations," Malone says. "There aren't a lot of mother-father situations at home. It's just not like that. I've got a lot of city kids."

Indeed, many of the players on the team live in one-parent homes or with a grandmother. The fathers have either never been around, haven't been around lately, or, in the case of at least one player, were murdered a few years back.

Most of the guys profess undying love for their mothers. For others, you can tell mom isn't much better than dad. Overdone as it may be, Malone offers a male role model.

"Growing up without a father is tough," says Al Miller, an effusive guard who's quick with a smile, a joke, and the ball. "Being alone makes you strong. My father was killed by some dudes around my way. You know. Or, I guess, no one knows. Just some dudes. I don't know.

"I just want to get away from all that. That's why I thank God we got this because in the city, things are crazy. Curtis, he does a lot of things for us. He's a good guy. Without him, we wouldn't be here. And I know a lot of kids on our team would be doing other things."

Added Derrick Payne, a strong forward who attended Oak Hill Academy in Mouth of Wilson, Virginia, in 1998–99, "Back home it's just me and my mother, Rosalyn. She's a great mother, I can't even tell you how great. But I don't want to be around D.C. This is great because everybody is like a family on this team. Whoever comes on this team, we're like brothers. We get hard on each other, but when it's time we'll step in and help too."

One player who has taken Malone's friendship further than most is Dermarr Johnson, who moved into his coach's Maryland apartment last year. Their friendship is why NCAA legislation can never stop the influence of grassroots basketball. You can try to take away the tournaments and you can try to take away the teams but you can't take away the relationships.

As Johnson, echoing a familiar sentiment, says simply, "Curtis is like a father to me."

It's game time and that means show time for the guys. Today's opponent is a team from Los Angeles and as Team

Assault runs through layup lines on a side auxiliary court here, Malone is a little worried about overconfidence. A few dozen coaches and scouts sidle up and grab seats while the players attempt wild dunks instead of fundamentally sound layins.

The small gym at NCAA Division II Cal State–Dominguez Hills is hot and stuffy. In an effort to keep costs down, the tournament's organizers, L.A.-based David and Dana Pump of Double Pump, Inc., won't turn on the air conditioning. The Pumps make money here by charging each of the seventy-five teams an entrance fee of $175. They also charge all college coaches $50 for a week's pass and a coach's pack, which includes team rosters listing each player, his height, position, high school, and occasionally home phone number.

The pack is not worth the money but the Pumps, like every other tournament organizer around the country that does the same, know places like the University of Kentucky or North Carolina can afford it. Because as many as three hundred coaches from some 175 schools will march into the bandbox gym, it's a profitable source of income.

Media and scouts enter free, while the public must pay $5 a day to watch. Not that it matters. There is virtually no media coverage, basically only some scouting services and a basketball magazine or two. Fans are few, local parents or the occasional hoops-obsessed fan who likes watching a dizzying array of games unfold on three courts from 9:00 A.M. to well after midnight.

The Pumps also get sponsorship money from adidas to hold the event, which is just one of the reasons the company's banners are hanging throughout the small gym. It's also why almost every team here is sponsored by adidas. Just a few miles south on the San Diego Freeway, on the campus of Cal State–Long Beach, is a Nike-sponsored tournament that features most of the swoosh's stable of top teams. There are only a few tournaments annually—the Bob Gibbons Tournament held each Memorial Day weekend in Chapel Hill, North Carolina, and the Spiece Run 'n' Slam, held in early May in West Lafayette, Indiana, to name two— where top teams from both companies compete.

"If you are sponsored by adidas, Sonny wants you here [at the Pump tournament] and at the Big Time in Las Vegas," says Jimmy Salmon, coach of the Tim Thomas Playaz, a Paterson, New Jersey, based team that receives donations from not only its namesake and most famous alum, but adidas. "Other than that, he says play where you want."

For Assault, adidas' sponsorship deal pays the entrance fee and the cost of travel, hotel rooms, and food. In a sense, this week is a lot of adidas money shuffling hands.

The first half of game one plays to Malone's fears. He sits his first unit and starts some of the younger kids who haven't gotten much playing time recently. In their chance to impress the coaches, they stumble, falling behind 27–12.

Malone calls timeout and lays in on them.

"If you think you are just going to go out there and win because you are Team Assault, then you're wrong," he shouts. "This team is pretty good. They're from L.A., so you know they are going to play hard."

Later in the half he subs in go-to guys, such as Johnson, Payne, Brown, Miller, and others. The tide turns quickly as Assault applies a full-court press. This team boasts guard play that is relentless. Brown, Miller, Troyce Haynesworth, Brian Chase, and junior Cliff Hawkins are as good on-the-ball defenders as you can find, and when they apply the press most opposing guards cannot advance past half court.

The result is a swarming, in-your-face attack that resembles a hurricane. This leads to a parade of breakaway dunks.

The half ends 47–40, in favor of D.C. Malone still isn't happy, mainly because the hotdogging had already begun. On an open break 6-6 junior Bernard Robinson gets too fancy and blows an easy basket.

"Come on, Bernard," shouts Malone during one sequence. "Forget the finger roll, dunk the fucking ball!"

His halftime speech isn't pleasant.

"They scored forty on you guys! They shouldn't have done that, let's get after it. You young guys, I'm putting you back in but I expect you to play. Don't blow this in front of all those coaches. This is why you are here."

They don't blow it. The second unit—led by underclassmen Robinson, David Holmes, Hawkins, and James White—pour it on. The L.A. guards are harassed into a series of turnovers. The lead stretches to 56–40, then 60–40, then 64–40. An East Coast thug style has taken over and banging, bumping, and aggressiveness is everywhere. The L.A. coach is furious, screaming at the refs for fouls. At one point words are exchanged between an L.A. player and the D.C. bench. It's not so much threatening as humorous. Most of Assault laughs. No one is intimidated. It's clear they don't fear any fistfights.

Eventually L.A. calls timeout so the coach and the ref can get into it. The L.A. coach is a big man, the ref isn't so big. Voices keep getting raised. Malone gets up and walks over to investigate, the L.A. coach shoots him a glare. Malone comes back to the bench.

"I ain't messing with that," Malone says with a laugh. "That coach is too damn big."

The bench cracks up. Play resumes and finally, ten and a half minutes into the second half, L.A. scores to make it 66–42. It's as close as L.A. would get. Malone praises his younger players and puts in the first unit. The game deteriorates into a D.C. dunk show and playground track meet. College coaches sitting across the way, there to evaluate, roll their eyes and pass the time gossiping.

Malone is a youthful presence on the bench who wears adidas sandals, a pair of black adidas shorts, and a gray adidas T-shirt. The cell phone in his pocket rings more than once and he talks briefly on the phone while the game goes on. His goal is to become a college head coach. On the bench he likes to yell, but also laugh. And he can coach the game. When needed, he runs some set offenses and knows how to use his personnel well.

Maybe most important, he also knows how to motivate what he has. The kids want to play one-on-one and showcase their ability. Malone allows for that as long as it takes place in a somewhat controlled system of play. If he tried to run set offenses 100 percent of the time there would be a mutiny.

"This is supposed to be fun," Malone says. "People take AAU ball too seriously."

By game's end a dozen college coaches stop Malone as he tries to make it off the court to offer a "Good game, coach." Or a "Curtis, by the way, that sophomore, what's his deal?"

For Malone, that's the question he loves most to hear.

The Best of the Summer Tournament takes place during the NCAA's July evaluation period, which means college coaches can watch an unlimited number of players and teams during the three-and-a-half-week stretch. When Team Assault plays, they do not lack for onlookers. Which is the point.

"The best thing about this team is getting a kid who

doesn't get seen a lot a Division I scholarship," says Malone. "It makes everything worthwhile."

The player who needs the least amount of showcasing is Dermarr Johnson. Since he played for Team Assault in the Bob Gibbons Tournament as a freshman during the spring of 1996, he has been considered the nation's top recruit in the class of 1999.

At 6-9, the smooth Johnson has uncanny ball-handling skills, foot speed, and wingspan. He can beat almost any player his size off the dribble and has the kind of talent that makes people stop and watch. You need not be a college coach or full-time scout to watch his fluid game and realize he has gifts the other kids don't. Because of that he has topped every recruiting list out there and, thus, received an incredible amount of scrutiny. Johnson has been put through the wringer the past few years while critics pick apart every flaw in his game—too skinny, too selfish, too unmotivated. Johnson actually sat down this summer with one of his harshest critics, Clark Francis of *HoopScoop*, who is so down on Johnson's game that he rated him the thirty-second best player at ABCD Camp.

"He told me that he did that just to motivate me," Johnson said. "He said he just wants me to live up to my ability and said he had written some bad things about me but not to take it personally."

Easier said than done.

"They say all sorts of stuff," Johnson said. "Last year they said I was too weak, too skinny. Now that I've been lifting they say that sometimes I don't play hard. I don't know, I think I play pretty hard and then I hit a peak and they see something special, and then I come down from the peak. So they think I'm slacking. It's hard to say. I'm just playing, trying to have fun. This isn't that important."

The pressure has been oppressive. The game here that Johnson seemed most relaxed at was one he sat out in an effort to nurse a groin injury. He wore a bright smile as he cheered his teammates on.

"I never thought things would blow up so big," says Johnson one night on the way back from the gym to the hotel. "At first it was good. I didn't know anything about rankings and I thought it was great people thought so highly of me. But now, it's crazy. The hype just built up and I get a lot of criticism. All the good stuff has just turned around.

"If I could do it again I wouldn't be known until before my senior year," Johnson said. "I'd be like Tracy McGrady. Just come out at the end. Then no one gets on you."

Johnson is an easy-to-like kid. He is well spoken, down-to-earth, and very quiet. On the court he plays a fierce game. He isn't afraid to scowl, bump, or take it at his opponent, but off the court he is very low key and private. One of the reasons he moved out of his grandmother's house—where his mother also lives—and in with Malone is because it's quieter.

"At my old house there were so many people around," says Johnson. "It's quiet at Curtis's house."

He doesn't drink, smoke, or really even hang out. Back in Maryland he basically stays out of trouble by spending time with his girlfriend. But he has become so big in prep basketball, you'll hear all kinds of stories about him.

"I've read all sorts of rumors about me," Johnson says, a little disgusted. "Some say I've already signed with an agent. Some say I have some kind of big car, like a Range Rover. I'm like, 'Where?' I don't have any car. Or they say my grades are bad. Or everyone says I am going to the NBA directly out of high school.

"I've never once, not once, said I was going to do that,"

Johnson continues. "Everyone thinks they know me but no one even talks to me. They just make it up because they think they know me. Everyone has been saying I was going to the NBA since I was in tenth grade."

The rumors have hurt Johnson. The past two years he had attended the Newport School, one of the better academic high schools in Metro D.C.—a school where most students strive for the Ivy League. While Johnson admits he was never the best student, he did qualify for an athletic scholarship at the University of Cincinnati, where he eventually signed. By 1999, he was attending Maine Central Institute, the New England prep school with the powerful basketball program.

Still, the talk of the pros, being the next adidas player to go to the NBA directly out of high school, à la Kobe Bryant and Tracy McGrady, has surrounded Johnson since he was a sophomore. Part of that is because of his skills and part because his game is the kind Vaccaro covets—an athletic wing player—and might drop a multimillion-dollar endorsement deal on.

For his part, Johnson said, emphatically, that he would attend college. But he thinks the perception that he won't has scared schools away from recruiting him.

"My favorite school has always been North Carolina, because of Michael Jordan," said Johnson. "I've always wanted to go there. They sent me letters up until last year but I haven't heard from them. I guess they aren't recruiting me."

The nation's number one player not recruited by his dream school?

"They all think I'm going to the NBA," said Johnson. "One ACC [Atlantic Coast Conference] coach said he wouldn't waste a stamp recruiting me. Why?"

That leaves Johnson with an interesting mix of schools on his recruiting list, as of midsummer. There was Georgia Tech ("I'm pretty cool with the assistant coach Dereck Whittenburg, and I like their style of play"), Michigan ("A big-time school and their coach Brian Ellerbe, is from D.C."), Pittsburgh (Panthers assistant Troy Weaver is a former coach of Team Assault), UNC-Charlotte ("Dalonte Hill [a sophomore] and I are like brothers"), Maryland ("It's the local school"), and Utah ("They just came on the list. They might have the best coach in the country."). Ironically, the school he would sign with, Cincinnati, wasn't in the picture yet.

And so those six come and watch, but not as closely as you might think. Weaver, the Pitt assistant, is a constant. As a former coach of Assault he has known all of the players for years and is recruiting a few of them. Since Malone is his best friend, he often spends half the day hanging around in his hotel room or eating meals with the team. He doesn't need to bump into kids because he is always around.

Likewise, assistants from UNC-Charlotte, Utah, Georgia Tech, and Michigan are almost always courtside during games.

"But I haven't seen too many head coaches coming to watch Dermarr," Malone says one afternoon while hanging around in the hotel room.

"What?" interrupts Weaver, who's hanging around also. "Ralph [Willard] watched him a half dozen times. He watched every one of his games at ABCD."

"Yeah, I guess he did," says Malone. "But not many other guys."

Johnson's recruitment has been tame by big-time standards. Part of that comes from Malone, who as coach and house mate is handling the recruitment. He is not someone who seeks the glad-handing and attention that others do. He turns down a half dozen dinner invites a night from coaches to eat at Subway with his kids. He doesn't like to give the impression that he is too close to any school.

"I'm not into that stuff," says Malone. "I want to be a college coach someday and I don't want to burn any bridges. Anybody who wants to recruit one of our kids can. I even ask kids who they like and go out and tell those coaches to start recruiting."

Utah is the perfect example. Malone asked nearly everyone in basketball who they thought were the best coaches at the college level and why. When the name Rick Majerus kept being brought up, he discussed it with Johnson and then approached surprised Utes assistant coach Donny Daniels and told him Dermarr would like Utah to recruit him. Majerus called the next day.

One thing Malone says he won't do and never has done is sell a player.

"I know I could get some money for a kid like Dermarr, I know there are schools that would cheat for him, but what would that be saying?" he says. "I'm better off in the long run playing it straight. I don't want to teach Dermarr that's the way things are done. I don't want to go through the negative stuff. One day maybe I'll be able to move on to the next level and coach and make some money that way. If I took money now, I know I'd never be able to do that."

In fact, Malone says there really isn't a good way to recruit him except by being straight up.

"The last two highly recruited players that I handled are Kevin Lyde and Mark Karcher," Malone said of the two former Assault players. "They both went to Temple. Now everyone knows John Chaney isn't going to pay for players. He just comes in and recruits. But I think he's a great guy, an honest guy, and Temple was the best situation for those kids."

For Johnson's recruitment, things are still in the slow-simmer mode. He doesn't read much of his recruiting mail and only occasionally talks to coaches on the phone. He says he doesn't even pay attention to who watches him play.

"I'll deal with all of that later," he says with a shrug. "I want to sign late."

By March his list had changed, with the only original team still in contention being Maryland. Cincinnati and Connecticut had both been added. And even with the specter of the NBA still there, Johnson wound up attending UC.

A slightly lesser recruited player on Team Assault is Brian Chase, a 5-9 point guard who shoots the ball very well. He attends Washington (D.C.) Dunbar High and coming into this tournament was being recruited by a couple dozen Atlantic Ten, Big East, and Colonial Athletic Conference schools.

One of those schools is Virginia Tech, which had assistant coach Dean Keener in attendance to keep a close eye on Team Assault. Although Chase was aware of Tech, he didn't know much about them until this week.

On Sunday Night, Keener spoke with Chase's mother, Catereda Lloyd, back in Washington and made a very favorable impression. When Chase called home early in the week his mother told him about the conversation and what she had heard about Virginia Tech's academic programs. Chase told his mom that he had noticed a Virginia Tech coach watching him play and would see if the Hokies kept the interest up. They did.

The next night as Chase drained a couple of long threes, Keener stood silently under the basket jotting down notes.

After the game Keener hung around where the team was milling about, hoping to make eye contact with Chase and ascertain what Chase's room number at the hotel was so he could call him directly in a few hours. The NCAA allows schools to engage in one phone conversation per week with a recruit, but during July, finding the recruit is a challenge unto itself. Keener, however, got his number. That night coach and recruit spoke for half an hour.

"He's a real nice dude," said Chase after the conversation. "He was straight to the point, he let me know what was going on. He had called my mother and father and they really liked what they heard about Virginia Tech so I was waiting for him.

"He said that they have a point guard who will be a senior when I'm a freshman and it'll be up to me to push him for playing time. But then after that, the job is mine. I'll be the oldest point guard on the team. He said I was their number one target. He was real cool. They shot right up to the top of my list.

"I called my mother after and we decided we'll drive out there in August for a visit. He had told her that the campus is so beautiful that once someone visits, they usually sign. If everything is as he says it is, I might do just that."

But now, however, Assault wants to win this tournament before heading home. As the week plays out, the games tend to blur. After some up-and-down play early in the week, Assault begins hitting its stride and games quickly become blowouts. It seems no one can handle the full-court press.

This allows Malone to play his entire bench. Johnson plays only sparingly in one game and sits out another to rest his groin. Assault doesn't need him. By tournament time it blows through the competition before meeting up with the New Orleans Jazz in the finals.

The Jazz are big, which is trouble for D.C. Leading the way for Jazz coach Thad Foucher is 6-11 Jonathan Bender, a silky star from tiny Picayune, Mississippi. ("The town's pretty little," Bender admits. "I hate to say any hometown because no one's ever heard of it. It's pronounced Pick-EE-ooon.")

Call it what you want, but team Bender up with 6-11 Wesley Slocum and the Jazz have a serious height advantage. Malone has to play Johnson inside—not his normal position—and count on the 6-6 Payne, also more of a small forward, to battle Slocum on the boards. A more serious problem, however, is the Jazz guards, who can handle the ball and, at the direction of Foucher, know how to beat a press. Still, Team Assault's confidence is high to start the game.

"Come on guys," says Brown. "Let's get this done." The team breaks its huddle with a "One, two, three, D.C."

The Jazz, however, prove to be too much. In front of a fair-sized crowd and scores of coaches, they jump out to a big lead and the Assault has all it can handle just to keep it within twenty. Bender is brilliant and the Jazz dominate the boards. Johnson begins asserting himself in the second half and the guards drain some long jumpers. With three minutes left the New Orleans lead is six, but down the stretch the Jazz hit virtually all their free throws and pull away, winning the title 85–70.

Foucher and Malone, two prominent adidas coaches, shake hands at game's end, knowing they'll lock horns again soon enough. The players, meanwhile, are upset. Defending their home city—chests full of regional pride—is a big deal.

Still, some good came out of the week. Each player got

a chance to show his stuff in front of coaches who can provide the free college education that puts them one step closer to getting out of the nation's capital. And they saw the sights—Hollywood, Beverly Hills, Venice Beach, even where the L.A. riots began ("Yo, doesn't Snoop Dog live 'round here?"). And they had fun creating friendships that will last.

But there is also reason for suspicion. The kids were used all summer as corporate billboards, pawns in an ego-driven test of wills between not only Nike and adidas, but George Raveling and Sonny Vaccaro. Their brash, talented, and cool persona was just the kind of walking advertisement adidas covets to sell shoes, something few of them realize.

Summer basketball's reputation has never been worse. Much of that is deserved. Some opportunistic coaches, some less-than-honest shoe companies, and too much money have created a scene where underhandedness is, if not prevalent, at least much too common.

And the pampering of kids is open to debate. Is giving city kids a taste of the good life positive, or is flying them around the country based solely on their basketball skills giving them an unfair idea of how one gets ahead in life?

By July, star players Haynesworth and Payne, two of Malone's six seniors, were still not academically qualified to earn a scholarship to a Division I institution. And it was likely neither would make it, forcing both to seek other options. Each is a talented enough player that they would have been offered scholarships with or without the exposure D.C. Assault provided.

So wouldn't they have been better served in summer school, trying to qualify for scholarships instead of playing basketball on the Vegas Strip and here in crime-ridden Carson?

The only thing for certain is that during the summer of 1998, Team Assault, the loudest AAU team in the country, sold shoes for adidas. And on one July night, had fun giving Rodeo Drive a culture shock on wheels.

CHAPTER 13

The Best Billboards Money Can Buy

T he weathered plaque just outside the front door of Miami Senior High School alerts all that the architecturally spectacular building is a historical landmark. The first ever high school in Miami, it was once the centerpiece of the cultural and economic growth of the area. The school's opulent auditorium was the site of operas, concerts, and plays, drawing governors, business leaders, and Miami's upper crust. Its classrooms were the learning ground for scores of future elected officials.

The last thirty years haven't been so kind to Miami Senior. As Cuban immigrants flocked to Miami, the fabled neighborhood of Little Havana grew up around the once-famous school. Instead of hosting the city's elite, the area became famous for violence, theft, and failure. The Cadillacs that once parked on the street during Broadway road show productions now drive out of their way to avoid the area.

So Miami Senior went about building a new reputation. "We know that athletics is one way for us to bring positive attention to our school," principal Victor Lopez said. "And athletics is a real source of pride here. I can't deny it is a focus for us and it keeps us in the news."

A half block south of the school's main entrance, a giant basketball painted in the street marks the entrance to the school's gymnasium—dubbed The Asylum by opponents who can't stand up to the craziness inside. Hanging two rafters deep are banners telling all entrants that The Asylum is as historic as Miami Senior's school building, home of a state record seventeen basketball championships in Florida's large-school division.

The storied Miami program was dominant in the first half of the century, regularly winning Florida state championships. But other schools caught up and teams throughout the state started beating the Stingarees at their own game. Then along came a well-connected coach who restored the luster to Miami Senior.

Winning didn't come easy at a school where the neighborhood was both crumbling and teeming with young men who had played little basketball in the past. But coach Shaky Rodriguez knew the answer. He would use his relationship with Sonny Vaccaro, then Nike's director of grassroots basketball, to draw support for his financially strapped club and then he would take advantage of the county's majority-to-minority (called the M&M) transfer rule. The rule, designed to avoid busing mandates handed down by the courts, allows students to easily transfer to a school where they would be the minority. "That M&M rule was our main advantage," Rodriguez, now the coach at Florida International University, said. "Immediately, any black kid from north of downtown could transfer in uninhibited. That benefited us tremendously."

Since Miami Senior was now a nearly all-Hispanic school, putting African-American students in Stingarees uniforms was made a lot easier. Putting them in stylish uniforms designed for the team by Nike made it easier still. Throw in new shoes, travel bags, practice jerseys, and money to attend big-time tournaments around the country, and Miami Senior became a magnet school for basketball prodigies. "Absolutely we became the place to go," Rodriguez said. "We had kids who were good who we couldn't make room for."

The Stingarees became such a magnet that you could begin nearly every season from then on by penciling them in to the state championship game. Beginning a year after Rodriguez inked his first deal with Nike, Miami Senior went on a championship tear, winning the state title in 1987, '89, '90, '91, '93, '96, '97, and again in 1998—but more on that last one later. Rodriguez said that during the ten years before he left in 1995, the team never lost more than three games in a year and never won fewer than thirty. They even had a three-and-a-half-year stretch when they didn't lose a game in the state of Florida.

Sonny Vaccaro first signed Miami Senior to a deal while he was at Nike, then convinced Rodriguez to switch to adidas in the early 1990s when Vaccaro joined Nike's competitor. But when Rodriguez left to become head coach at Florida International University in 1995, so did the personal bond between adidas and Miami Senior.

The door open, George Raveling called new coach Frank Martin on a regular basis. Martin said, "asking if we were happy and promising to take care of us if we weren't." Upset that adidas hadn't given his team the new uniforms it had promised, Martin returned Raveling's call and in 1997 made the big switch (though a public records request to school principal Victor Lopez couldn't produce a copy of the contract with Nike).

"I went to Oregon, to where they have Nike headquarters, and they made it clear we were going to be one of their signature programs," Martin said. "They promised we'd have the best. That's what I wanted for my players. That's what got me."

Indeed, if you ask Raveling about the high schools Nike sponsors, he'll tell you Miami Senior is "one of five or six of our top programs." In exchange for shoes, gear bags, all-new uniforms, practice outfits, and money for travel expenses, Nike bought the right to put their logo on nearly everything the successful team touched.

As impressive as the championship reminders aloft in The Asylum are, the banners that catch the eye of most aspiring Stingarees today hang just a little lower, tacked to the walls behind the basket on The Asylum's south side. Fifteen feet high, the black banners carry only the Nike swoosh, the official shoe of Miami Senior High School basketball.

"That shoe thing is important to players, no matter who says what," said Jemel Davila, a member of Miami Senior's 1998 championship team. "I mean everyone knows Miami Senior has it going on with Nike and before that with adidas and that means something. Is it why I went there? Not totally. I wanted to play winning basketball. But that's what you get when you win. You get the gear."

The relationship between winning and shoe deals on the high school level is not lost on either the teens or the adults.

"Their shoe deals gave them an advantage," one rival Dade County coach said. "It may sound silly to you and me, but kids identify with that and they love the idea that Nike was paying for their stuff, buying their shoes. You'd have to say they were Nike's dream school too, in a minority neighborhood in a big market, winning all those championships. It made Miami Senior the place to be and, in a lot of people's minds, had a lot to do with the trouble they got themselves into. You can't blame all their problems on Nike, but that deal sure made them feel like they were invincible, like they were too big for the rules. They got out of control there and didn't think anyone could take them down."

On the court, that was true. But a reporter with *Miami New Times,* a weekly tabloid, did what opponents couldn't. The reporter, Robert Andrew Powell, heard the rumors that Miami Senior's run of championships was fueled by players who had little reason—other than basketball—to be attending the school.

On the eve of the 1998 state championship weekend, a *New Times* cover story questioned the legitimacy of Miami Senior's Dream Team, with the headline: "How Did the Folks at Miami Senior High School Create a Killer Basketball Squad? Simple. They Cheated."

The Stingarees went on to win the state title that weekend—their third straight—but returned to find an investigator from the Florida High School Athletic Association snooping around. The FHSAA confirmed the *New Times* report, documenting that five of the team's players, including superstar Udonis Haslem, didn't live in the district and that all fifteen players on the varsity roster had transferred into the school from somewhere else. Haslem, who would go on to attend the University of Florida, didn't even live in the county, which would have made him ineligible to enroll in Miami Senior, a Dade County public school.

Like its historic confines, Miami Senior High School's basketball program became part of history too. After months of wrangling, the FHSAA ruled that Miami Senior's 1998 state championship should be forfeited and that the team be declared ineligible to compete in the 1999 tournament. The punishment was the harshest penalty ever handed down by the FHSAA, whose commissioner declared the case "one of the most, if not the most, blatant violations of FHSAA rules against recruiting that I have ever encountered."

A few weeks before it was stripped of its title, Miami Senior received a $1,800 check from the city of Miami to pay for another state championship banner and for championship letter jackets. The money, arranged by then Miami city commissioner Humberto Hernandez, arrived as the city was teetering on the brink of financial ruin. A few months later, Hernandez was charged with illegal recruiting of absentee voters and Miami High penalized for recruiting basketball players. The banner was never purchased, the money was never returned.

Left with the skeleton of a one-time nationally ranked program, the Stingarees still finished the 1998–99 regular season 18–1. But there were no road trips to Hawaii, no national holiday tournaments. And the team with a half dozen major college prospects was left with one player hoping to get a scholarship from Duquesne.

In the spring of 1998, Greenbrier High School in Evans, Georgia, became the focus of national attention when senior Mike Cameron was suspended from school by principal Gloria Hamilton. Cameron and his 1,200 schoolmates had been herded into the school's parking lot where they were supposed to stand in lined-off areas that would spell the word "Coke." Each class had assigned spots: seniors were to spell the letter C, juniors the letter O, sophomores the K, and freshmen the E. A photographer was brought in and hoisted on a crane to capture the moment and enter it in Coke's national contest for Coke in Education Day.

As nearly two dozen Coke executives watched with glee, the photographer snapped away until Cameron peeled off his jacket to reveal . . . a Pepsi shirt.

Cameron was yanked into Hamilton's office where the principal suspended him not only for being disrespectful, but for "potentially costing the school a lot of money," according to media reports. The principal admitted she was worried that Cameron's action would cost her school the opportunity to win a $10,000 national prize offered to the school that developed the best marketing plan for Coke-sponsored promotional business discount cards. The local Coke distributor promised to throw in another $500.

When reporters started calling about the suspension, Principal Hamilton refused to back down. "I don't apologize for expecting my students to behave in school," she said. Her boss, Superintendent Tom Dorhmann, backed Hamilton, saying he was "flabbergasted" by the media attention. "The kid [Cameron] is preying on the press," Dorhmann told the *Washington Post*. "He's used you."

But around the country, the question became who was using who? The director of the Atlanta chapter of the American Civil Liberties Union told the *Atlanta Journal-Constitution*: "This concerns me because basically, it's pimping our kids. Is it worth $500 for students to be out there hustling Coke?" Newspapers from coast to coast offered:

"Without even knowing it, der furious fuhrer [Greenbrier principal Gloria Hamilton] was imparting to the students a civics lesson in obsequiousness and greed. It is disquieting to think that a kid could be kicked out of school for refusing to regard an impersonal multinational corporation with the same reverence that the principal does." (*Raleigh* [North Carolina] *News and Observer.*)

"What exactly is a school doing sponsoring a 'Coke in Education Day' anyway? Promoting a commercial product to its captive audience of young people?" (*Omaha World-Herald*)

This incident taught students "that money is more important than freedom of choice. It taught them that silence is more desirable than dissent, that conformity is better than being different. And it taught them there is no shame in selling out if the price is right." (*Miami Herald* columnist Carl Hiaasen)

"Schools shouldn't be in the position of selling captive students to advertisers, whatever the excuse. They are entrusted with children's minds and they have no right to sell access to them. Even a quick glance at the sales pitches made by marketing companies peddling promotion ideas to schools makes it clear the whole point is to make money for advertisers, not to help kids." (*Chicago Tribune*)

But while Cameron's story sparked national debate about the propriety of allowing soft drink companies to buy their way into public schools, little of that outrage has found its way onto the playing fields of high school sports.

"A lot of attention has been paid to these schools that sell advertising space to soft drink companies or accept computers for grocery receipts," said Alex Molnar, a University of Wisconsin–Milwaukee professor of education and the nation's leading expert on the subject of corporate sponsorship of public education. "But no one seems to be asking these questions about schools renting space on the bodies of their students for advertising purposes. In many ways, these apparel/shoe deals are much worse than what is happening with soft drink companies because Coke doesn't get a spot on the jersey worn by the football or basketball team. Coke may buy a spot on the scoreboard, but that's not the billboard that a team jersey is. Nike's spot on that jersey is the best billboard money can buy.

"It looks so pure for Nike to give money to a high school, helping kids, but they do it for a reason. They know that kids are the greatest economic force out there and that kids look up to athletes, even the athletes that are their peers."

In a 1998 study of businesses—including shoe and apparel companies—and their influence in America's public schools, Molnar made this point: "The justification for the sponsorship agreements most often used by educators is the need for money. Money also drives the corporate side of the equation. It is estimated that children between the ages of four and twelve purchase or influence the purchase of goods and services worth nearly $500 billion a year." David Siegel, general manager of Small Talk, a division of Sive/Young & Rubicam, notes that advertising directed at children has increased twentyfold in the past decade to $2 billion. Small wonder marketing professor James McNeal describes children as "the brightest star in the consumer constellation." According to McNeal, "Virtually every consumer goods industry, from airlines to zinnia seed sellers, targets kids."

Vaccaro admits it was economics—not necessarily good old community spirit—that was behind his thinking when he developed the high school sponsorship program at Nike and then again at adidas.

"Sponsoring high school teams is a big part of keeping adidas visible to the people who buy our product," Vaccaro said in a 1998 interview. "And the people who we're trying to stay visible to are kids. I admit it is unfortunate that we have to put high school athletes in the middle of this. They're just the pawns in a big corporate fight. But Nike is not going to stop. So we can't stop, either."

A few education advocates have begun to ask questions about the appropriateness of letting shoe companies shape the minds of children while reshaping the competitive balance of public school leagues.

"These relationships really create haves and have-nots in athletics, and I don't think anyone can agree that is good," said Barbara Fiege, director of the California Interscholastic Foundation's City Section. "The advantage some schools get at the expense of their rivals is not healthy."

A greater problem is that schools become addicted to shoe money, Fiege said, and have a hard time adjusting when they don't have the marquee players that attract Nike or Reebok to invest in their programs.

Raveling, in an interview with the *Los Angeles Times,* bristled at the charge that Nike's money was tilting the playing field, turning some sponsored programs into juggernauts at the expense of competitors. "The worst thing that ever happened in athletics is this thing about how it's got to be a level playing field," Raveling told the *Times.* "It is ludicrous for anyone living in the United States to think that everything is equality."

But the *Sacramento Bee* proved Fiege's point, showing that by 1993 more than one fourth of the California Interscholastic Foundation's five-hundred-school Southern Section's $1.1 million budget came from corporate sponsorships. Thus, when Reebok, which had signed a multiyear $2.8 million sponsorship agreement with the CIF in 1991, decided two years later to cancel the agreement, the CIF was sent scrambling for dollars.

Raveling says all that concern is misplaced, that Nike's efforts are mostly about helping public school systems replace lost tax dollars.

"The first thing that everyone in America needs to understand is social dynamics and the role that big business plays in social dynamics," Raveling said. "What has happened is that most people are ignorant of economics in America today. Because what has happened is, when I was growing up as a kid, municipal and state governments provided young people with opportunities to grow and prosper in sports. They provided playgrounds, they provided summer leagues, they provided materials for them to wear for the leagues. They ran the leagues. But like most of what has happened in American society today, many municipal and state and federal fiscal responsibilities have been transferred to the private sector and so big business is being asked more and more to assume what are governmental responsibilities.

"But then, what happens in this dynamic—when you transfer that responsibility to big business, they now become criticized for being civic-minded. We're asked to keep the libraries open later, we're asked to donate computers, we're asked—all over America today, foundations are giving money to education to help tutoring to do all kinds of situations like that. But then when you do them, then people say you have some sinister motive. So, on one hand, while government wants big business to be participatory, but then when you become participatory what they say to you is you have some ulterior motive for doing it. The ulterior motive is civic pride. Okay, we make profit. We put money back

into society. What we do—and I can only speak for Nike—
is we try to provide opportunities for kids to fulfill their
dreams. If that's not as American as apple pie and mother-
hood and the flag, then I don't know what is. And why we
should be criticized for trying to help young people—all
these kids that we provide these opportunities here, right
now—if all this was to be shut down, what would those kids
be doing? A lot of those kids would be out in mischief right
now.

"So I think that we provide a useful service for society.
And why we have to apologize for that, or why we have to
be subjected to criticism—I guess maybe, years from now,
historians will debate why big business was asked to do this
and then when they took it on, they were subject to criticism.
Maybe you can explain to me why this dynamic has come
about. You want us to help, but then when we help you say
we're bad guys for helping.

"Besides, the media is making such a big deal about the
schools that we sponsor and we sponsor more than a hundred of them. But I promise you, 60 percent of them aren't
the caliber of a Miami Senior or a Los Angeles Crenshaw.
That 60 percent, they don't have all the stars that you guys
in the media focus on, saying we're buying their loyalty.
These are just teams we sponsor."

Asked to back that statistic up, Raveling, though, would
not release a list of the schools Nike sponsors. "That's private information," he said. "Nike is a private company. I
don't ask you for private information."

Miami Senior, on the other hand, is one of the schools
Nike doesn't mind mentioning . . . even though the Stingarees would seem to be tainted by 1998's scandal and the loss
of the state championship trophy.

"We have always stood behind all of our teams as well as

our athletes," Nike's Paul Murphy told *New Times*. "We stood behind . . . I can't think of her name, that figure skater . . ."

"Tonya Harding?"

"Yes! Tonya Harding. We stood behind her and we have always stood behind all of our teams."

CHAPTER 14

Free Speech for Sale

Bob McChesney can't figure out if he should be shocked, outraged, or depressed. A committed free speech advocate, he was proud to lead the fight in 1996 when the University of Wisconsin–Madison signed an exclusive five-year, $9.1 million contract with Reebok to tattoo that company's vector logo on everything right down to the university mascot, Bucky Badger. What Wisconsin traded for that money was marketing rights to clothing designed like the university's athletic wear and, more important to McChesney, "the right to free speech."

"There was a clause in that contract that, once we found it, sent the faculty through the roof," said McChesney, now a professor at the University of Illinois. "The clause declared it a violation of the contract for anyone at the university to 'disparage' the Reebok brand name. We couldn't believe it."

By pure happenstance, the discovery of the "no disparagement" clause coincided with national and international protests over the treatment of Asian employees who were responsible for manufacturing most of the shoes sold by the two largest sneaker companies—Reebok and Nike—in the United States. Several independent studies showed that subcontractors working for the footwear giants were forcing employees to work overtime—often up to seventy-five hours per week—while paying them $2.45 per day in Indonesia and less than $2 a day in China. Stories abounded of employees working as slaves and children as young as twelve working all day building shoes.

"Their labor practices make Dickens's England look like the classless society," McChesney told *The Chronicle of Higher Education* at the time.

McChesney and his colleagues went on a tear. They used the faculty e-mail system to start a petition. They worked with the local media. They found sympathetic politicians who agreed to hold press conferences. The state attorney general agreed to investigate whether the clause violated the faculty's free speech rights. "If the University of Wisconsin advertises a firm like Reebok, it accepts the conditions under which Reebok profits," McChesney and a fellow professor wrote in the campus-wide e-mail.

They had everyone asking how any university—the bastion of free speech in America—could negotiate away the right of its employees to "disparage" a shoe company. "You talk about a question people had to squirm to answer," McChesney said. "Try that one on the front page."

Add the fact that Wisconsin, the signature university in a liberal state where many citizens are decidedly pro-union, seemed through this contract to be squelching debate over the Asian labor issue, and Reebok found itself in a no-win situation.

Under siege, Reebok amended the contract and dropped the clause.

McChesney felt he had made a difference, "and after all,

isn't that why we teach?" he asked. *The Chronicle of Higher Education*, the bible of education periodicals, did a two-page feature on the victory in Wisconsin, and several faculty members appeared on radio and television shows. "I believed our message was out and I guess I just assumed faculty at other universities wouldn't stand for this kind of clause either," McChesney said.

He assumed wrong. McChesney might have won in Wisconsin, but a review of a handful of contracts between major universities and shoe companies shows that "nondisparagement" clauses still clutter the landscape of American universities and no one seems upset about it. "I thought we had started something," he said. But the fire apparently never caught.

"It's depressing," McChesney said after reading the contracts. "Actually, it is shocking and it should be shocking to anyone. It should be outrageous. It's depressing that these clauses apparently aren't as shocking to others as they are to me. Maybe the problem is, it's the sort of thing when people hear about it who aren't connected to universities, I think they say the debate is ridiculous. But we live in an age in which everything's for sale, we're in an era in which the traditional notions of integrity and public service are collapsing because of the commercial tidal wave. And in that context, then, I guess people don't understand what is wrong with these kinds of contracts.

"Maybe nobody cares today about these issues, about labor practices and free speech," McChesney laments. "Maybe Americans are so happy about the economy and low unemployment and wage increases that, right now, those things don't matter. But when our institutions of higher learning, the places we must count on to keep the fight for basic rights alive, find nothing wrong with negotiating away the free speech right of any employee, that's a path I don't think any of us should be comfortable with. Just throw a 'For Sale' sign up front and let's make our position obvious. It's a very sad state of affairs when universities will take corporate cash and sell their silence. That's what they're doing."

There was a day, when Sonny Vaccaro started signing major college basketball coaches to endorsement deals for Nike, that the media and some college presidents voiced objections to the practice of coaches shilling for shoe companies.

"We had little groups of objection around the country," Vaccaro said. "But we sold people on the fact that we were saving the universities money by not having to buy shoes and we were saving them money by contributing to the salaries in the athletic program. Like always, universities were strapped then, always looking for money. We painted it as just another source of money."

Despite the need for money, when Sonny's deals became known, academics started questioning who a coach would ultimately be loyal to—the shoe company or the university. As the shoe deals grew in size and number, the questions grew louder. The NCAA even formed a group to study the problems of college basketball and put coach-shoe contracts at the top of its agenda.

"When our committee was formed, there was a growing feeling among at least some segments of people involved with college athletics at that time that athletic apparel companies, shoe companies in particular, held too much sway over the coaches at NCAA institutions," said Patricia Vivierto, commissioner of the Gateway Football Conference and chair of the NCAA's committee. "There was a fear too that those shoe companies were getting more and more involved in identifying prospects at earlier and earlier ages. Kids in the eighth grade were suddenly Nike's kids, not kids. We made a suggestion, and the suggestion was that we treat representatives of athletics manufacturers in the same way that we treat our boosters, move to keep them at arm's length from the athletes.

"I think at that point in time there were people that thought we were being overly paranoid and that there wasn't a need for intervention," Vivierto mused. "I'm sure if you took a poll today, no one would have that feeling."

The committee's recommendations for distancing young athletes from shoe representatives never got off the ground. One member of the committee groused privately that too many schools were in bed with shoe companies to make any move that impacted the companies' bottom lines. And the committee's final report didn't even get into the money coaches were accepting from shoe companies. "On that one, we knew the genie was out of the bottle," Vivierto said. "Shoe money was such an integral part of so many coaching deals that taking that money away was impossible. This money, and all the baggage that comes with it, had become a part of our culture. By the mid-to-late 1990s, faculty weren't paying attention to these contracts, the media wasn't paying attention to these contracts. What happened at Wisconsin became lost. It just became par for the course that universities would take this money and give it to coaches and accept the quid pro quo that comes with the money— and that is that you'll never speak ill of a shoe company."

Indeed, when the University of Tennessee signed an all-sport agreement with adidas in 1997, no one objected to paragraph 13: "DISPARAGEMENT OF PRODUCTS: University shall not during the contract term, and for a period of two years following the termination or expiration of this agreement, disparage the adidas brand name, adidas products or adidas. This paragraph shall survive the termination or expiration of this agreement."

"You're kidding me," Professor Mark Miller, a Faculty Senate member, said when a reporter gave him a copy of the contract three years later. "How can they do that?"

Tennessee president Joe Johnson, who said he also was unaware of the nondisparagement clause, added that after hearing it, he was sure it was unenforceable. "I can't imagine any clause like that that could limit the free speech rights of forty thousand students or twelve thousand faculty and staff," Johnson said. "I remember reading the dollar amounts of that contract, but didn't go over it paragraph by paragraph. I don't think we can sign away those rights. And if adidas wants to cancel the contract they can do that. We'll go out and find someone else."

Robert Erb, director of sports marketing at adidas, agreed with Johnson . . . sort of. Erb argues that despite the vague use of the term "University" at the beginning of the clause, "it was never intended to cover faculty." He said the contractual wording is necessary to protect the company from criticism within the athletics department. He compares the contract to other endorsement deals with similar restrictions.

"It shouldn't come as a surprise that faculty wouldn't be aware of that contract clause," Erb said. "Why should they? The disparagement clauses are in there talking about something completely different. It isn't about free speech and it isn't about whether or not people can protest or not protest workforce issues, or any of these other matters. I mean frankly I would welcome the dialogue. And I think most people within our industry feel the same way that that isn't really an issue. What it's really talking about is more along the lines of—you're going into a relationship with a partner. And let's forget for a moment that it's a university and let's assume that it's you and me, okay? Or maybe it is Nike and Michael Jordan. And everyone is entering into an agreement and here's the agreement. You're going to, in exchange for compensation, we're going to trade your publicity rights for product and cash. And in exchange for that, we're looking for an endorsement. Implied within the endorsement is that you're going to help us create the best product possible to play. What happens if during the contract period you say publicly, 'I don't like these products,' even though you had entered into the agreement and even though you had worked to help create the product? Wouldn't you agree that it would probably destroy the value of your endorsement?"

But is it a fair analogy, Erb is asked, to compare a contract between two private entities with a contract between a private company and a public employee like a university coach?

"Of course I see a distinction," he said. "But do you see professional coaches, even though they are 'public employees,' as being able to sign contracts and earn private money? Yes, these coaches are university employees, but they are earning this money in a private contract. My point is that effectively that's what it is, it's the same thing. Each of the individual coaches and the athletic director, to some extent that's who the agreement's with. It's with them, it's not with the individual athletes, or with the student athletes, or with the student body or with the faculty.

"Nobody gives up their First Amendment right to anything. A disparagement clause has nothing to do with a First Amendment right. They can say anything they want," Erb said. "Sure, the contract can be made worthless, but that doesn't restrict you from saying anything. They're being paid for an endorsement of product. Let's go back again for a second to Michael Jordan. Michael Jordan gets in front of the cameras and says, 'After twenty years and a great deal of introspection, I've decided that Nike sucks.' Nobody is depriving Michael Jordan of voicing an opinion. He just loses the money. We're paying for an endorsement among other things, right. If a person isn't endorsing, they're not fulfilling their end of the contract. It has nothing to do with the First Amendment, nothing. It is simply that—we're not stopping them from doing it, so that's where the First Amendment would come into play. We're not ceasing their ability to do it, and we're not telling them they can't voice opinions."

"Who is he kidding?" Professor Miller said. "He can argue until he's blue in the face that the wording of that contract doesn't technically restrict the First Amendment rights of the athletic staff. But when you make the point that millions will be lost through cancellation of the contract if someone steps out of bounds, that chilling effect is as good as an outright ban on free speech.

"Could you imagine if I, as a faculty member, entered into a deal with Coke that I would wear a Coke jacket to class every day in exchange for a few bucks and would promise never to say a bad word about Coke?" Miller asked. "Would that be right to sell the credibility of the university in that way simply for gain? The ethical constraints on faculty would preclude them from behaving in that way. Now, what if the deal I make with Coke says I'll make all my students wear a Coke jacket too, and I'll make sure no one says a bad word about Coke. I think any right-thinking person would object. Why should the athletic department of a university be different? Nonetheless it's routinely done. It's not done among faculty. It's routinely done within the athletic department, which represents my university. I understand the need for money, but imagine trying to make a few bucks for the university through my example. But right now people are accepting this in athletics. It is probably too late to change anything, but not too late to be bothered.

"It strikes me as a really strange thing for us to do when we claim that we are here to serve and help these young people, but by the way, if you happen to be an athlete, we'll tell you how you can dress and what you can't say. Student athletes are really vulnerable, I think, in these situations. They aspire to do what the coach wants, they hope for professional careers, so they go ahead and do this. And they also see it as common practice in professional sports. They're probably not worried about it, probably don't even think they should be. But there needs to be a distinction between a professional athlete selling this kind of exposure to a company and the university selling that young athlete."

Whereas adidas defends the clause and insists on its inclusion, Nike long ago recognized the potential for bad PR and has taken the opposite stance in recent contracts.

"We've taken the position that if the clause bothers any one of the schools where we are in partnership, we'll take it out," said Kit Morris, Nike's director of college sports marketing and a onetime university athletic director. "We want to work with colleges in a way that is respectful of their main business, which is education. There are two overriding values at universities: first, the freedom of expression, which is why they created tenure; and second, the search for the truth. No university will compromise either of those values. Besides, if we're doing our job right, they shouldn't have anything to disparage."

There are several universities where the clause in Nike's deals still exists, including super-programs Ohio State University and the University of Kentucky. Ohio State, in a deal signed in 1996, agrees that Nike can cancel the $10 million contract if "athletic department administration, coaches or staff disparages the quality of performance of Nike products or the brand." Kentucky's 1997 deal also only restricts the athletic department staff, noting that Nike has the right to terminate the agreement if anyone within the UK Athletic Association "disparages the Nike brand and/or Nike Products or takes any action inconsistent with the endorsement of Nike Products."

Those contracts are of great interest to a national network of student activists, led by Duke University's Tico Almeida, who are working to raise awareness of overseas employment issues.

"We are raising human rights questions every day on campuses all over America," Almeida said. "We are asking that these companies allow monitoring of their overseas plants and that they agree to pay employees a living wage. So far, we haven't had anyone try to tell us that we can't do that."

"And they won't," Erb said. "At least they won't from us. We'll never stop that. The student body can do anything they want, they're encouraged to say whatever they want. I would be excited and encouraging of all students to voice whatever opinions they want about our brand, or about our labor relationships, or about our relationship with the university, or the performance of our products on fields of competition. That's not what that provision is intended to stop."

Then why, Erb was asked, does adidas feel so passionate about keeping the clause?

"What this would stop is a formal statement by an athletic department to the effect that it was disparaging adidas," he said. "Can I imagine that ever happening? No, not really. But we have to protect the value of our investment."

"That's sad," Patricia Vivierto said, "when the leaders in the world of higher education—and I include athletic departments in that world—start worrying about the value of some corporation's endorsement. We didn't stop shoe companies from buying their way into universities. We didn't move to distance them from the young athletes and become an influence over them. What's left?

"I guess they won't be happy until we're tattooing them in the birthing room. 'Hey did that one get a swoosh, three stripes, or did he get a vector?' We'll just brand them on their butts before they ever leave the maternity ward. It's unbelievable. There's a trend here of this money and influence getting pushed lower and lower, from coach, now to young athletes. For some of us it is an insidious trend."

CHAPTER 15

Standing Tall

Longtime United States Senator Everett Dirksen of Illinois, discussing the ugly side of politics, once said that there were two things in the world you do not want to see made: sausage and legislation.

Senator Dirksen never attended any summer basketball camps or AAU tournaments.

While the action on the court is supposed to be the main focus, college basketball is made along the sidelines of basketball courts of the Nike All-America Camp in Indianapolis, adidas ABCD in Teaneck, and various AAU events around the country, most notably the adidas Big Time Tournament in Las Vegas, Nike Supershowcase in Orlando, and the Nike Peach Jam in Augusta, Georgia.

There in stuffy gyms, with shoe company banners hanging from the walls, college coaches and scouts, AAU coaches, high school coaches and parents, jostle for space to watch the game on the court. In such close proximity to one another, the recruiters and the handlers of the recruited, is where relationships are formed, hands are shook, and deals get done.

It's a long way from the glamour of the Final Four, where under the bright lights of national television in a sold-out dome stadium, America sees the final product. But without this, could there be that?

"It's a cesspool," said Sonny Vaccaro back in 1990, when he was Nike's director of grassroots basketball. "And we start the process."

These days, the process is going stronger than ever.

Naturally, the best players get the most attention. A top ten player nationally can have twenty schools courtside watching his game. The better the player, the more coaches watching the action, the more handlers hanging around. High school coaches, AAU coaches, assistant AAU coaches, and your proverbial "uncles"—the recruiting middlemen universally cursed, but oft courted, by college coaches.

"When I first started recruiting as an assistant in the 1980s," said Xavier coach Skip Prosser, "you dealt with the parents and the high school coach. Now there are so many people. AAU coaches, assistant AAU coaches, people with the youngster. It's not simple anymore. There are so many people. You don't know who to deal with sometimes."

At the 1998 Nike All-America Camp held in the National Institute for Sport and Fitness in Indianapolis, it was no different. With huge banners of Nike pitchmen such as Scottie Pippen, Ray Allen, and, of course, Michael Jordan flapping in the air-conditioned wind currents, players, their entourages, and college coaches mingled along the baseline and sat together in the stands. Everyone was working an angle.

The exception to the rule sat in the middle of a steel bleacher by himself, watching his son play on the court in front of him. James Taylor is a quiet, thoughtful, determined General Motors factory worker from Lansing, Michigan, and when it comes to grassroots basketball, he has his suspicions of everyone's intentions.

His son, Marcus, just happens to be a 6-3 point guard in the class of 2000 from Lansing's Waverly High School, and here at the Nike Camp, the only summertime event Marcus plays in, his son also happened to be the best player. His dad is the best player's entourage of one.

That's because Marcus Taylor does not play AAU basketball. He does not attend a big-time, talent-producing high school that jets around the country. He knows no sneaker representative. He has no "uncles," just a father.

Although they had generally eschewed any non–high school competition, in 1997, father and son decided that Taylor, then a sophomore, should give the Nike Camp a shot. Four days of basketball to judge where he stood with his peers. After that it would be back to Lansing for a dose of individual instruction, fundamentals work, and scrimmaging with the local college players at Michigan State.

As one of the few sophomores invited, Taylor was among the youngest campers, but it didn't stop him from dominating some of his older competition. By week's end he was deemed one of the camp's top ten performers regardless of class by the recruiting newsletter *HoopScoop*. Thus the Taylors decided to return in 1998 for four more days.

If there ever was a player an entourage would form around, a circus develop around, a shoe company court, an AAU coach shine up to, it was Marcus Taylor. Because here at the Nike Camp, the player regarded by most scouts to be the finest rising junior in the nation was killing not only his classmates, but the kids a year or two older.

His smooth ball handling kept turnovers to a minimum. He routinely broke into the lane for easy baskets. His jump shot was true from way behind the three-point arc. His court vision, decision making, and defensive intensity caused college coaches standing courtside to drool.

HoopScoop ranked him the number one player overall in the camp, an honor few juniors (Stephon Marbury, Felipe Lopez) have ever earned at either Nike or adidas ABCD.

"He's awesome," said Clark Francis, editor of *HoopScoop*. "He has a combination of ball handling, speed, quickness, athleticism, and outstanding shooting. Plus, he plays defense and is a great kid. He's got the complete package."

After one notable game, Taylor slowly walked off the court with other players, stopped, waved to his father, and headed into the locker room. With that, James Taylor gathered his belongings, got up, and walked out of the building. Alone. The Taylors have become the antithesis of summer basketball: a polite and outrageously talented player and a father who is very involved in his son's life. But more than that, they are the first family anyone can remember who turned their back on grassroots basketball.

With the exception of the time Marcus was eleven, and James put together a group of Lansing kids and played in a couple of local AAU tournaments, the number one high school player in the country never played for a traveling basketball team.

Despite dozens of offers from high schools near and far begging James Taylor to send his son off to some faraway locale for better exposure or a controlled environment, Marcus kept playing for his neighborhood high school, Waverly, whose supporting cast was merely average.

Despite an offer from Puma for Marcus, then just a sophomore, to appear in a print advertising campaign—unpaid, so as to be in compliance with NCAA rules—the Taylors said politely, "No thanks."

All the offers of expense-paid trips to Europe, Florida, California, and Las Vegas were turned down. The free shoes were mailed back. The Taylors bought their own warmup jackets at a Foot Locker in Lansing. The goodies, the glitz, and the glamour were left to the side. The addictive offers of fame, attention, travel, clothes, and Lord knows what else, which everyone seems to embrace, were declined.

James Taylor listened to every single offer—"I'll listen to anyone, but when it's all done I've got to do what's best for us"—and said no every single time.

Marcus Taylor was going to be a kid, his father said.

"Why does a teenage boy need to be flying to Las Vegas?" James Taylor asks. "Where he needs to be is home with his friends and family.

"The two most important things for Marcus are his education and the development of his game. I've yet to see how playing AAU basketball or traveling around accomplishes either of those. We drill him here. We spend time on his game. And he attends school and gets good grades. We have lots of scholarship offers. It's working fine."

And so as summer basketball continued to plunge to more questionable depths, the number one high school prospect in the country, regardless of class, became the first player in the history of modern youth basketball whom anyone can recall saying no to the entire thing.

The comparisons started early, maybe third grade. Which made James Taylor laugh. Here was his son, Marcus, nine years old, playing basketball in Lansing youth leagues. And while Marcus was, yes, taller than the other kids, and was, yes, running the point, and was, yes, certainly proving himself to be the best player on the floor, the comparisons were still outrageous.

The next Magic Johnson, they started saying.

Little Marcus Taylor was going to be the next gift to basketball from Lansing, a working-class town that serves as the capital of the state of Michigan. He was going to not only be good, like good enough to lead one of the Lansing high schools to a state title, and not just good enough to earn a Division I scholarship, and not just good enough to play in the NBA. He was going to be Magic Johnson good. One of the best of all time. A player who revolutionized the game by playing point guard despite having the 6-9 frame of a power forward. Marcus was going to be that good.

And he was nine.

"It was funny," said James Taylor of the hype surrounding his son then. "Living in Lansing I guess the comparisons were inevitable, but it was just funny. I mean, the kid was nine and people said he was going to be Magic Johnson."

Marcus remembers too.

"When I was younger I was much taller than everybody else and I was running the point guard spot so a lot of people were like, 'He's Magic Johnson,' " Marcus Taylor said. "You just laugh it off."

But not for too long. In fifth grade, Marcus attended Magic's basketball camp in Los Angeles and the old star of Lansing and the young star of Lansing became fast friends. The two had first met when Marcus was in second grade and Johnson, whose boyhood neighborhood is just three minutes from Taylor's, took a liking to the kid. At camp that year Taylor wound up back at Johnson's oversized house where he wandered off, as eleven-year-olds are prone to do, and got lost in the endless hallways.

"I started calling out his name to find him because I didn't know where I was," said Taylor. "It's a big house."

The two have remained friends ever since. Taylor was

even an outspoken fan of Magic's failed and oft-criticized 1998 nightly talk show, *The Magic Hour*.

"I watched it a lot," said Taylor. "I liked it. Some people didn't like it, but that's their opinion. I thought it was all right."

As Taylor's body and game grew, it became obvious that the kid was special. But Magic Johnson special?

"I knew he was good in third grade because he was competing against eighth graders and he was the best player in the group," said James Taylor. "He never played with kids his own age. The only time was when he was in eighth grade. He played with kids his own age then and he averaged forty. He averaged forty a game and about fourteen rebounds."

He was unbelievable. By age fourteen, he was a Lansing celebrity and the name of the future in national basketball circles. Even the cynics began to conclude that the Taylor kid was special. *HoopScoop* rated him the number one eighth grader in the country and already had him pegged for a college scholarship at Michigan State, where Magic played and the Spartans coaching staff had been leaving complimentary tickets for the Taylors since Marcus was in fifth grade.

When Taylor decided to attend his neighborhood high school, Waverly High, it made the newspapers. It also caused Sonny Vaccaro to invite a Waverly senior to play in his Magic's Roundball Classic in Detroit even though the kid wasn't a top three hundred player nationally.

The event of his first varsity basketball game as a ninth grader was deemed so newsworthy in Lansing that all three of the city's local sports anchors conducted the six o'clock sports live from Waverly High School. The game was a sellout. Marcus played great.

It was as big of a deal as it could be. And it could have gotten bigger had James Taylor said yes to anything. But for some reason, he never did.

James Taylor grew up in Benson, Louisiana, a small town outside Shreveport in the northwest part of the state. He played some basketball there, was an accomplished shooter, but was never an amazing talent.

"With my height," said the 5-foot-9 Taylor, "I couldn't play much. So I decided to get a job."

Like so many Southern blacks, James Taylor found that jobs were scarce in Dixie so he became part of the great 1960s exodus north, coming to industrial Michigan, where the promise of steady work at a union wage in the automobile industry seemed like heaven. Even if it was cold.

He wound up in Lansing as a repairman in the General Motors Body Plant Lansing Car Assembly. He married and had a son. He worked hard to build a small, tight family. And then his son became a superstar.

Like most parents, James Taylor didn't know a lot about the workings of amateur basketball, but he knew a hustle when he saw it and youth basketball had all the earmarks. Everyone wanted a piece of his son, pieces he didn't want to let get away.

Everyone wanted to treat him special, when James knew that could only cause problems. Everyone wanted him to grow up too soon.

So James held back. He turned down all advances for Marcus to play AAU ball, invitations that came as young as age nine. Instead, in an effort to check out the situation himself, James assembled his own team made up of Marcus and his friends and played in some local tournaments. Marcus was eleven. It was the last time he ever played in an AAU game.

"I got some kids from his high school, similar kids," said James. "He was going into seventh grade. I knew some of the kids wanted to play so I got them together. I wanted to see what it was all about.

"That was enough. I just don't think he needs it. I think some kids do, but he doesn't. And I think there are some good people in AAU. But he didn't need it. There were always people calling every day, every week or coming by and trying to get him to play AAU."

And not just local teams. As Taylor's name began appearing in recruiting magazines the offers from national programs flooded in also. From California. From New York. From everywhere.

"Oh yeah," said James Taylor. "Riverside Church [New York], Illinois Warriors [Chicago], I don't know. A lot of them. I get a lot of stuff in the mail."

To James it made no sense. The pitches were all the same. We're playing in Las Vegas, let Marcus come. We're going to Disney World, it'll be great exposure. We'll fly him in for a practice, the competition will be great for him. James listened to every story and kept saying no.

He felt a teenage boy would be better served in his own neighborhood than running around Vegas. As for competition, he signed him up for some local instructional camps, and because the Taylors lived just minutes from the campus of Michigan State, Marcus competed in pickup games with the Spartans, locking horns at a young age with players such as Shawn Respert, Eric Snow, and Mateen Cleaves.

"I used to say, 'He doesn't need the exposure—he gets more exposure than anybody I've seen," said James. "He plays with the best competition every day. He plays with college guys.

"Spending days and days each summer all around the country, he doesn't need that."

"He's right about that," said Francis, the *HoopScoop* editor. "He doesn't need the exposure. He could attend any college in the country. Everyone knows about Marcus Taylor."

"Everybody talks about exposure, but it's overdone," said Chicago Bulls coach Tim Floyd, who spent twenty years in the college ranks before going to the NBA in 1998. "We didn't miss too many guys in the 1970s. Trust me, colleges will find you if you're playing at a rec league somewhere. You don't need all that exposure." Not that the offers for Taylor ever stopped coming in.

"They give me a lot of respect because word's gotten around that I'm kind of careful," James Taylor says. "So if you want to approach me, you should approach me straight up. You know I'll listen to anyone, but when it's all done, I've got to do what's best for us. You know, his education and his development. He needs to go to school and make that a priority. And then he needs to work on his fundamentals. And so we drill him. We spend a lot of time working on his game. So he doesn't have a lot of time to be traveling around the country."

When Marcus was fifteen, Puma called asking him to take part in a print advertisement for its basketball shoes. There would be no payment, but the exposure in national basketball magazines, particularly in the hip-hop hoop bible *Slam,* would be significant. Any kid who didn't know Marcus now, soon would, Puma argued.

James Taylor said he didn't care who knew his son. Puma went with Chicago guard Imari Sawyer, another top ten player in the class of 2000, instead.

"There were some people trying to get him in a shoe commercial," said James. "And I said no. Right up front I said he's not going to do it but if you want to talk, I'll listen. And they talked and I knew the whole time they talked that there wasn't going to be a deal.

"Life is like coming up stairs and you don't want to skip a step. And that was what that was. Teenagers don't need to be in shoe commercials."

The funny thing is, despite that lack of exposure, the lack of national competition, and the lack of travel experience, Marcus Taylor has developed pretty nicely.

The Taylors work out individually. Fundamentals such as dribbling, shooting, and decision making were pounded home during sessions at the Waverly gym. As a point guard Taylor has become deft at controlling the game, seeing plays develop before others, calling for the ball in order to make the pass. And because of hours of shooting practice, his jump shot is one of the truest in the high school ranks. Where coaches often lament the lack of fundamentals and shooting touch, Taylor is an aberration. College coaches love him.

"The problem today is kids never practice by themselves," said Oklahoma State coach Eddie Sutton. "They are always playing in tournaments, playing in games. Guards just want to take it to the rim, they don't learn how to shoot.

"I grew up in Bucklin, Kansas, in the western part of the state, and learned to shoot by myself. A lot of coaches my age are like that. I think if you lined up all the college coaches and had a shooting contest with the college players, we might win. Even now."

Taylor's shooting stroke is so smooth that many observers think he'd be a twenty-point-per-game scorer in college if he switched to shooting guard.

"He'd be deadly," said one Big Ten coach, who can't publicly comment on specific recruits due to NCAA statutes. "I think he's a big-time scorer, but he's determined to play the point. And don't get me wrong, he's good there also."

So much emphasis is put on Taylor's individual training that even trips with the perceived neutral USA Basketball have been turned down. Before his junior year Taylor was invited to try out for a junior national team that would play a tournament in Moscow in July. Both James and Marcus decided that would take him away from home for too long so they politely turned the offer down.

"I told them that he wouldn't be able to go to Moscow because he had too much to do and they said come on out and try out anyway," James said. "I didn't want to lose four or five weeks of what we're doing. See, [summer] is the time we work on our things. This is a time of the year to get our work done."

Marcus did and enjoyed his week in Colorado Springs. But he didn't regret missing Moscow.

"I think to travel around the country or the world all summer, you don't have time to work on your game," said Marcus.

And it is more than the summer. Because the NCAA has opened up two windows outside of the traditional high school season for evaluation—one in September, and one in April—a proliferation of weekend AAU events have sprung up. The usefulness of these tournaments is open to debate. Most start on a Friday night and finish by Sunday, which means many players will miss at least one day of school and be gone from home for an entire weekend. In September 1998, Carlos Boozer, Jr., a top prospect in the class of 1999, flew from his home in Juneau, Alaska, to New Jersey for a weekend event. That same weekend some three dozen teams flocked to the campus of the University of Maryland for a weekend of games at the Charlie Webber Invitational AAU Tournament.

"And it's a waste," said one East Coast coach. "I'm not scouting anyone here. I'm only here so the guys I am currently recruiting see me. It's stupid. Most of the kids here aren't academically qualified yet. They should be home at school, taking SAT prep, going to a high school football game, being kids. Anything. But not playing more ball."

The only time the Taylors have relented and let Marcus step into the world of grassroots basketball was the Nike Camp. In 1997, both Nike and adidas offered invitations to Taylor as a sophomore. James Taylor figured Nike would be a better choice because Indianapolis was closer to home and the two could just drive down I-69 to get there. He also asked around and people said it was a well-run event. And so they came.

"We kind of sat down and said, 'Who do we know, who do we respect, and what's the best situation?'" said James. "We came here [as a sophomore] not really knowing and saw what their intentions were. They ran a good camp, pretty much as best as you can expect for this many kids."

Both companies again sent invitations the following year and both had middlemen make pitches about their respected virtues. James Taylor decided to stick with Nike.

"I am not one of those guys who says we should be jumping around and try this or that," James said. "There's always people trying to get you to switch because there is this thing between those two [Nike and adidas]. But I'm not caught up in that. I'm not trying to degrade adidas or anybody. If we weren't satisfied with the Nike Camp, then maybe we'd try adidas. But this is fine."

To gain high-level game experience not always available at the high school ranks, Taylor has been a regular at pickup games at Michigan State's Breslin Center. From the time he was a preteen he got his head beat regularly by the Spartans players. Although increasingly he held his own, stories of him dominating Cleaves, a two-time All-America, or NBA star Steve Smith in pickup games were nothing more than Lansing urban legend. He learned by failing against the best.

"It's tough, but I used it as an experience," Marcus said. "I can learn a lot from those guys and I have learned a lot from those guys. Offensively, defensively, and from a mental standpoint. They've taught me a lot about basketball and life and the decisions you have to make in college. It's a different level of game. Playing with the Michigan State guys, that's how I get better."

But although there were some tough times in Breslin, there were days he shined. Springfield, Illinois, talent scout Stephen Wacaser recalls working Tom Izzo's summer basketball camp in East Lansing when Taylor was in eighth grade. Each night in Breslin the MSU players scrimmaged. Wacaser watched one night and was impressed by a small but skilled guard.

"I asked Tom, 'Who's that kid, he's unbelievable. Where's he from?'" Wacaser said. "I thought he might be [future Spartans starter] Thomas Kelly or one of their other freshman. Tom says, 'That's Marcus Taylor, he's in eighth grade.' I was like, 'Don't give me that.' And he was like, 'Seriously.'"

To a lesser degree, way down in Childersburg, Alabama, Alice Wallace is making her own stand against grassroots basketball. Although her son Gerald had been playing basketball since he was just six years old, Alice never knew he was any good until she watched him in eighth grade and all those gangly limbs began to know where to go.

"He used to not be able to dribble," she said. "The men who coached him told me he was real good and I could see it."

The next year Gerald Wallace entered Childersburg High School and by 1998–99 he was a slashing, dashing 6-foot-7 wing forward who some considered to be the finest basketball player in the class of 2000 in not only the state of Alabama, but maybe the nation.

Wallace had spent the last few years playing AAU ball with Kenny Harris, coach of the adidas-sponsored Birmingham Ice. The idea that little Childersburg would attract anyone's basketball attention is alone noteworthy. The tiny town of 4,300 on the banks of the Coosa River about thirty-five miles southeast of Birmingham has never produced a Division I basketball player. Most of the locals are enthralled by auto racing, what with famed Talladega International Speedway sitting just ten miles to the north. And the town's school population is so small the high school and the middle school share a building.

But Gerald Wallace and his quick first step were putting the small town on the basketball map.

So on the map that by February of 1999, rival AAU coaches had descended on Childersburg to recruit him, George Raveling himself came to Childersburg High School to work a sponsorship deal, and everyone had an opinion on what summer camp Gerald should attend, adidas ABCD or Nike. All of that caused Gerald Wallace to complain to his mother that all this shoe stuff was affecting his concentration in school.

And that's when Alice Wallace said enough is enough.

"Basketball should be something he enjoys doing," said Alice. "It's a fun game. And he is in high school and that's all he should be worrying about, his high school team. It's something he should be enjoying with his friends."

But as Alice Wallace tells it, things began getting interesting in central Alabama on January 18, 1999, when Childersburg was playing at Jemison High. Sitting in the bleachers she was approached by Tony Acklin, an assistant coach of the Alabama Lasers, the Nike-sponsored team organized by Huntsville businessman Mark Komara that gained local acclaim for having star center Marvin Stone.

The two began talking about basketball, the Lasers' program, and Gerald's future. Acklin told Alice Wallace that the Lasers were one of the premier AAU programs in the nation and Gerald should switch from the adidas-sponsored Ice. He also talked up the virtues of the Nike All-America Camp in Indianapolis. And he said the Lasers could be good for Wallace.

"He told me that Gerald plays good ball," Alice Wallace recalls. "Gerald should be at a higher level than he is now. That if he came with them he could get more exposure. And he told me that it [was no longer] time for Gerald to [be] playing ball just to be playing ball.

"I was like, 'What do you expect a sixteen-year-old child to do, except playing ball just to play ball?'

"And I looked at him kind of funny and he said, 'You know, Gerald should be making money playing ball.' "

Alice said she was taken aback.

The conversation came to an abrupt end but not before Acklin handed Wallace a business card and told her they'd be in touch.

"He gave me one of his little cards with 'Alabama Lasers' on it and told me some big man from Nike would be calling and contacting me and talking." Wallace threw the card out immediately. Acklin acknowledges speaking with Alice Wallace that night but denies suggesting that Gerald should be paid to play.

On January 22, Mark Komara approached Alice at a Childersburg High game, and engaged in a brief conversation, before Harris, the Birmingham Ice coach, walked up.

Within days Nike's George Raveling had flown into Alabama from Los Angeles and along with Mark Komara and William "Wig" Pearson of the Lasers arrived in Childersburg and met with basketball coach Chad Slaten. The arrival of Raveling was big news as the word swept through the school.

"All I heard was that they were there, everyone said the head folks were there," said Gerald.

That day Slaten came by the local Winn Dixie Supermarket where Alice Wallace works as a head cashier and told her "the Nike people" were in town.

"He said they were going to have a meeting at another man's house and they would love me to sit in on their meeting," Wallace said. "And I said, 'Okay, I'll think about it.' But I didn't go."

Slaten says he, Raveling, Komara, and Pearson sat and talked at the high school. Raveling told Slaten about the virtues of the Nike Camp, the exposure Wallace would receive along with the SAT prep and life skills classes. He also told Slaten about how Gerald could work at the Michael Jordan Flight School that summer. The Jordan School is an instructional camp held in Los Angeles in which top Nike high school players—including Korleone Young, Jaron Rush, Corey Maggette, and Marvin Stone—annually work. Compensation can be up to $1,000 per week and the players have a chance to not only meet MJ himself, but scrimmage with him, Slaten was told.

Just in case Slaten had any reservations about the Jordan School or the Nike Camp, Raveling offered him the chance to work both events himself as a counselor.

The group also discussed the possibilities of Nike agreeing to a five-year sponsorship deal with Childersburg High, Slaten said, in which the company would provide shoes and gear to the team. They never mentioned that Gerald Wallace had to attend Nike Camp.

"That never was said," Slaten said. "But hey, I wouldn't even ask for the shoes if I didn't send the kid to the camp. I'm not a dummy, I knew about shoe contracts. I had heard that [a contingency deal] may happen, but as far as this coach goes, it didn't happen here."

Slaten said the whole thing was eye-opening. The twenty-nine-year-old Childersburg native led his team to a 28–5 record in 1998–99. Slaten said he had no opinion on what camp Wallace should attend and he has taken steps to make sure no one thinks he is pushing his player to the Nike Camp. When Nike sent him three pairs of free shoes, he gave them to his assistant coach. Another goodie package containing sweatsuits and gear remained unopened for weeks.

"I don't want to open it until I find out what we are going to do with Nike Camp," said Slaten.

Slaten also says while he was excited to meet a coach of Raveling's stature, he was concerned with the appearance of Komara and Pearson.

"I made it known quick that I didn't want to talk to AAU," said Slaten. "I don't get into AAU. Gerald has got a team he plays for and I'm not going to ask Gerald not to play for his team. I told him that, if you're trying to get me to persuade Gerald to play for this team here [the Lasers], you can forget about that. I told Coach Raveling I don't know if it's a good idea Wig [Pearson] came. I didn't want him coming. But they assured me that wasn't why they were here."

He said his views on shoe company sponsorships have

changed. He first learned that Nike was offering high school sponsorship deals when he read a newspaper account on Nike's involvement with Marvin Stone's high school, Huntsville Grissom. Slaten says he was shocked Nike was interested and then that a school would agree to such a deal.

"I couldn't believe they would do that," said Slaten. "I couldn't believe they would do something like that as far as getting stuff."

He feels differently now.

"But then, when you have an opportunity to do that, and you have a budget like we do at Childersburg High School, and most high schools do, and it's legal, my opinion on it changed immediately," Slaten said.

"And I think a lot of coaches say no, no, we wouldn't do that. I think a lot of coaches would change their mind if they had the opportunity to do so. And it may be jealousy, whatever. It would be hard not to. But at the same time, Gerald, he's going to be successful with or without Nike. He's going to be successful with or without adidas. Nor does Chad Slaten need it.

"But it's a business. Nike didn't get to be Nike by sitting back and selling tennis shoes. I do realize that if we didn't have a Gerald Wallace here and he was ten miles down the road, then they're going to be down there. But it's a business. You look at, in my opinion one of the greatest athletes to play any sport is Michael Jordan. And he's Nike."

Gerald Wallace said the business is too big and too confusing. Why, he wonders, would they be so interested in him that three people, including someone as famous as George Raveling, would come all the way to Childersburg just to invite him to attend one camp and work at the Jordan Camp? He'd prefer if everyone went away.

"My coach asked about [the Jordan Camp]," said Gerald

Wallace. "He asked if I even knew anything about it. If I wanted some information about it. I told him I'd get back to him, but I didn't. I really haven't wanted to get involved in this."

Gerald Wallace also declined an opportunity to meet with Raveling, Komara, and Pearson.

"They said the head folks from Nike were here," said Gerald Wallace, a shy sixteen-year-old. "I didn't go. I didn't have time."

When Alice heard about it and talked things over with her son she was concerned.

"Gerald had told me he got asked about [meeting Raveling] and he said he was having problems concentrating in school," she said. "I said, 'Why are you having problems in school?' And he said, 'Well, they want to know, do I want to talk to 'em or do I want to go there.'

"I [had] told him that if anybody wanted to talk to him or approached him, speak to them, ask them how they are doing and say nice to meet you and if they want to talk about anything else then tell them they have to talk to his momma."

So she called assistant principal Alex Stewart and told him to make sure no one bothered Gerald and that he shouldn't have to meet with Nike representatives if he didn't want to. Wallace said Stewart was sympathetic.

"I talked to the [assistant] principal about [it] and told him Gerald felt nervous about it," Alice said. "I said to him, 'No one can just walk into your school and take [Gerald] out of class and talk to him.' He said he understood and would make sure that no one would bother him while he was at school."

What further concerned Alice Wallace was speculation that the Childersburg High deal with Nike hinged on her son attending the Nike Camp during the summer of 1999. Although that was never specifically mentioned by Raveling, Slaten said, Alice Wallace raises a skeptical eye. She's aware of other schools agreeing to deals like that.

One of those is Tampa (Florida) Prep. That school began receiving over $2,500 a year in shoes and gear from Nike in 1997, the tradeoff being that 6-foot-10 star player Casey Sanders, then a high school sophomore and now a freshman at Duke, would attend the Nike Camp that summer, Tampa Prep coach Joe Fenlon told the *St. Petersburg Times*.

"I didn't feel real good about getting stuff because I never believe people give you something without wanting something," Fenlon told the *Times*. "So I felt very uncomfortable. My wife and I had many nice discussions about the whole thing. But when it really came down to it, it was an economic decision," Fenlon said. "I do not have the most affluent kids on my team, and ultimately we would have had to go out and raise that money to pay for this stuff that we could have been given."

For his part, Sanders told the *Times* that he saw nothing wrong with Nike's donations being based on his presence at the Nike Camp.

"I do understand that the shoe companies are trying to build a sense of loyalty with the player by giving them stuff," Sanders said. "But for me, that would never make me sign a contract with that shoe company down the line.

"You need to be careful because I know that nobody wants something for nothing. Everybody is looking for something in return. This is what I've been taught and this is what I believe.

"I know that some kids might not take all this like me and they may feel the pressure from these shoe companies. I can definitely see how that could happen. And what I would say to them is, 'Don't ever expect something for nothing.' "

The Wallaces don't. Which is why Alice is concerned about schools receiving sponsorship deals from multi-billion-dollar corporations based on the efforts of their students. She argues that Childersburg High works for her son, not the other way around, and it is not his job to earn a sponsorship deal for the school by attending a certain camp.

"I don't think it should be based on that," said Wallace. "I think a lot of what he told me, when he said, 'Momma I can't concentrate in school.' The thing that was bothering him, I got the impression, [was] he's a child and he don't know.

"Somebody came along and said, 'Well, if you do this and that, we'll get this and that.' And I think he felt like he'd let his school down. [He was thinking] 'I don't want to, but this is something I need to.' And I don't think this should be put on a child.

"This is what I think. If Nike just gives Childersburg High something, then that's fine. That means well. But not if it's you don't do this and you don't do that, then we're not going to do this."

Gerald Wallace said he was surprised there was this much interest in where players attend summer camp. The endless discussion about the offering of the contract and the visit from Raveling were the talk of Childersburg for a couple of months.

"I don't see no purpose in it," Gerald said. "I don't see the matter in it. It's just a camp to learn. They shouldn't have the right to tell anybody where to go."

Or maybe it's more than just a camp, he shrugs.

"After this, I think there must be something else [to it]."

Alice shakes her head also.

"You're cutting out a child's childhood," she said. "He's not having a time to be a child. This is a time, his junior year of school, where he should be enjoying his classmates and do the things a sixteen-year-old child would do."

Gerald Wallace attended the 1999 adidas ABCD Camp and played basketball for the Birmingham Ice, shunning Nike and the Lasers offers. Although Nike says Wallace's failure to participate in Nike summer basketball was not a factor, Childersburg High School never got its deal from Nike.

For that, Alice Wallace, who stood up to the offers, feels proud.

"He's happy where he is and I'm happy where he is," she said.

Despite stories like that of the Wallaces, some parents and coaches view people such as James Taylor as overprotective, overbearing alarmists. They disagree there is inherent harm in playing summer basketball. They say that letting a kid play in one tournament, letting him go on an overseas trip is not going to ruin him.

James Taylor sees validity in this, he just chooses to do it his way. He says he was more protective when Marcus was younger and more impressionable.

"I'm not so worried about him at this stage because he's come along really well," James said. "When he was younger and didn't know much and didn't know right from wrong, then I would worry about [outside influences]. Sure, it's possible he could have gotten around some kids who could have influenced him. Now I don't worry about that. He just doesn't need it.

"People think it is so easy [being a young star]. He just goes out there and makes plays. But it is tough. And especially when you are on top. Everything is blown up. Everybody is watching. That's the microscope he's been under since third grade. The next Magic Johnson. It was a community thing, then a city thing, then state and now national. Most people don't get that until they are seniors in high school, so it's not a long period of time to do that. But not us. I just wanted him to enjoy days outside of the microscope."

Hanging around those bleachers, and standing courtside at Nike Camp, he's heard the horror stories like everyone else, although he won't talk about it.

"I don't have anything negative to say because I don't know anything about that stuff," James said.

But he thinks there wouldn't be as many problems if parents were as close with their sons as he and Marcus are.

"I think parents need to be more involved," James said. "I've heard, 'Let the kid do what he wants to do, go where he wants to go.' You tell me, when you were fifteen or sixteen years old, what kind of decision were you going to make? You don't know anything.

"So what you do is get his okay to help him. If he trusts you, then it's okay. But it has to be something you build. If he doesn't trust you, if he doesn't know you and you haven't proven yourself to him and he doesn't know you are on his side then it won't be okay. And I don't let anybody else in."

James Taylor realizes he is unusual these days. So many young players come from broken homes where unsuspecting mothers trust the wrong people. While many AAU coaches pass themselves off as father figures, it's nice for Marcus Taylor to have an actual father.

"Well, the problem is not about us," James Taylor says. "Marcus is covered, he had a mom and dad around him. There are a lot of kids who don't have that dad to protect them. A guy who has been around the game a long time, who knows what to expect, knows people in the business. So I knew all along that it was nothing I had to worry about.

"But a lot of parents, single parents, they don't know a lot of people. They have no idea. Nothing has surprised me so far. So I had an idea what to expect but most people don't. And I hate that. Then there are a lot of people without, they have so little and they get offered anything and they'll take it. So, it's tough. That's the problem I don't like.

"It can be ruthless. So that's why I'm not in no hurry for him. He's comfortable. He's all right."

And he's number one in his class.

CHAPTER 16

Taking Responsibility for This Mess

There are few things in the game of basketball today that can be said without debate. This is one: The deepening battle to become the "sole influence" over the best American twelve-year-old is bad for the game. It is bad for the twelve-year-old. And it will ultimately be bad for the companies trying to win his affection.

This effort to find the next Michael Jordan—and don't let anyone fool you, that's what this is—guarantees only one thing . . . simply by trying so hard to find the next Jordan, we are assured he won't be found. What made Michael Jordan was that he worked so hard to overcome failure, that he, as he said at his retirement press conference, "stayed true to the game." He was not spoiled by shoes and sweats and gear bags and sunglasses at age fourteen. The time that today's next Jordan spends on airplanes enjoying the adulation of multinational corporations, the Real Jordan spent on courts in the blazing sun working on his game. Jordan became who he is because he wasn't spoiled by this system. The Next Jordan almost assuredly will be ruined by it.

We understand this is not a time when the concept of individual responsibility is very popular.

It is, instead, the days of me first. Where getting mine and protecting it is everything. Where victims, even those suffering from self-abuse, are heroes and no one is more than a Barbara Walters tell-all away from forgiveness. These are the days when no one dares cast the first stone, even when a boulder is called for.

That said, there is simply no easy solution, no snap-your-finger circumstance, no single piece of legislation to reverse the damage corporate America has inflicted on the game of basketball as it waged its unnecessary, personal, and bitter war in search of the next great American sports personality.

There is another truism about which there is nearly universal agreement: The current system must change. For the good of the game and the players. Anointing twelve-year-olds the next Michael Jordan is no way to help a young player develop. But there is a better way. Although it starts with individual responsibility.

Shoe companies deserve their share of blame. But the list of culprits is long. There is the NCAA, which legitimized the summer recruiting season when at its 1988 convention it attempted to "level the playing field," by limiting the time coaches were allowed to evaluate high school talent. The reasoning from the less wealthy members of the association was that if Ball State or Holy Cross or Sacramento State could not afford to fly in and see a star athlete's every practice, then those that could, Duke, Kentucky, and the rest, shouldn't be able to either.

The legislation, like so many NCAA laws, created more problems than it solved. By limiting evaluation during the winter months, but creating an unlimited live July recruiting period, the NCAA made the traveling team coach, unregulated and occasionally unsavory, the star and the gatekeeper of its recruiting process. In doing so, it made the traditional high school coach virtually obsolete.

The very people the NCAA despises today are truly of its own creation.

So is the system, so intense each summer that confused parents and players think the only road to a college scholarship is to play eighty or a hundred basketball games in a month and hope your legs and your jump shot hold out long enough to sign a college scholarship. So desperate are the NCAA's future student-athletes that even those who don't think the current system makes sense, those that consider passing, saying enough is enough, wouldn't dare because they worry it might limit their future.

Part of that comes from the creation of the early signing period, another well-meaning NCAA rule that has backfired. The Association created a week-long signing period in mid-November to allow seniors to sign a binding national letter of intent with a college. This was designed to allow players to end the recruiting process before their senior season and eliminate the distraction. However, it wound up pushing the season for verbal commitments up, now into the spring of a recruit's junior year. It is now common for a college program to have all its scholarship slots filled by the end of August or prior to the first day of class.

This has placed added pressure and importance on the summer recruiting season and, worse, on the completely useless spring and September traveling team season, which takes kids out of the classroom and onto the recruiting trail in the hope of attracting college attention. It has, in essence, continued the deemphasis of high school basketball. It has also shortened the period for college coaches to evaluate players, which leads to more mistakes and more kids playing at schools above their level. And that leads to dissatisfaction and transfer.

It is the NCAA that needs to reevaluate its role in the problem and not stand by idly.

Equally adept at creating an enemy they now bemoan are the nation's state high school federations, which prevent high school coaches from running summer travel teams. By blocking their own coaches from taking part in what is now the most important part of the recruiting calendar, the federations have cut high school coaches off at the knees. And given power to the travel coach.

Then there are those summer coaches themselves, so quick to defend a system, to point to the small positives without looking in the mirror and asking honestly what they are in this game for. Is it the attention college coaches pay you? Is it the money shoe companies provide? Is it spending the summer jetting around the country? Or the ego trip of being on the inside of the glamour world of college basketball? Of having Tubby Smith or Roy Williams or Jim Boeheim know your name? And you knowing their home number?

Traveling team coaches hang their morals on two key ideas: that getting their kids off the city streets assures short-term safety and that providing exposure for unknown players facilitates the earning of athletic scholarships. Both arguments have little merit. Surely a coach doesn't need to fly a kid three thousand miles away from home to keep an eye on him. The same effort to help a boy become a man could be made in their own neighborhood. The same time could be spent back home teaching a kid right from wrong. Sure, some players have tough backgrounds, but are they the first? Is teaching a child that their athletic skill is their most, or only, valuable commodity, the way to help them out of poverty?

And with the horrific percentage of players struggling to earn basic high school diplomas, or achieving even moderate scores on their standardized tests (you can't blame cultural bias for a 240 on the math portion of the SAT), it is difficult to believe July wouldn't be better spent in summer school or SAT prep. A kid can take a Kaplan Course for less than the price of a plane ticket from New York to L.A. Plus, isn't instilling the idea that school is actually more important than another tournament worth achieving? And don't bring up the shoe camps' public-relations-driven academic classes as sufficient scholastic pursuit, you know as well as we do that your own kids mock those as a joke.

As for exposure, we can only wonder how college basketball managed to stock its rosters and fill its scholarship slots in the ninety-some odd years before the proliferation of talent camps and AAU tournaments. Somehow, they did. The idea that a wave of lesser recruited players would fall through the cracks is laughable. How many low Division I players attend a college more than a hundred miles from home? How does a marginal Baltimore point guard benefit from playing in front of the coaching staff of UCLA, when only Coppin State and American University will ever recruit him? Isn't there such a thing as useless exposure?

But don't forget the players themselves, the hustlers with their hands out who ignore what they know is right and do what is wrong. Kids who use the system because they pretend to know how the system is using them. Want to use the system? Ignore it. No player in the country has upset the system more, caused more brows to wrinkle, caused more befuddlement and more panic than Michigan's Marcus Taylor. He's just too cool for shoe companies.

Then, of course, there is America's education system, from junior high right through to Old State U, which is so desperate for money, so short on ethics, so consumed by getting their share, that they sell their students, sell their morals, and sell their freedom of expression to the multinational which offers the most cash. High schools that will agree to shoe company contracts on the basis that one of their students effectively earn the money by performing at a certain all-star camp need to reevaluate their priorities. Are they too desperate for Nike's or adidas' approval or gear to realize that it is not the student's job to work for their school, but rather the school's to work for the student?

Cities and towns across the country engage in boisterous debates about whether a Coke machine should be allowed in municipal hallways but turn a blind eye to using sixteen-year-olds as moving billboards to sell product. To everyone we offer the advice of our favorite San Bernardino philosopher, the esteemed Elvert Perry: "Buy your own goddamn shoes."

And you can't let the college coaches completely off the hook. As they complain, as they cast insults, as they decry the loss of ethics in the recruiting game, they are rare to blow the whistle, to stand up and be counted, to name names, and, most importantly, to do their own business honestly. Will a shoe company back down from their campaign—which coaches themselves call hurtful to the game—if not forced? Of course not. But what if the most respected members of the coaching profession made them? Embarrassed them into it. Stood up on national television and in front of the nation's print media and said, enough is enough, something has to change, shoe companies need to get out of youth basketball. The same things they whisper to reporters off the record.

What if Mike Krzyzewski and Dean Smith and John Thompson and Rick Majerus and Nolan Richardson stood together and said it? For the good of the game. For the good of the kids they profess to worry about. Or does a shoe company own their voice too? All have grown rich off the shoes their players wear. They've become millionaires. Are they not now rich enough? Will a coach out there dare to give back the money and say, "From now on, I buy my kids shoes? And I think this is wrong. And I think the actions of this person have escalated the problem." Will they say it on the record? Will they?

And then there are the shoe companies themselves. They spend millions of dollars each year to chase little kids who can dribble a ball around the country so they can sell more shoes. Does a shoe company care if one of their players becomes an NBA bust with barely a high school degree? Does a shoe company worry about Ronnie Fields, once the star of the Chicago prep world, who felt he was ready for the NBA out of high school and now struggles to stay in the CBA? Nike once flew him around the country, showcased him at their all-star camp, and treated him like the next Jordan, which he thought he'd become. But then he got hurt and although he still thinks he's the next Jordan, Jordan never played for Rockford.

Of course, the first step to recovery, like with an alcoholic, is admitting your problem, and shoe companies are a long way from taking that first step. To his credit, adidas' Sonny Vaccaro admits he is one of the people who keeps the cesspool of amateur basketball bubbling. But he says he isn't stepping back until Nike does. Which is like waiting for gravity to take a day off.

And George Raveling and his bosses at Nike? They are lost in a delusional world where they have repeated the same public mantra about helping society by acting as corporate saviors so many times that they may actually have begun to believe it. Finding people who think the current system of youth basketball needs fixing is easy. People are frightened by the dishonesty. They claim the system is in disarray. They say too much power is in the wrong hands. They worry that too many temptations are hurting the kids. And they point out that the vast amount of shoe company money flooding amateur basketball has brought out a new breed of opportunist, looking not for glory, but fat payouts.

Who are the people? Take your pick. College coaches. College administrators. Conference administrators. NCAA investigators. Social scientists. High school coaches. Parents. Players. Even most AAU coaches, who claim the worst of their ilk are sullying all of their images. Even Vaccaro.

But not Nike.

"I refuse to get caught up in all of this make-believe stuff that is constantly being promoted by the media," says Raveling. Make-believe stuff?

Raveling admits that it wasn't make-believe stuff when on February 14, 1997, he told his stable of traveling team coaches during a teleconference that, "The wise man changes before he has to."

He said that, he admits, to encourage his troops to beat adidas at its own game by creating personal and long-lasting relationships with younger and younger athletes.

The game can only wish he'd listen to his own advice. Surely it is suffering. The quality of play the NBA is putting out each night is not up to the aesthetic levels of the past few decades. The level of boorish player behavior, however, is at a record high. The league's newest generation of players, the ones weaned on a steady diet of free gear and AAU ball, is generally regarded as pushing the game to new depths. The worst are vocal defenders of their individual rights. They are shocked when informed marijuana is illegal, hustle is demanded, off-season workouts are expected. They talk on their cell phones a lot. They don't dive on the floor very often.

Consider some of adidas' signature players. Tim Thomas, traded after two disappointing seasons in Philadelphia; Jermaine O'Neal, struggling to crack the line-up in Portland; Tracy McGrady, playing listless in Toronto; Antoine Walker, one of the most despised athletes in Boston for his hotdogging style, fat contract, and lazy on-court attitude that proud Celtics fans have always despised.

We understand these are not the days for individual responsibility. We very much understand that.

These are the days of individual rights. The right to do as you please. The right to be a hypocrite. The right to violate any rule you disagree with. The right to make your money any way you know how. The right to take only a cursory interest in academics. The right to employ a former crack dealer to baby-sit kids because he's effective. The right to give six figures a year to a high school coach with a shaky academic program because he delivers kids. The right to sell out your school because $7.1 million goes a long way in Lexington or Knoxville or Chapel Hill. These are the days for those rights.

But with every right should come a responsibility. And the vast majority of the people in college, high school, and grassroots basketball do profess, and legitimately have, a love for the game of basketball. Most have a similar interest in the development of young people. Most are good people caught participating in a bad system. Most also are concerned about the future of their sport and are quick to pass on stories about how this current system is causing harm. All of them have the right to do what they wish with the sport. All have the right to lead the children in their charge as they see fit. All of them have the right to seek their own self-interest, their own personal gain, their own personal glory.

They also may have the responsibility to do something else.

Epilogue

The play that made the NBA's collective eyes pop out, the one that made the scouts and the general managers certain that Lamar Odom had that special something that separates great talents from Hall of Famers, came in the closing moments of the 1999 Atlantic 10 championship game at the Core States Spectrum in Philadelphia.

With the game tied at 59 with 7 seconds left, Odom's Rhode Island Rams had a final chance to beat Temple for the title. The 6-10 sophomore from Queens took the ball thirty feet from the basket, held it calmly for a few seconds, then slowly but deliberately dribbled left. He beat his man off the dribble before stopping at the last second and popping from behind the arc. He had timed it perfectly, so that as the shot hit mid-arc the final buzzer sounded, and when it swished through the net, the Rams were conference champs for the first time in school history.

"Even your great college player rushes that play," said a scout for the Denver Nuggets. "Lamar never panicked, he knew how much time he had and he won it. It was a Larry Bird, Michael Jordan, Magic Johnson–type play. Let's forget for a second that he was 6-10 and playing guard. That play is a play very few people can make."

To those who had known him best, it was a performance of greatness no better than when he was just a skinny sophomore at Christ the King High School and poured in thirty-six points to lead CTK to the New York Catholic League Championship. It was that performance that truly burst Odom on the national amateur basketball scene. Between that title game and the Atlantic 10 one, five years had passed. And everything had changed for Lamar Odom.

The amateur basketball journey of Lamar Odom is one littered with broken promises, bad blood, and allegations of underhandedness. Few who were once close to him still are. He attended three high schools and two colleges, twice entered the NBA draft and twice tried to opt out, went from star to pariah of his AAU team, went from best friend to hated enemy of a Las Vegas dentist who gave him thousands of dollars, and left two colleges wondering out loud if he was ever worth the trouble.

"One of the most screwed up situations I've ever seen," said none other than Jerry Tarkanian, who after failing to recruit Odom to Fresno State found himself in a heated war of words with UNLV, the school he once coached and Odom originally signed with.

"Lamar Odom probably ruined the greatest basketball life of this generation," said Sonny Vaccaro, who befriended him soon after the Catholic League championship game but by the time draft day arrived had little to no contact with him. "He was going to [have that life], which doesn't mean he couldn't change. But he's screwed it up."

Screwed it up so much that despite a long and loyal relationship between Vaccaro and Odom, Sonny swears he had no interest in signing the player to an endorsement contract with adidas. Screwed it up so much that although universally hailed as the talent of the 1999 draft, Chicago, Vancouver, and Charlotte all passed, leaving him for the Los Angeles Clippers at the fourth pick.

"Lamar has too many flaws," said Vaccaro. "Which doesn't mean he isn't the best talent of his class and he isn't one of the ten best talents of this decade. I don't want to downplay what his ability is. I've seen kids with problems, I've seen kids screw up, but I've also seen kids bounce back and play."

The question becomes, did Lamar Odom's problems exist before the adulation or is he a product of the crazed, use-or-be-used environment of high school and college basketball? Will he become the player for the next millennium, or will being the product of basketball at the millennium forever hold him back?

It had started early, the fame, the pulls, and the mistakes. The New York City Catholic League is the nation's finest and most competitive high school basketball league, and in a city that worships star power, particularly young star power, Lamar was the king at sixteen. They write books and make movies about those who were teenage stars on the playgrounds of New York, and Lamar the Star was the latest Goat, latest Helicopter, latest Sweet'Pea Daniels. Everyone wanted a piece of him. People, Odom says now, who used to claim they were looking out for his best interest. Except, he says now, he doesn't believe they really were.

"I got a lot of bad advice," he says. "I listened to the wrong people. In some cases, growing up in New York is not easy. I pretty much let [the success] go to my head. I was not focused on the right things."

The basketball journey of Lamar Odom has been told and

retold enough. It requires little more than a brief synopsis here, but what emerges from his days at Christ the King, through the three-high-school senior year, the two colleges, the allegations of academic fraud, and the mind-boggling erratic personality shifts, are two simple facts.

First, from the age of sixteen Lamar Odom never had to deal with the full consequences of his actions, because in today's world of amateur basketball there was always someone else willing to bail him out of a jam. And second, like the street savvy New York City kid he is, Odom may have figured out how to play the game to his advantage, because it's not easy to find someone who was once close to the player who still is.

Take Vaccaro and Gary Charles, Odom's AAU coach on the adidas-sponsored Long Island Panthers.

Wasn't Odom Vaccaro's prize New York recruit to the adidas ABCD Camp? Didn't he become the star of the Panthers, one of adidas' flagship programs? Wasn't he such an important commodity that when the Panthers found themselves short a point guard during the summer of 1996 Vaccaro answered by encouraging talent scout Tom Ostrom, now an administrative assistant at the University of Florida, to send Minneapolis guard Khalid El-Amin to Gary Charles? All to keep Lamar happy.

Weren't Vaccaro and Charles with Odom every step of the way during his senior year of high school—through the thick and the thin of all three high schools he attended? The last one Odom attended was St. Thomas Aquinas High in New Britain, Connecticut, which was coached by Charles's long-time friend Jerry DeGregorio.

Odom also stood by adidas. He was Mr. adidas in high school, even announcing he would attend the University of Nevada–Las Vegas at an impromptu press conference before

Vaccaro's Magic's Roundball Classic. It took place in the Detroit Pistons locker room, with Dick Vitale acting as unofficial MC. The move gave adidas and the Classic airtime it otherwise would never have earned. (In a funny twist, George Raveling told ESPN "that Odom was overrated and overhyped.")

And when *Sports Illustrated* questioned the validity of Odom's standardized test score—detailing how Odom, ranked 312 out of his CTK class of 334, amazingly improved his test score by the equivalent of 400 points on the SAT—both Vaccaro and Charles defended Odom, going on television to declare his innocence.

Charles even helped Odom after UNLV dumped him, guiding the player to Rhode Island, which would soon begin to wear adidas shoes and by then had hired DeGregorio as an assistant coach. DeGregorio is now the Rams head coach.

But by the summer of 1999, Odom no longer spoke to Vaccaro. Or Charles, who he once called a father figure.

"And that's a shame," says Vaccaro. "Gary and him don't talk. Not a word. That's much worse than anything with Sonny Vaccaro. All that Gary did for him? Gary was wonderful to him."

Odom doesn't want to talk about Charles, but he isn't afraid to admit when things started getting crazy for him. "I should never have left Christ the King," he says. "If I could do it again, I'd stay there. I should have kept it simple."

"It's hard when you are young and everyone knows what's best for you," Odom said. "You are just going to make mistakes."

How about the strained relations Odom left at UNLV, where his original signing was supposed to signify a true rebirth of Rebels basketball? During his recruitment, Odom developed a close relationship with the Rebels' youthful coach, Bill Bayno, and with assistant Greg "Shoes" Vetrone, a New York native. But when the school decided to part ways with Odom following the allegations of test fraud, Odom bristled that Bayno didn't fight hard enough for him and was angry when he was informed of the school's decision not by the coach, but by one of the program's administrative assistants.

"It was the worst day of my life," he says. "They could have done more for me."

Bayno and Odom haven't spoken since. Neither have Odom and Vetrone, who no longer works for UNLV. The one Vegas person Odom did stay in contact with, at least for a little while, was UNLV booster David Chapman, a local dentist who talked regularly with the player even after he transferred to URI. That changed last spring, however, and the two no longer speak. The NCAA is currently investigating Odom's recruitment to UNLV and in connection with its inquiry has questioned Chapman, who sources in Vegas say was a longtime supporter of UNLV basketball. Chapman says he was just "helping a friend" when he gave Odom thousands of dollars. UNLV will not comment on the ongoing investigation.

With so many busted relationships and so little trust surrounding Odom, one has to wonder just what happened or if the real truth could ever come out. What is clear is that as sure as the system is designed to use players such as Odom, the kid figured a way to use the system right back. But was it really to his benefit?

"I think I just had too much happen too soon," the well-spoken Odom said. "I was young and everything came so quickly. I'm much older now. I've been through a lot. My grandmother, Mildred Mercer, I'm very close to her. She's taught me a lot and she's seventy-five years old and she always says, 'Old people know best.' Maturity and experience help the decision-making process. I've gone though a lot of adversity. I've gotten older and wiser."

How much wiser is open to debate. He said this not long before he showed up late for a private workout with the Chicago Bulls, then he fired his agent and tried to return to college. The Bulls, who were dying to find a reason to take a chance on him with the number one pick, drafted Duke's Elton Brand instead.

"Let me say this about Lamar," says Vaccaro. "He's one of the nicest kids I've ever been involved with, in terms of being around him. But I really think he's got two personalities. There are two Lamar Odoms. He is unbelievable. Warmth and smiles and hugs, and I think he's sincere when he does these things.

"It's a shame what happened to him," Vaccaro continued. "I really think Lamar Odom is scared of success. I really think that's the problem. He takes the easy way out of every situation he's ever been in in his life. "

Odom could be the poster boy for the modern basketball phenom. Discovered at an early age, he was given anything and everything because of his immense potential. A kid from a broken home—father Joseph wasn't around much, mother Kathy passed away when he was twelve—he was flown around the country. He was outfitted. He was tended to. He was doted on by the New York hoops community. He was on the back page of the New York tabloids before he could drive. And a shoe company was by his side the entire way.

When one school didn't work out, he went to another. When a conflict arose at that one, he was off to yet another. When a standardized test seemed an insurmountable hurdle, his scores incredibly improved. When seemingly no school wanted him, one bended its academic standards to take him.

He took everything they gave him. Time will tell how great the great talent will wind up becoming. But the funny thing about Lamar Odom is, NBA rookie or not, he is already a generation removed from today's reality. In his day, say 1994 when he was a high school sophomore, he was still somewhat of an unknown. He hadn't yet burst on the national scene. He hadn't yet crisscrossed the country to play in national AAU events, or national talent camps.

In his "day," when he was fifteen or sixteen, life was pretty simple.

But today, a sixteen-year-old without a national rep is nobody.

It's a hot summer day in Atlanta and to the kids, the preteens, the seventh graders, and the rest, basketball is on their mind.

This is the Junior ABCD Camp, a talent camp run by Wallace Prather, coach and organizer of the Atlanta Celtics AAU team. And these are some of the best young kids in the Southeast.

Dozens of those in attendance make it clear they are already competing to prove they are the best.

When Lamar Odom was twelve, he said he was hanging around his neighborhood playing basketball with friends.

When Michael Jordan was twelve, he was hitting lazy fly balls on a Wilmington, North Carolina, baseball diamond.

When those that would be next are twelve, they are already in a talent camp, a junior meat market, sponsored by a multinational apparel company, watched closely by one of the nation's most prominent traveling team coaches.

It's just part of the trend.

Vaccaro makes no bones about hoping to find the best players at the youngest possible age and establishing a relationship with adidas. Raveling, for his part, has encouraged his summer coaches to contact him in writing with the names and phone numbers of the best young junior high level players in their areas.

While top competition—in the form of national traveling team tournaments—has long been available for players as young as eleven, the all-star camps and shoe-company-sponsored events are new.

Prather began his camp in 1998 as a way of identifying and motivating high-quality young players. It was also a way to weed out the players from the pretenders because, as you might expect, getting an accurate scouting report of a thirteen-year-old isn't easy.

Vaccaro says that despite what the name Junior ABCD implies, he does not consider Prather's camp to be a true warmup for Sonny's ABCD Camp. More accurately, Vaccaro admits, Junior ABCD is a way for Prather to find young players for his Celtics organization.

"Wallace does that with very little support from us, maybe $5,000," Vaccaro said. "It's not a very big thing on my agenda. He wants to get seventh, eighth, and ninth graders involved, all Southeastern kids."

In fact, Vaccaro said, he thinks events like that push the boundaries of positive experience and he doesn't think he should be involved.

"That's too young," he said. "The misconception now is [that he's interested in expanding the adidas grassroots system]. The only thing I'd do at adidas is the [ABCD] camp, the Big Time [AAU] Tournament [in Las Vegas], and to give [traveling teams] money to go play."

Not to be outdone, Nike continued its sponsorship of two tournaments run by Mae Fisher, a Las Vegas woman who runs basketball tournaments in the city. Fisher organizes not only an Easter weekend tournament held at UNLV but also the Mae Fisher Las Vegas Classic in August.

The two tournaments bring hundreds of kids, some as young as twelve, and their parents to the glitz and glitter of Vegas for a weekend of basketball, entertainment, and complimentary product handouts, most with the Nike swoosh on it.

Then there is the growing Phenom Camp held in Lansing, Michigan. Run by Kenny Drake, a twenty-six-year-old former player at Central Michigan University, the Phenom hosted 160 kids from twenty-seven states at the inaugural event in August of 1998.

"I had wanted to run an all-star camp," said Drake, "but I knew you can't compete with adidas and Nike. So we went with the younger kids. I think the camp is a great idea; we give kids a chance to compete with the best, see where they are at nationally, and then head home and work on their games. They need to know. And a lot of kids realized that. And they loved it. And they needed it."

Drake shrugs off criticism that kids age twelve to fifteen are too young to compete in national camps. Although players of that age have long had the opportunity to play in national AAU tournaments, talent camps have always been considered true meat markets, a place where the best lock heads in front of college recruiters. Even players are often critical of the system.

It has been said that such camps weren't good for kids of such a tender age. "I disagree with that," said Drake. "Look at gymnastics and tennis. You've got kids playing as pros at thirteen, fourteen years old. Why should basketball be different? I understand there won't be any professional basketball players at that age, but I think they are old enough to compete nationally.

"The kids playing basketball train just as hard, work on their games just as hard. Why shouldn't they get the recognition too? I think it's fair. Most of our guys are going to be freshmen in high school."

Courtney Goldwire is one of Drake's partners and is planning on running a regional Phenom Camp in Atlanta. A regional camp in San Diego is also in the works, and Drake says he hopes to begin running similar girls' camps by 2000—although Philadelphia camp organizer Mike Flynn has been doing just that for years. Drake began facing regional competition in August of 1999, when Chris Grier, coach of the adidas-sponsored Michigan Mustangs, began running a Junior ABCD Camp in Lansing.

Like Drake, Goldwire says the kids are old enough to handle the pressure of the national competition. He says he isn't the one who starts a process that so many in basketball criticize.

"Some people say we're baby killers," Goldwire said. "I'm like, 'what's new?' It's been eons since freshmen and younger were playing varsity basketball. I'm not trying to blow a kid's head up. There's a lot of freshmen who don't get a chance to go to adidas or Nike. I think players that can play should be able to.

"I know there are going to be people out there who don't understand what we are doing or criticize us," Goldwire continued. "Hey, I don't want to be a baby killer. I think there is a safe way to do this. It's the same thing as junior nationals [AAU], so what's the difference?"

Goldwire, who once tried his luck publishing a youth basketball magazine called *Full Court* and is a longtime summer basketball observer, used his contacts around the country to help stock the Phenom Camp with decent talent.

The problem with dealing with junior high talent is that

word of mouth is essential to finding players. There are only a few scouting services for players that young. And even players with big reps arrive untested.

While to most basketball fans, the idea seems ludicrous that someone is ranking the top fifty sixth graders in the nation, it's happening. Among basketball junkies and throughout the junior high hoops world names such as Shaun Livingston of Peoria, Illinois, Sheldon Williams of Midwest City, Oklahoma, Chad Moore of Alabama, Carl Marshall of Chicago, Richard Cobbs of Los Angeles, and Sebastian Telfair and Klinky Klingsdale of New York City are, amazingly, household names.

"I was talking to one of Shaun Livingston's people in Peoria and telling them about the camp I wanted to run," said Drake of the diminutive but skillful thirteen-year-old guard. "And he was describing Shaun and he said, 'The kid's a phenom.' And I said, 'I've been looking for a name for the camp, and that's it. Thank you.'"

While Drake and Goldwire certainly facilitate the promotion of the young players, many kids and their families promote themselves. During the fall of 1997, for instance, Livingston's family sent one of the authors a copy of a home video of then eleven-year-old Shaun tearing it up in a fifteen-and-under Gus Macker Tournament in Champaign, Illinois.

What made that tape memorable was not that it was sent—top scouts and media regularly receive such videos—but that Livingston's crossover dribble was so developed for a player with such a lanky frame. It was clear, even to a non-coach, that the kid had game.

Ironically, the criticism that Drake and Goldwire feared most was not that their camp might exploit kids, but rather that they were associated with a shoe company. Apparently that's how far the image of Nike and adidas has dropped in recent years. Which is why the Phenom Camp is proudly independent.

"I don't have any ulterior motives," says Drake. "I don't work for Nike. I don't work for adidas. When they called— and believe me they both did—I didn't play favorites. Sonny Vaccaro called during camp and George Raveling did too. And I gave them both information. Sonny wanted a list. That's all he wanted. I faxed it to him. He just wanted to know who's who. And George did too. He wanted to know who played well.

"I don't favor either one. And I really don't care. I don't want to get involved in that little war they're having."

Goldwire says that even if Nike or adidas wanted to fund his camp, he wouldn't be interested.

"I wouldn't take their money for sponsorship," Goldwire said. "We're looking for an organization to sponsor us. What would happen if Nike or adidas came in and helped us is it would look like a pipeline to their grassroots system. We don't want that.

"We're holding it in August, in the dead period, so no coaches can come," Goldwire continued. "I'm not inviting coaches. I don't want to be known as the initial flesh peddler."

The dinner party was supposed to be an evening away from the endless grind of the business of basketball. It was at the stately Sarasota, Florida, home of Dick Vitale, who on the occasion of the 1999 Final Four in nearby St. Petersburg had invited many of his friends in the game to relax with a catered meal by the pool and a tour of his lavish home and his impressive collection of sport memorabilia.

Leisurely eating his dinner at a corner table, Brian

Ellerbe was doing just what Vitale wanted. The young Michigan coach had just completed a stressful year. His Wolverines, undermanned following a scandal involving his predecessor Steve Fisher, struggled through the season while Ellerbe worked day and night putting together a top five recruiting class that should improve his fortunes in the seasons to come. So with recruiting temporarily suspended due to the NCAA-mandated no-contact period, this was a chance to unwind, to get away from the rigors of running a Division I basketball program and visit with old friends.

No such luck.

"Coach, how we looking for that game next November?" asked basketball entrepreneur David Pump in lieu of a greeting as he hustled up to the table. "We on or what?"

Ellerbe looked up from his food, nodded, and told Pump he had received the information and would get back to him. "Pump, I'll let you know, I'll see what we can do."

"I'll be in touch, soon," said Pump, before quickly darting to another table.

For most in college basketball, the Final Four is the climax of the season, a time when the game gathers together, crowns a champion, and those not competing reflect on the past year, angle for jobs, or get in a round of golf with friends from around the country. But for Dana and David Pump, owners of the Los Angeles–based Double Pump, Inc., it's business time.

After securing an invite to the Vitale party—Sonny Vaccaro got the twin brothers in—this was a chance for the Pumps to do more than just round up coaches' complimentary Final Four game tickets. This was a chance to shore up their newest business deal—scheduling their exhibition basketball team, the California All-Stars.

For decades, college teams have sought the chance to

tune up their squads in games that provide good competition but do not count in the win-loss column. The NCAA allows two such exhibition games, and since the 1970s independent teams such as Marathon Basketball (once called Marathon Oil) and Athletes in Action, a Christian group, have put together teams of former college stars to crisscross the nation and play such games.

"There was a time in the 1980s," says Marathon Basketball owner Glenn Sargent of Joliet, Illinois, "where our team would play twenty-eight of the thirty nights in the month of November. After a game, we'd load up and drive to the next campus for another game the next night. *Sports Illustrated* did a story on us, the title said, 'They Drive by Night.'"

Sargent's operation is a classic ragamuffin outfit. Now seventy years old, the gruff, tough Sarge, as he's known throughout the game, still takes nine players, packs them into a van and an old station wagon, and on a shoestring budget rolls over the nation's interstates providing very good competition.

"The thing about Sarge's teams is they can play any way you want," says Ohio State coach Jim O'Brien, who's played Marathon since the mid-1980s when he coached Boston College. "They always had some good talent, and if you asked, they could slow it down or play uptempo. Whatever best helped your team. And it was not uncommon for them to beat us. Which I thought was good."

For Sargent, running a team meant more than just staying involved in a game he's loved since playing in the 1940s in the old National Industrial League and for the Washington Generals against Abe Saperstein's original Harlem Globetrotters. "I was the dumb white point guard who would always fall for the hidden ball trick," he says with a laugh. Running a competitive preseason team also meant money.

Since most schools include exhibition games as part of their season ticket package, the bigger programs can have 15,000 or 16,000 tickets sold. The payout for Sargent's team can be as much as $15,000 a night. O'Brien's Ohio State program, for example, pays $10,000 for a game.

Since he began running the Marathon teams in 1972—Marathon Oil, Inc., dropped sponsorship in the mid-1980s—Sargent and others like him have been viewed as a quaint, innocent corner of the game.

But like everything else in 1990s basketball, shoe companies and recruiting have moved into this onetime simple aspect of basketball.

The Pump brothers—identical redheaded twins that virtually no one can tell apart, causing most coaches, upon seeing either, to declare simply, "What's up, Pump?" in an effort not to be wrong—are involved in nearly every aspect of amateur basketball. They annually put together a number of Southern California AAU teams (called Pump 'n' Run), operate the July Best of the Summer AAU Tournament at California State University at Dominguez Hills, and also host a couple of high school tournaments during the year at the same site. All of their events and teams are heavily sponsored by adidas. "They are close business associates of mine," says Sonny Vaccaro.

In 1998, the California All-Stars fielded two teams that played nearly three dozen games, including dates against high-powered and high-priced operations such as Kentucky, Kansas, Maryland, Georgia Tech, and others.

"We had a great year," said Dana Pump. Each brother traveled with an all-star team but hired coaches to handle sideline duties. "Playing all those big-name schools was fun."

And profitable, which is why both brothers combed the

Vitale party to shore up loose dates. Ellerbe has only one open date on his Michigan schedule, because the Big Ten mandates that he play a foreign team the conference contracts with. In 1998 he filled the open night with Athletes in Action, a Christian group that uses sports to promote their religious beliefs. Ellerbe would have scheduled the California All-Stars immediately, if not for some of his other offers.

That included an exhibition team sponsored by EA Sports (the video game company) and run by Darren Matsubara, a Fresno, California, AAU coach. Matsubara, a mustached twenty-eight-year-old Japanese-American and former point guard at California State–Northridge, runs the Elite Basketball Organization, a high-powered adidas outfit that has featured such highly recruited national stars as Juneau, Alaska, native Carlos Boozer, Jr., (Duke) and St. Albans, West Virginia's Brett Nelson (Florida) as well as swingman DeShawn Stevenson, among the top talent in the class of 2000.

Matsubara and the Pumps weren't alone in trying to make the most from exhibition games. New York AAU coach Mickey Walker began running an exhibition team in the mid-1990s. And legendary Five Star Basketball Camp owner Howard Garfinkle of New York City has put together a team. Garf, as he's known, has access each summer to literally a thousand high school players and has long established relationships with college coaches who once worked for him.

"There are a lot of offers; I'm not sure where to go, who to play," said Ellerbe, who eventually went with the Pumps.

It's a line oft repeated. UCLA coach Steve Lavin, who is particularly reliant on recruiting California players, can't afford to snub either the Pumps or Matsubara. When confronted with one date and two teams, he got everyone together and tried to work it out. He'll play the Pumps in 1999 and Matsubara in 2000.

"I want to help both guys out," says Lavin, who claims that he doesn't expect anything more than a good game in return from either group.

To many coaches, even the ones scheduling these AAU-type teams for exhibition games, this is distasteful. The idea that a once simple part of their job is now another potential recruiting headache is something they don't want to deal with.

"Everybody is always looking for a recruiting edge," says Ohio State's O'Brien, who has stuck with Sargent and another outfit he has played for years. "And this is another chance for people to get an edge by using the exhibition game. It's a little bizarre. And it's not so much that coaches think people can help you in recruiting, as much as they are concerned that someone can hurt you. And the general feeling among coaches is, 'If I don't play these guys, can they hurt me? Why take the chance?' It's a little sticky and I wish it wasn't like that, but that's the way it is these days.

"But we have always sold loyalty and that's why I like what we are doing. Glen Sargent has always brought in a very good, competitive team and I see no reason to change. He's old school and we like to consider ourselves old school. So we deal with him."

Recruiting favors, if they exist, could be only the tip of the iceberg. The idea that a school is presenting a check, sometimes with as many as five figures, to a person who is also closely involved in the coaching and recruitment of top prospects is a possible conflict of interest that makes even veteran coaches shudder.

What would prevent a school from upping the guarantee for an exhibition game from $10,000 to $25,000 or

$100,000 in exchange for a star player? The money would be above the table and perfectly NCAA legal.

All of the coaches running both AAU and exhibition teams deny they would ever make such a deal and there is no evidence that it has ever happened. Yet, considering that there will likely be an explosion of such dual interests as more AAU types realize the dollar potential, does college basketball need this?

"Obviously it could happen," says Saint Louis coach Lorenzo Romar, who, coincidentally, spent nine years running Athletes in Action after becoming a born-again Christian during his NBA playing days. "It could come to the point where someone says, 'Hey, Player A really likes St. Louis, and if you give a little more, you'll get him.' If that were to happen, that would not be good for the game."

"In the recruiting business," says Ole Miss coach Rod Barnes, "it's always something. People are always trying something, so opening up a potential avenue for that is not good."

Closing that avenue is something the NCAA may eventually look into, but the Association is notorious for its slow-moving bureaucracy and is no match for those who operate outside of its jurisdiction.

In their defense, no one is breaking any NCAA rules. Because of that, don't blame adidas or Nike because their summer league coaches have figured out a way to make extra money, says Vaccaro. Blame the NCAA for allowing a system that is ripe with abuse.

"This is the stupidity of the NCAA because they leave themselves open to this. As long as this is legal, they are allowing all the spectators and all the speculators with opportunity to do just that. If I was a college coach who didn't have those teams playing me, or I was a school that couldn't get a Pump guy or a Mats or a Garf guy or a Mickey Walker guy then I'd be concerned. But it's their rules."

One person who is not sweating the increased competition for games is Sargent, who has beaten back all comers for nearly three decades and doesn't fear AAU types. He views this as a short-term threat to the game and to his business.

"I've had coaches who have dropped us say that these other teams are saying, 'If you play us, we will help you recruit our players,' " says Sargent. "But there's not that many players. You sing a song like that and it will catch up with you. Let's say they play twenty-five or thirty games. They don't control twenty-five or thirty players. It can't happen. They can't numerically provide that many blue-chip players. I wish those teams all the luck in the world. And if colleges want to chase that carrot and play an exhibition team that they can beat by thirty and not give them good competition, then go with it.

"In thirty years of doing this I've seen all types of bandwagon jumpers. The only thing you have in this business and in life is your word. And I've always been able to say that anything I say that I'll do, I'll do it. I back up my word."

Whether the new breed of traveling team owner will last as long as Sargent is still to be seen. What is likely, however, is that as long as the NCAA allows this, expect more teams to form and the relationships between college programs and summer basketball to grow murkier.

The ability of an elite, likable athlete to move huge amounts of product, to build companies, to change the way the *Fortune* 500 works is a truth that is now self-evident. Michael Jordan proved it.

In the shoe and apparel industry, the cutthroat competition to overthrow Nike from its $9 billion industry leader pedestal is also indisputable.

And to win the war among competing companies to find that next great pitchman who might change the pecking order, the "next Michael Jordan" who can surge a company's sales tenfold in ten years, is clearly an established corporate goal—reiterated by none other than shoe god Phil Knight.

The only thing not clear is the damage being done to the young athletes who dare to dream of being the next Michael Jordan. The next six-time world champion. The next role model to a generation.

Michael Jordan, Larry Bird, Magic Johnson, the three greatest basketball players of the past two decades, all grew up in basketball obscurity. All attended their local high school. None played national AAU basketball. Each bought their very own pairs of shoes. All held part-time jobs to earn a little spending money. Each developed a hunger to be the best, an obsession to be a champion.

That obsession is what made those players great.

No young player today—invited to a Phenom camp at twelve, ranked nationally by thirteen, babied, never disciplined, never punished, never taught the consequences of bad grades, of a poor attitude, of talking back to a coach—has to be so similarly obsessed to be considered great.

Today's young players defy authority. They can strangle their coach in the NBA because they are taught as teens that there is always another coach out there willing to take them. There are never too many mistakes to be made. There is always an easy road to walk.

"Too much, too soon," says Lamar Odom, whose history in modern amateur basketball made some NBA teams doubt he'll ever reach his enormous potential. "I got too much, too soon."

He was sixteen when America's grassroots system took him in. Old by today's standards.

The awful truth is this: Corporate America's obscene search for the next Jordan—led by Nike and adidas—has practically ensured he'll never exist. Their coddling will ruin him before he ever gets a chance. Even Nike pitchman Jordan has to regret that.

Index

DAN WETZEL is the managing editor of *Basketball Times*. In each of the past four years, he has received national investigative reporting awards from the United States Basketball Writers Association.

DON YAEGER is a writer and associate editor for *Sports Illustrated*. He is the coauthor of the *New York Times* bestseller *Under the Tarnished Dome* and the critically acclaimed *Pros and Cons: The Criminals Who Play in the NFL*.